Cabbageu

by

Sue Brown

Copyright

Copyright 2014 Sue Brown

Lulu Print Edition

ISBN: 978-1-326-02986-9

The moral right of the author has been asserted.

All rights reserved. Apart from any fair dealing for the purposes of research or private study, or criticism or review, as permitted under the Copyright, Designs and Patents Act 1988, this publication may only be reproduced, stored or transmitted, in any form or by any means, with the prior permission in writing of the copyright owner, or in the case of the reprographic reproduction in accordance with the terms of licences issued by the Copyright Licensing Agency. Enquiries concerning reproduction outside those terms should be sent to the publisher.

With Thanks

To **Roger** for your love and laughter ...
and **James and Emma** for refusing to let me give up on this writing lark! For all the days when I wanted to hide and admit defeat ... I thank you for picking me up and giving me the confidence to carry on writing. I couldn't have done it without you!! Love the bones of all of you!

Just to say ...

To Siobhan Durkin for your friendship and faith. Helen Thomas ... Pat Mcguckian ... Gary finn ... Gabby Basara ... Carla Spooner ... Michelle Alder ... Brenda Turner ... Mia Bibby... Gemma Moore ... Wendy Lloyd ... Jools ... Carrie ... Katie Rowlett ... Mo Brander ... Annette Rowe ... Dougie Doodle ... Paula carter ... Steve & Val ... Marc Anthony and Julie on Goodreads ... Yvonne Wareham ... Jo Mcdonald ... Samantha Bygrave ... Ty Mcdonald ... Andy Morris ... Rob Holt ... Pat Gulley ... Cath Emery ... Paul Harper ... Addie Nicholson ... Sharron Smith ... Paul Maddocks ... Catherine Hanmore ... Susan Mitchell ... Nicole o ... James Armstrong ... Lisa Walker ... Salma Ayas ... David Rowe ... Catherine Robson Smith ... Linda & John Stokes ... Dawn1971...Ditto!!

And for those of you I have worked with in jobs that suck the very soul out of you ...
Never ... Ever ... Give up on your dreams!!

For Finn

Contents

Introduction 9
Chapter One 11
                           … Ladies Night at the Nut Hut
Chapter Two 27
                                      … Name that Tune
Chapter Three 39
                                          … The G Spot
Chapter Four 46
                               … Place Your Bets Please
Chapter Five 60
                                        … One Cool Cat
Chapter Six 71
                           … Unidentified Flying Footwear
Chapter Seven 82
                               … The Suicidal Scotsman
Chapter Eight 97
                               … Situation Very Vacant
Chapter Nine 106
                                    … Lenny The Leg
Chapter Ten 115
                                        … Orville & I
Chapter Eleven 126
                 … A Severe Case Of Foot & Mouth
Chapter Twelve 136
                                           … Open Wide

Chapter Thirteen 144
...Wiggy

Chapter Fourteen 154
...Lob The Builder

Chapter Fifteen 161
King Dong & The Dahlias

Chapter Sixteen 172
...Roll Up! Roll Up!

Chapter Seventeen 183
...The Tattooed Lady

Chapter Eighteen 191
...Piling Into The Pound Shop

Chapter Nineteen 200
...Is There Anybody There?

Chapter Twenty 210
...Kenny & The Cornflakes

Chapter Twenty One 217
...Love Thy Neighbour

Chapter Twenty Two 230
...Alan & The Anti-Christ

Chapter Twenty Three 238
...Mazel Tov Mrs Morgenstein!!

Chapter Twenty Four 260
...Don Corleone & Date Expired Food

Chapter Twenty Five 270
Here Comes The Bride ...With Ken Dodd By Her Side

Also by Sue Brown 287

About Sue Brown 288

Introduction

Mary appears to have morphed into Madonna overnight.

She's wearing a Marks & Spencer dress with a Playtex bra over the top.

She's either been watching MTV again or it's the Prozac her GP prescribed.

Prozac! I ask you! For a ninety-three year old! Whatever next?

No wonder she's Cabbaged with all the medication she's on. Capsules for her heart … tablets for her wheezing lungs and a positive plethora of pills for all her other ailments.

We are a Cabbaged community.

Pete's cabbaged on Carling Special Brew and drugs to stop his liver exploding.

I am in a permanent state of Cabbageness … not because of drugs … that's just my normal state!

I shall have to coax her out of that bra.

Far too provocative for bingo at the day centre.

God forbid that some randy pensioner thinks he's onto a promise …

Chapter One

... *Ladies Night at the Nut Hut*

Don't get involved Tilly told me. Walk away and let other people sort out their own problems. Which is fine I suppose. If you have a heart of stone or until you find yourself confronted by Alan ... wearing a plaster over one lens of his NHS glasses and asking if you'd go along to his fiancee's hen night. Not so much asking actually as pleading.

That doe-eyed rabbit look ... albeit with one eye ... that breaks your heart and makes it impossible to refuse him anything. Alan in his anorak and Aston Villa bobble hat.

The very same Alan who only met this young woman a few months ago and after a quick shag in Tesco's car park pledged his undying love for her. I have to say I worry!

And there's the rub as they say. Alan is not my problem. I have a son of my own to worry about and apparently a mental health problem at the moment, so enough said. I truly have tried to distance myself but without much success.

The mere sight of Alan's shredded socks is enough to get me reaching for the adoption papers.

I have lost count of the times ... during our therapy sessions ... that I've had to fight the urge to grab hold of him and just give him a cuddle.

A great big chobbly cuddle just to let the lad know that somebody does care.

Except I can't. You just can't go around grabbing men and hugging them can you? He's so frail anyway that one of my crusher cuddles could kill him.

He must weigh all of seven stone ... soaking wet. See what I mean? Add to that his boils and now that bloody plaster on his glasses and well ... it speaks for itself.

I can do this for him anyway. Pitch up for Tracey's hen night. Just show willing and make a discreet exit when nobody's looking.

I've only ever seen her from a distance. Jack and I saw her collecting trolleys at the supermarket last week. She wasn't wearing a leg calliper or anything so I remain optimistic.

Just for once I want something to go right for Alan. Just once. Not much to ask is it?

After a lifetime of quite obvious despair I feel the lad deserves a break. Perhaps Tracey is it.

Maybe she's the one. The soul mate he's been searching for. Apparently she has quite a gift for oral sex so at least they should remain happy in that department. It's not something I'd normally discuss with a stranger but Alan made a point of extolling the virtues of Tracey's … erm … gift of the gob so to speak … at one of our therapy sessions. Bless him! I suppose when you're still a virgin at twenty-eight and some girl comes along and pops your cherry you're bound to get a tad excited!

Let's not go there shall we? I'm no expert. Married for almost thirty years to the same man … and I can honestly say … hand on heart … that I have only ever seen the one … erm … willy that is!

It's true! Cross my heart and call me a tart but I swear it's true. Met Jack … fell madly in love … married and remained quite content with his undercarriage thank you. I know it's twee and considered dreadfully old-fashioned but tough! Besides which, he is extremely well endowed in that department. Or so he tells me. What would I know?

Although, to be perfectly honest I suppose technically speaking I have actually seen two.

I raised a son, Tom, and he's twenty-seven now so yes, it's two. Although of course, it's been about twenty years since Tom decided he was a man and started covering himself up. Which is quite right of course.

I'm all for respecting people's privacy. God forbid that any poor unsuspecting soul should accidentally get a glimpse of my dangly bit's. That's enough to put you off dairy products for life!

So anyway ... I'm on my way to the hen night. It's only local. Although to be fair I think Tracey could have chosen a more lively venue.

We're to meet at the Nut Hut on Oakham High Street.

That's what I call it anyway. Vegetarian restaurant. Lots of bearded people, men and women wearing Shared Earth t-shirts and all that. The correct name of the restaurant is Pasta & Pine Nuts ...

***

Hmm ... are you getting my drift here? Pretentious & Pricks would be more appropriate I feel.

Don't get me wrong. If you choose not to eat anything with a face then fine. Just don't be so sodding sanctimonious about it!

Just because I enjoy the occasional steak doesn't mean I'm the devils seed, so fuck off basically! Go chew on a lentil or something instead of lecturing me on animal cruelty and showing me leaflets with baby calfs on. Like I say ... fuck off!

Not really getting the hang of this Anger Management thing am I? Hey-ho! I shall have to ask Tilly if I can have some extra sessions.

Ladies Night At The Nut Hut. This should be an experience and I'm all for trying something new.

Apart from bondage of course. I don't go there. I get claustrophobic in B&Q so the chances of me ever being trussed up in chains with a leather gimp mask on are highly unlikely.

Jack sulked for a while when I first dismissed his suggestion but he's over it now ...

"Have you got everything Cass?" he suddenly asks, pulling up outside the Nut Hut.

"Think so." I tell him, falling out of the car and landing in a heap on the pavement.

"You okay Cass?"

"Fine thanks ... just caught my foot in the seat belt."

"Call me later. I'll come and pick you up."

"Thanks."

And with that he's gone. Dashing back home to catch the last few minutes of the American Open. Tiger Woods is in a mood and lashing out at spectators.

His balls are going in all directions apparently.

What can I say? I'm married to a man who's obsessed with the sport.

A man who himself has experienced problems with his balls on several occasions. Nuff said.

***

Tracey and her hens are seated at one of the window tables. I say hens in the lightest possible sense.

There appear to be just the two of them ... and Tracey ... and me of course. Oh well here we go ... smile girl ... make it look as if you're up for this even if you'd rather be at home waxing your pubes.

"Hi Tracey, thanks for asking me." I grin, heading for the table.

She is nothing if not polite and viewing me with a certain amount of suspicion, gets up to greet me.

"Who are you?" she asks, extending her hand in greeting.

"Cassie ... erm ... Alan told me to pop along." I tell her, my face pink with embarrassment.

"Oh right, " she smiles, "Thanks for coming, Alan's told me all about you."

I plonk myself down in the one vacant seat, and find myself seated opposite an extremely elderly woman wearing one of those joke Rastafarian hats. You know ... the sort you can buy on the sea front in Blackpool.

Huge knitted contraption with yards of knotted dreadlocks glued to the base.

The word bizarre springs to mind but I hold my tongue for the moment.

"Cassie, this is Ruby my Gran." Tracey explains, gesturing over to the woman opposite.

"Nice to meet you Ruby ... nice hat!" I tell her, hoping to break the ice.

"Where's your hat?" she growls back at me, with a certain amount of menace in her voice.

This is not going well. I don't do hats. Especially ones which make me look like a fuckwit.

"Sorry ... I didn't know we were supposed to wear one." I smile back.

"Alan should have said." Tracey laughs, adjusting her policeman's helmet, "It's just for fun."

Here we go again! Poor kid. Her hen night and she seriously believes an assortment of weird hats will make the party go with a bang. Bless!

"I could have a bash at making one." I tell her, "Maybe use some of those bread sticks" ...

I am nothing if not eager to please and desperate to try and make Tracey's hen night an enjoyable one.

Lord knows Ruby's not up for it and neither is the waspish looking woman on my left.

"This is Felicity ... my social worker." Tracey informs me, as if reading my thoughts.

Oh bollocks! I've walked into a caseworker session with Social Services. Ruby is quite obviously living in sheltered accommodation and now I have Tracey's problems to worry about.

What the hell would a young woman in her twenties need a social worker for?

Drugs ... prostitution ... the mind boggles and my heart goes out to her ... and Alan. Whatever is he getting himself into?

"Felicity Farquharson actually." she snaps at poor Tracey, "Get it right you silly girl."

Fuck you Farquarhahahahahahahson! Twat! Like I said ... Anger Management not going too well at the moment. Sorry, I do try but one look at old Feliciteeeeeee and I get the overwhelming urge to kick her in the chuff.

Sorry ... that's not nice but so true. I have no idea why people like Felicity wind me up but they do. It's just that way they have of looking at other people. That patronising sneer. The nose wrinkled in disgust. Another Alicia but younger.

Ugly and bitter. Wafting their way through life ... trampling on people as they go.

She will try to put me down but I don't go there anymore. And anyway, how on earth could I be intimidated by a woman out in public wearing a Darth Vader hat?

Bet she spent hours deliberating over that one.

How inventive! A hen night and I bet she dashed into Twats-R-Us to buy that on the way here.

"Cassie." I tell her, not even bothering to extend a hand in friendship ..."Cassie Ryder."

Silence hangs heavy in the air as we eye each other suspiciously. Fliss is quite obviously used to being in control ... of Tracey and probably her Gran as well ...

... Ruby The Rastafarian. And a very disgruntled Gran at that!

If looks could kill, I would be dead right now as Ruby glares at me across the table. For fucks sake! What have I got myself into now?

***

Okay, calm down girl. Try to get things into perspective. Step into their shoes for a second.

Ruby is obviously miffed at being forced into doing Bob Marley impressions. Well, you would be at her age wouldn't you?

Tracey is out of her depth poor sod. And as for Fliss ... well ... can't be easy can it? Dandruff and a Darth Vader hat? See ... it's all making sense now.

"Shall we order...I'm starving...I could eat a horse." I waffle, trying to make conversation.

Maybe not the right expression to use whilst seated in a vegetarian restaurant. I can feel at least a dozen pairs of eyes burning holes into my back and I wish I'd kept quiet now. Oh shit!

"I don't touch animal flesh." Fliss informs me, fiddling nervously with her right earring.

An earring that could only really be worn by a vegetarian social worker. One of those dangly wire earrings with what looks like a piece of coal welded on the end. An arty farty earring, no doubt purchased from a Fair Trade shop.

She has the necklace as well. A matching set. I bet the money she paid for it was enough to provide food for a family of five in Mombassa for a year.

"I fancy a Giant Hawaiian." Ruby suddenly pipes up, taking me by surprise.

The prospect of old Ruby wrestling with a Polynesian in a grass skirt perks me up no end and I begin to relax.

Sadly, one glance at the menu tells me it's actually a pineapple platter with herbs. Not to worry, it was a jolly mental image, if only very briefly.

"I'll have the same as Gran, it looks lovely." Tracey smiles.

"Me too." Fliss chips in, "But no olives on mine thanks."

I am at a loss as to what to order. Pasta makes me gag and pineapple gives me sore gums. Even the menu itself is grey. Bit like the food.

Probably made from recycled paper of some sort.

From trees especially grown in the lower regions of the Umkoko River.

Whatever ... I appear to have a choice of black bean burgers or lentil lasagne. I can't have those ... I'd be farting for a fortnight.

The waitress is hovering in the background looking bored. I would be too, having to serve tossers like this all day long!.

I'm panicking now as all eyes focus on me, waiting for a decision.

17

I don't function well under pressure, which is the only explanation I have for what comes out of my mouth next ...

"Sirloin ... very rare ... served on a crusty bap with chips and peas please." I giggle nervously.

The sharp intake of breath surrounding me is quite audible as the other diners rise up in indignation.

Fanny Farquarrrrrrhaaaarrrr actually gasps as if she's about to keel over.

"I think you'll find most of us can't tolerate meat ... or wheat." she tells me quite sharply.

"Funny that, cos I can't tolerate people who wear cardigans knitted out of badgers hair." I snap.

I know! That was nasty and uncalled for but true! She's sitting there, wrapped up in what looks like a badgers bum-fluff jumper, telling me what I can eat!

I don't think so!

"We do a nice tofu steak." the waitress intervenes, fearing a fight may break out. Bless her.

She's trying her best and all for six pounds seventy an hour. I smile sweetly at her and turn my attention back to Fliss.

"Tell me Fliss ... what exactly is tofu?" I ask her in all innocence. I truly would like to know.

It's something that's bothered me for quite a while actually and I feel now is the time ... and the place ... to clear the matter up.

Fliss is flummoxed and it shows. Her brain is racing into overdrive. I can tell by the twitch that's developing in her right eye.

"Well ... it's a vegetable of course" ... she waffles, playing for time.

"Really? I've never seen any on the allotments ... or in Tesco." I tell her.

"No ... I ... erm ... it's more vegetable based I believe." she snaps, changing direction.

"I think it's cheese." Ruby joins in, nodding her dreadlocks vigorously.

"No ... it's definitely not a cheese." Fliss bites back at her, quite viciously I feel.

"I think Gran's right...I seen it on a menu somewhere...tofu on toast." Tracey tells her.

Fliss is obviously not used to being questioned on her knowledge of tofu and suddenly explodes ...

"For goodness sake...listen to me...tofu is not a cheese!" she bellows at the top of her voice.

Now, as far as I'm aware, vegetarians are renowned for their calm disposition. No red meat cursing through their veins and inciting them to violence. Another myth exploded!

The waitress looks close to tears and I step in to put an end to this farce. I started it so it's only fair really I suppose.

"Never mind...I'll just have a large Jack Daniels...no ice thanks." I tell her.

"Sorry, but we don't serve alcohol, just herbal teas and soft drinks." she quivers.

It gets better! No food and apparently no booze either. No wonder vegetarians look so fucking depressed!

If I'd known, I would have secreted a bottle of Jack's about my person ... an art I am quite adept at I have to say. Now it's my turn to take a deep breath and I do, while at the same time trying not to physically break down and weep into my napkin.

"No problem", I grin "I'll have an orange juice."

"Anybody else for drinks?" the waitress asks, backing away from our table.

"Mineral water all round I think." Fliss jumps in, "We none of us drink."

Oh shit! Tofu and teetotal. Any minute now I'll wake up in McDonald's with a quarter-pounder in my hand and realise all this was just a nightmare.

How do they do it I ask myself? Survive the trials of life without the odd roast beef dinner or a night out on a bender?

That's what life's all about surely? Enjoying yourself?

Were we really put here to punish ourselves? Deprive ourselves of all the lovely things that give us pleasure. Things like ... well ... fags and booze and falling over now and again after a night out with the girls.

All good clean harmless fun. Unless you're a veggie of course. I'm learning.

It takes me a while but I get there in the end. I'd like to tell Fliss to loosen her knicker elastic and live a little but now is not the right time.

This is Tracey's night after all.

"Do you drink a lot?" Farsquarrrr suddenly pipes up, smirking at me.

"Yeah loads." I tell her with a sarcastic grin.

"Mm" ... she mutters in a condescending tone, smiling knowingly at Ruby across the table.

Right, that's it! The gloves are off Fuck face! Call me anything you like but don't infer that I'm an alcoholic just because I like to enjoy life. I've lived next door to Pisshead Pete for twenty years.

I KNOW what alcoholism is!

"I'm assuming that you don't then." I snap back, daring her to continue.

"Never touch the stuff." she gloats, "It is indeed Satan's succour."

Do what? Satan's what? Oh for fucks sake ... a bloody bible-thumper as well! Here we go.

This is about to kick off big time. I'm pretty sharp where rumbles are concerned. Mainly because I seem to be in the middle of most of them lately.

"Bollocks!" I tell her, keeping the conversation short and to the point.

"Pardon?" she gasps.

"You heard, I said bollocks ... big dangly things ... bit like your earrings."

She is gobsmacked for a second and I glance across at Tracey, hoping she will not be too upset by the fracas, but oddly enough Tracey appears to be quite amused by it all. Her eyes are twinkling and her expression is one of amazement, not horror.

"I think we should say a quiet prayer." Fliss suddenly whispers, bending her Darth Vader head towards the table top.

Ruby does as she is told, her dreadlocks swiping me in the face as she lowers her head in reverence. I can see exactly where this is going. Outside ... into the car park ... with me and Darth slugging it out to the death. Sanctimonious sod!

I swore and now we all have to pray to God for my salvation!

Well I've got news for you love ... he's busy! Large amount of famine and war going on in the world. I don't think bollocks even come into it do you?

"No need to pray for me love ... he's got more important things to do." I tell her.

"The good Lord listens to all our prayers." she hisses.

"Well if that's the case I will join you." I whisper back, lowering my head,

"Dear God ... please do us all a favour and tell Felicity to fuck off!"

All this proves too much for Tracey who suddenly lets rip with a stonking great belly-laugh.

Deep from within the soul. A laugh that lights up my life and indeed the entire room. She really is a very pretty girl underneath all that shyness and deference. Enormous hazel eyes and beautiful auburn hair. Me thinks Alan may get his happy ending after all.

"Lord forgive them for they know not what they do." Old Fart face continues to herself.

Excuse me? I know exactly what I'm doing thank you! Making a stand against bossy, self-opinionated twats like you for a start!

Give me strength! And save me from these so-called churchgoers who only wear their Christianity Cardigans on a Sunday. You know what I mean?

21

Out comes the posh cardigan for church, where they ask to be absolved from all their sins, then they troll off home and behave like spiteful bastards for the rest of the week.

No thank you! If that's what being a true Christian is all about then I don't want any part of it.

I myself have an absolute overwhelming faith. I do! The difference being that my faith is in here.

Inside. I don't need a church to prove that He exists.

I'm of the opinion that you do what you can on a daily basis for your fellow man and that's about all you can do. Like The Lighthouse Family say ... he's out there doing what he's gotta do ... And I have no doubt of that. He is. Nuff said.

I think the Buddhist's have it all wrapped up actually. I like their philosophy. They believe that we all have a warrior within us. Deep down.

A warrior who can rise up and take on any challenge when called for.

Only in my case it would have to be a worrier. Imagine an army of Warriors ...

striding along, in preparation for battle. Followed closely behind by a small army of Worriers ...

"Ooh ... it'll be dark in a minute ... what was that noise?"

Something along those lines anyway. I really should stop listening to those ruddy programs on Radio 4.

That's where I get all this rubbish from. Radio 4 and the Daily Sport of course.

They do some fascinating articles on the most bizarre subjects. Elvis working in a chip shop in Clacton ... whatever ... you get my drift.

"Amen."

At last! She's finished, silly tart! Good job too as the food's just arrived.

Well, their food. I shall have to make do with a glass of juice I suppose.

"Three Hawaiians ... one no olives" ...

"That will be mine." the Reverend Felicity tells her, taking the platter.

"And mine's just the juice."

"Can I get you anything else?" the waitress asks, handing me the glass.

"No, I'm fine thank you."

Ruby still has her head lowered onto the table and the dreadlocks dangle dangerously close to her pineapple platter.

I hope she hasn't keeled over and died during the rumble. That's all we need.

A Rastafarian with rigor mortis.

My fears are unfounded as she suddenly gets a whiff of food and rallies round. Perhaps having a nap.

I bet that bloody hat's giving her a migraine. Must weigh a ton. Poor old sod.

"Delicious!" Tracey tells us, biting into a piece of pineapple.

"Scrummy!" Fliss agrees, nibbling on a tiny sliver of tomato.

My life! We appear to be having an Enid Blighton moment here. Scrummy! Do people actually use words like that any more?

Not where I come from they bloody well don't!

Reverend Rollocks would be laughed out of our chippy I can tell you.

George The Greek has enough trouble with the English language without confusing him with words like scrummy!

"So Tracey, when is the wedding?" I ask her.

"Not till September but I'm going into hospital next week for an operation."

"Oh dear."

"Wanted to get this out of the way ... give me time to recover after the op."

Blimey! Must be something serious. It's only June 24th today.

"I hope it's nothing too serious." I ask.

"Gallstones ... the lot's gotta come out ... big op they told me."

"I'm sorry ... still ... be better when it's over." I reassure her.

"Dairy products." Fliss sneers, "It's a well known fact."

"It's a wonder babies don't get them then ... since they survive on a diet of milk." I bite back.

She's ignoring me completely now. Choosing to defy the fact that I exist. Suit's me.

The sooner she fucks off back to the Millennium Falcon the better.

"They give them to you after you know." Tracey informs us.

"Really?"

"As a keepsake like."

"Maybe Fliss could have some jewellery made ... nice pair of earrings." I giggle.

Tracey giggles too and surprisingly enough, Ruby joins in ... her mouth gaping and exposing a large chunk of chewed fruit as she does.

Why do elderly people do that? Yet another one of life's mysteries that drives me mad. They chew ... and chew ... and chew ... then open their mouth for everyone else at the table to examine exactly what they've been chewing on for the past hour!

I'm not sure if it's my last comment or the sight of some severely masticated pineapple but Fliss suddenly decides she's had enough and jumps to her feet.

Feet which I might add are encased in the most hideous pair of straw sandals I have ever seen. Handmade I should think.

Probably did them while on a craft holiday in the Snowdonia mountains.

"Sorry but I have to dash ... I have Sunday School in the morning."

"Are you sure?" Tracey asks, getting to her feet.

"Positive ... thanks ... it's been nice."

Nice! Is she on drugs or something? I'd say it's been a disaster so far. What with me and her at each other's throats.

And the food. And no booze. And the bollocks bit. I can think of better words to describe this evening.

"Good night Ruby." Fuckwit Farquar snaps, her face burning with rage.

"Night."

"Night Tracey."

And with that she's gone. Wafting through the door onto the High Street in her badger jumper and straw shoes.

Rushing home to be in bed by nine after bathing her face in Witch Hazel. Sad.

She's in such a rush to escape she's forgotten the Darth Vader hat is still perched on top of her head.

That should make for a few comments when she passes the Pig & Whistle.

If Pete's outside he'll think he's hallucinating again.

***

"So Tracey what would you like to do now." I ask her.

"Not sure really ... what about you Gran?"

"Yes, do you have any ideas?" I chip in.

"Let's get pissed." Ruby suddenly says in mid-chew.

"A girl after my own heart Ruby!" I laugh.

"Gran!"

"Lighten up girl, that snotty cow will have you old before your time." she laughs

"Exactly my sentiments!"

"It's not my fault ... she latches on ... you know what she's like Gran." Tracey whispers.

I am intrigued. Here was me thinking the old Social Worker was obliged to be there as part of her professional duties but apparently not.

"What do you mean Tracey?"

"She used to be my case worker ... years ago ... when Mom died ... now she just keeps turning up."

"Bolshy bitch!" Ruby snarls through clenched false teeth.

"What a damn cheek!" I am indignant on Tracey's behalf.

No life of her own so she butts in on other people's.

"Come on, eat up Ruby ... I'll take you to a little bar I know." I tell her.

"Do they sell stout?" she laughs.

"Course ... anything you want."

"Gran, remember what the doctor said." Tracey warns her.

"Yes ... he said I'd be dead in six months ... that was two years ago ... got that wrong didn't he?"

I have to say, Ruby turns out to be a star! Several bars later and after copious amounts of stout and Jack Daniels have been consumed, I finally fall into the hallway, landing directly in line with Jack's bare feet.

He's used to me by now and simply squats on the bottom stair with an amused smile playing on his lips.

"Good night was it?" he grins.

"Excellent."

"Tracey enjoy herself?"

"Absolutely."

"Where did you end up?"

"Can't remember."

"Been dancing ... or your version of dancing?"

"Of course!"

"Where did you get that bruise on your chin?"

"Fell off the wall outside the chip shop."

"Who bought you the hat?"

"What hat?"

"The one on your head."

"Ruby the Rastafarian gave it to me."

"Bed?"

"Please."

"Spliff?"

"No thanks."

Chapter Two

... Name that Tune

He's still got that ruddy plaster on his glasses. Only now it's gone all dirty with what appears to be a tuft of cat hair stuck to it. Jesus!

What am I going to do with that lad? I lie awake at night just worrying about him and it's none of my business. He has Tracey to worry about him now. Time I learnt to butt out but every week during these sessions he seems to lurch from one crisis to another.

Last week it was yet another boil. Right smack bang on the end of his nose. I was afraid to look in case he got embarrassed.

At one point he scratched his nose and I put up my umbrella in case it burst. Poor diet you see. Leads to all sorts of problems.

Scurvy ... rickets ... he'll be in hospital before that wedding ... mark my words. Fresh vegetables. That's what Alan needs.

Plenty of roughage. That would clear his bloodstream. I shall bring him a bag of green beans and spinach next week. Tell him I grew them on my allotment. Not that I've got an allotment.

He'll never know. Sprinkle a bit of mud over them and he'll never guess.

He's making a list of some sort. Scribbling away on the back of an old lottery ticket with a pencil.

Probably the guest list for the wedding. Jack and I are invited. He gave me the invite as we came in today.

Bless him. One of those photocopied jobs that people make themselves.

It's at the Registry Office on Temple Street with a reception afterwards at the Hogs Head.

Alicia's got an invite too and since she does actually have a hogs head she'll fit in nicely. She's very quiet today.

Sitting opposite me with her standard shit face expression. Nothing changes.

Tilly hasn't arrived yet. Must be running late.

Since they are both deep in thought I might as well have a mooch round. Never really taken a good look at this room.

We just file in and file out again every week. Not much to mooch around.

Basic chairs and an oak desk with Tilly's timer on. Few magazines. An incredibly dead pot plant and a very dead wasp on the windowsill.

The usual sort of stuff. Hang on ... what's that hanging behind the door? A megaphone of all things.

How odd. Either it's for particularly hard of hearing inmates or fire and safety I should think.

"Do you have to move around so much, I'm feeling a bit delicate today." Alicia snaps at me.

"Sorry ... just bored ... not feeling well?"

"I've been awake all night with an ... erm ... upset tummy."

"You got the squit's?" Alan shouts across the room, sending her into a tizzy.

"Do you mind!"

"What?" he protests, unaware of the delicacies involved with a lady like Alicia.

"It's not the ... whatever ... it's a delicate tummy."

"I hate the squit's. Makes your bum-holey burn." He continues on full throttle.

"Alan!" Alicia Squitia screams at him.

"Especially if you've got that cheap bog roll." He elaborates.

Alicia is looking green around the gills now and I turn away in case she sees me laughing. I love that lad! He tells it like it is.

No side to that one and I like it. It's honest and quite refreshing in this day and age. What you see is what you get with Alan. Boils and all.

The devil in me refuses to lie down and without taking a breath, I grab the megaphone and raise it to my lips ...

"Attention please! Alicia's got the squit's!" I bawl ... not realising the damn thing is turned on.

My life! What have I done? Just announced at around seventy decibels that Alicia has the squit's!

I bet they heard that in the Alps. Oh my life! How awful.

"Alicia ... sorry ... I really am." I grovel.

Yet again I am saved as Tilly suddenly bursts through the door, laden down with a CD player and an assortment of boxes.

"Afternoon everyone." she smiles, depositing the heap onto her desk.

"Alicia's got the squit's." Alan informs her, still scribbling away on the lottery ticket.

"Oh ... really ... sorry to hear that." she winces.

Alicia is beside herself with shame and simply shakes her head in despair. I hang the megaphone back on its hook and smiling apologetically at Alicia, take my seat next to Alan.

"Right everyone, sorry I'm late. Been sorting out the stuff for today's session."

"I got my CD." Alan tells her, rooting around in his Lidl carrier bag.

"Good ... and how about you ladies ... did you choose a piece of music?" she asks us.

We nod and Tilly starts setting up the CD player. Music today. We were asked to select a piece of music that means something to us personally. Where do you start? I adore music.

Every variety ... Mozart to Meatloaf ... give me a beat and I'll dance to it. Well ... I'll have a damn good try.

Dancing not being one of my specialities as you know.

Although, I have to say, my Irish dancing is coming on a treat.

I've been practising in the lounge with my Riverdance DVD.

The polished wooden floor's taken a bit of a bashing but there you go.

The main problem being that Levy gets all excited during my dance sessions and invariably ends up diving onto my back and wrestling me to the floor.

For a dog, he's not a bad little mover.

Tends to slobber a lot during a salsa but there you go ... so do I.

Burning Bum-Holey has a CD in her hand, waving it about in a frenzy to get Tilly's attention.

Might as well let her go first or she'll only sulk. Tilly obviously has other ideas as she suddenly turns to Alan and gently takes the CD he's holding from his hand.

"Okay, let's start then. See what choice Alan's made." she smiles.

The CD clicks into gear and after a few seconds the familiar sounds of We Wish You A Wombling Merry Christmas blasts forth.

Bless him! It obviously has some relevance in his life.

Who are we to criticise? To each his own I say.

Alicia looks mortified. Nothing new there then. I do wish that silly woman would let go of her inhibitions and open herself up to some new experiences.

Bum Holey is quite obviously a box person.

Her whole life filed away in neat little boxes with labels on. Fuck that! No wonder she dislikes me so much. I'm a total mess.

Everything in my life is chaotic and jumbled and I like it that way! I like chaos. It keeps you on your toes.

Alan is tapping away to the beat, his fingers drumming out the rhythm on the edge of his seat.

I join in and tap along with him and before long we have quite a little jam session going.

Tilly smiles warmly at us and as the CD finishes she raises her hands and gently claps.

"Lovely Alan, what an interesting choice."

"Me Gran got it for me." he tells us, fiddling nervously with his broken glasses.

"Well tell her we all enjoyed it." I smile at him.

"Can't ... she's dead." he volunteers quite matter-of-factly.

Oh blimey! Talk about putting your foot in it! Wish I'd kept my gaping gob shut now.

"Died eighteen months ago ... found her dead in the chair." he continues.

"Sorry ... I really am." I whisper, tears welling up in my eyes.

Even Alicia looks touched, which is a first, and sympathetically nods her head at him ...

"Was it old age?" she asks.

"No ... Cadburys Creme Eggs." he suddenly blurts out.

Not for the first time am I stunned by something he's said. He comes out with the most bizarre things but this has to be the best yet!

How on earth could somebody die at the hands of a Cadburys Creme Egg?

Unless she tried to swallow it whole and choked to death.

"Sorry?" Alicia squeaks.

"She was a diabetic ... couldn't stop her eating um ... she loved the bloody things." Alan sighs.

"Oh dear." Tilly gasps.

"Easter see ... one of the neighbours gave her a boxful and she ate the lot."

"Goodness!"

"Found her in the chair...wrappers all round her feet ... diabetic coma they said." He continues.

My life! I wonder how they explained that on the death certificate? The mind boggles.

Only Alan could have a relative killed by a chocolate egg. Or a dozen chocolate eggs. Maybe more.

Those boxes hold about twenty-four I think. Nice way to go though. Better than being run over by a furniture lorry.

Things are beginning to slot into place now. Alan must have lived with his Gran. Granny Reared as Ma would say.

He's never once mentioned his Mother so I suspect my theory is true.

Raised by his Gran … hence the somewhat old-fashioned dress sense … and the lack of social skills.

I'd make a good detective. Problem is, I don't own a mac.

"Shall we press on ... time's running out?" Tilly whispers, "Alicia ... your CD?"

Bet your life it's a classical one. Something morose and dark. Something suitable for a drama queen.

True to form, Mahler's Fifth Symphony wafts it's way around the room with Alicia closing her eyes to achieve full dramatic effect.

Her fat face contorted in angst. Silly tart!

Now I quite like Mahler. I have to be in the right mood for it but I do like some of his works.

Not to be recommended if you're suicidal but in small doses it's fine.

I'm so busy concentrating on She Of The Squit's that I almost miss the fact that Alan is crying! Oh no!

I can't bear this. Switch the bloody thing off! The lads got enough problems.

I try to catch Tilly's eye to warn her but she's focusing on the notebook on her lap. Hurry up!

Finish for God's sake! He'll be swinging from the light fitting in a minute! All I can do is watch in despair as hot, salty tears cascade down his cheeks.

The one remaining lens on his glasses steaming up with the heat.

This is unbearable. Why didn't she bring something jolly along?

And in her present delicate condition Burning Ring Of Fire by Johnny Cash would be more appropriate.

After what seems like forever, the CD finally ends and I reach across and gently touch his hand. What do you do?

I can't bear to see another human being in distress. He smiles back at me and roughly wipes the snot off his nose onto the sleeve of his jumper.

Tilly finally clicks as to what's going on and offers him the box of tissues she keeps on the desk. I have a lump in my throat the size of a gob stopper and have to bite hard on my lip to stop myself from joining him.

He's a born survivor our Alan. Within seconds, he's his old self again and the matter passes without a trace ...

Apart from the trail of green snot up the sleeve of his jumper.

"Very moving Alicia ... any reason why you chose that track?" Tilly asks.

"Daddy loves it ... it's one of his favourites." she sighs dramatically.

That would be the Daddy you dumped in a rest home then? The rest home that's hundreds of miles away?

The same Daddy that you don't get time to visit? Heaven help us! The fact that you live alone and could easily take him in appears to have escaped you. I rest my case.

"I can't remember the exact segment but it's Mahler." she trills in a superior tone.

"Mahler's Fifth ... the Adagietto" ... I tell her in an even more superior one.

"Of course, it was on the tip of my tongue." she snaps.

Yeah right! I'm not fussed. I just happen to have a photographic memory where music is concerned.

Can't remember my own name most of the time but still.

"And you Cassie ... let's have your track shall we?"

Mine's nothing special. Just a particular track that I happen to play a lot. Simply Red ... the *Sunrise* Track.

It's actually the remix version at the end of the CD. For some reason it just lifts my spirit's and whenever I hear it I'm forced to hurl myself around like a lunatic, bopping away to the beat.

This fact came as somewhat of a surprise to the staff in Asda last week as I threw myself into it with a vigour amongst the feminine hygiene products.

True to form, as the rapid bass thumps around the room, I find myself on my feet and giving it large.

Oh fuck it! I'm nothing if not impulsive and far too old to worry about embarrassing myself.

Who cares? Not me for sure. And Alan certainly looks as if he's enjoying my efforts.

I grab his hand and surprisingly enough he gets to his feet and joins me. Give it some welly lad!

Let's kick Mahler up the arse and enjoy!

I don't think Tilly's ever seen anything quite like it. Her pretty face a picture of joy and fascination.

Bet she's never witnessed anything like this in her sessions. Whey-hey!

Alan is well into it now, his arms and legs jerking in spasms along with the beat. To be perfectly honest, he bears a striking resemblance to Brains out of Thunderbirds but what the heck ... at least it's cheered him up.

Old Squit shit remains rooted to the spot. Her face carved in stone.

Expressionless and unmoved. Please yourself! Brains and I are having a ball!

Sadly, the track ends before we can really get into it and as silence descends we both flop down onto our seats, exhausted from the effort.

Who'd have thought you could have so much fun in therapy?

Depression's not all doom and gloom. It's about doing whatever you can to lift yourself out of that depression. Climb your way back out of that black hole.

And if that means jigging around a Mental Health Unit on a wet Wednesday afternoon, then so be it.

"Splendid!" Tilly beams, That was most enjoyable."

"My pleasure." I tell her, panting from the effort.

"Can I borrow that Cass?" Alan asks excitedly.

"Sure, take it, I have the CD at home."

He'll be doing the clubs next. At last! We'll have this lad actually enjoying life soon.

Can't have been much fun being raised by his Gran ... assuming my theory is correct of course.

Gran's are wonderful cuddly creatures who give you Smarties and sloppy kisses. Not much use on the old Garage Music front though ... or giving a young lad street cred. I imagine Alan's street cred went out of the window when he bought that anorak.

"I was going to play my track ... Happy by The Lighthouse Family." Tilly says,

"But let's chat for a while about what makes you happy shall we?"

"That made me happy ... dancing." Alan suddenly pipes up.

"Good, I could see that." Tilly smiles.

"Buying a new hat does it for me." Alicia butts in.

"Right ... erm ... a new hat." Tilly looks stunned.

"My spirit's soar after an hour in the hat shop." Alicia crows.

"I see" ... Tilly looks perplexed.

"Christos ... at Chic in the village ... does some wonderful things with feathers." Fuckwit gushes.

What would that be then? Strip you naked and tickle your tit's with one? I doubt it somehow!

"And Cassie ... how about you?"

"Where do I start ... Mars Bars ... music ... rolling in mud with Levy" ...

"Who's Levy?" Alan asks looking puzzled.

"My dog ... black labrador."

"Does he bite?"

"Only if you bite him first." I giggle.

"Has he ever bit the postman?" Alan asks.

"No ... never!"

"I bit the postman once." he informs me quite casually.

"What on earth for Alan?"

35

"Cos he punched me in the face."

Now, I have to go there don't I? You can't just leave a statement like that hanging in mid-air.

"Goodness ... whatever for?"

"He wouldn't give me the post ... said he needed proof of me identity."

"Right ... er ... so?" I ask ... afraid of what's coming.

"I tried to grab the letters and he went mental and punched me." he laughs.

"I see."

"So I bit the bugger ... on the ankle ... right through his sock."

Okay ... let's summarise shall we. Alan wants the post. Postie refuses and punches him. Then what? Where does the ankle come in?

"Sorry ... I don't understand ... why the ankle?"

"I fell over ... when he punched me ... knocked me down onto the grass."

"Got it!"

"Bastard reported me to the Post Office ... we had to collect our post from the Esso garage after."

Oh my life! Where does all this end? What the fuck has an Esso garage gotto do with it?

"An Esso garage?" Tilly asks enthralled.

"Yeah ... Gran knew Phyllis on the pastie counter." Alan tells her.

Phyllis? On the pastie counter? I think I'm having a seizure!

"Phyllis?" even Alicia is agog now.

"She's left now ... but we've got a new postman so it don't matter." he shrugs.

Thank God! I feel quite exhausted after all that. Bloody hell ... talk about a trauma.

"Right everyone ... time's up I'm afraid." Tilly giggles.

Alicia is up and gone before we even put our chairs away. Must still be feeling crook.

Alan meanwhile remains seated and looks reluctant to leave. Bless that boy. Probably wants another session on the dance floor.

"Cass ... erm ... can I ask you something?" he stutters nervously.

"Course, ask away." I smile, scooping up my bag.

"You know about music. I need a song for the wedding...for me and Tracey to dance to." he blushes.

"You mean the first dance kind of thing?"

"Yeah ... Harry at the Hogs Head says I have to pick a song."

"Blimey Alan! There are hundreds to choose from."

"I know and I've only got a few old tapes."

"Leave it with me ... no problem ... I'll sort you something out." I promise.

"Thanks Cass."

"No worries ... is there anything else I can help you with?"

"We could do with a wedding cake" ... he suddenly says walking away.

"Erm ... okay ... fine ... leave it with me." I gasp.

"Cheers Cass! I'll tell Tracey."

And with that he leaps up and runs off to catch his bus. Tilly is waiting to lock up and smiles at me sympathetically.

"What did I tell you about not getting involved?" she whispers.

"I know ... but he's so bloody sad ... and well ... all alone."

"No he's not ... he's got you for a start off!" she laughs.

I laugh along with her as we make our way to reception. Did it again didn't I? Instead of walking away I jumped right in with both feet and now apparently have committed myself to buying a wedding cake!

At a rough guess I'd say they cost about five hundred pounds. Oh shit!

It's no good. I shall have to make them one. I can do that.

***

CAKE CRISIS I

Take 2 dozen eggs and break into bowl.
Add 6 tubs of Stork.
Mix.
Add 4 kilos of sugar.
Change to bigger bowl.
Stir in 8 kilos of plain flour.
Put welly's on.
Open litre bottle of Jack Daniels.
Throw darts at Delia's photo.
Taste mixture.
Put head down toilet bowl.
Write to Mary Berry.

***

Chapter Three

... The G Spot

I can't understand what all the fuss is about. All this uproar about The G Spot. For goodness sake! Not exactly rocket science is it? My life!

Jack discovered mine on the first night we met ... no problem!

If you believe all you read in the glossy magazines it's almost impossible to locate. What bollocks! No wonder men feel inferior and women are all under the impression that they're missing out. The power of the press you see.

A very dangerous thing. This constant barrage of pressure to perform. Ridiculous!

Sea lions perform. Humans are a far more intricate machine. Is it any wonder over half the population are taking tranquillisers?

I blame Cosmopolitan. They've got a lot to answer for.

Anyway, like I was saying ... this G spot. In my case it refers to my Giggle Spot.

Possibly the most important part of a woman's psyche.

Hit that on the button and you've got it made.

Jack has been making me giggle throughout our entire married life. Indeed, I have been known to experience several G's in one night.

I can tell you're impressed!

I don't normally do advice. Why would anyone want to take advice off me?

But ... in this case I'll make an exception.

Ladies ... look for a guy who can locate your Giggle Spot. Find that and all the rest will follow. Trust me, I know about these things. Sex is great. I'm not disputing that.

It's just that everybody seems to take it SO seriously.

I can't go there because I'm not really very good at it!

I do try but ... as with my dancing skills ... I have no sense of rhythm.

I have a theory on all this. I believe that I have a missing chromosome. The girly chromosome.

The one that gives you a natural flair for all things girly. Mine is definitely missing. I'm quite certain of that.

The female of the species is supposed to have a natural aptitude for ... well ... girly things! Dancing for one. Can't do that. And cooking. Can't do that. Knitting. Nope. Sewing. No. And shopping?

What hell on earth that is! I absolutely hate to shop! See ... told you!

There's something definitely wrong with me. I can manage the grocery shopping. That's okay.

But shopping for girly things like clothes and shoes and make-up. Forget it! Security guards home in on me as soon as I enter the store.

Probably because I'm invariably covered in dog-snot and fag ash but still.

Should I need a new outfit, Jack will come along with me and make sure I don't knock over any display stands.

I shall be needing something decent for Alan's wedding so that should be fun.

Shall have to steer clear of the Armani shop in the City Centre. I blundered into there just before Christmas and made a right prat of myself.

I'd forgotten my glasses you see and Jack went off to buy some gifts for me.

I was left with strict instructions not to wander away from the Brasserie so I just waddled along, looking in shop windows.

Well, I thought it was a charity shop. God knows why!

They're all so bloody posh now ... charity shops.

All chrome and colour co-ordinated.

Anyway, I waddled in and wafted around ... closely followed by a huge geezer in a peaked cap. I'm thinking what good quality all the gear is and piling things over my arm like a lunatic.

Trousers ... jumpers ... couple of shirts for Jack. Then I caught sight of one of the price tags!

£279 for a pair of trousers? Fuck me...things must be bad in The Third World!

Thankfully, at this point in the proceedings, Jack arrived and after he'd finished laughing he replaced all the goods and escorted me from the store.

The geezer in the peaked cap was a bit miffed as he'd obviously primed himself to pounce but there you go. Like I say ... hopeless.

I can't play the piano either but it's never held me back.

And this is my point you see. It's fine to be flawed! It is ... really!

I blame that Mrs Miniver. A generation of women raised in the belief that you simply must light your husband's pipe ... run him a hot bath ... and bake shortbread biscuit's on a daily basis.

What crap! Greer Garson has a lot to answer for in my opinion. Have you seen that film?

An entire generation did ... in the fifties ... and life has never been the same again for women of Ma's generation.

Mrs Miniver ... and this is true ... actually stands in the rubble of her bombed-out house ... it's a wartime epic of course ... and insists that everything will work out and not to be discouraged!

There's no roof for fucks sake! And everything will be alright!!!

Unbelievable! And it gets worse. Her son is sent off to war ... he's a fighter pilot of course in the RAF ... and she just waves him off with a stoic smile. Fuck that for a lark!

If anyone ... and I mean anyone ... dared to try and send Tom to war, I'd fight them to the death.

I don't care how big you are, you're not having my son! Go fight amongst yourselves and leave my boy out of it

He's almost twenty-eight and still my ovaries throb when he's within a five mile radius of home.

No wonder we are a cabbaged society. It strikes me that if you're not perfect then society considers you a reject.

Expectations you see. Too high and too many. I don't have any which helps.

Maybe I've got a few brain cells missing as well as a chromosome cos I really don't give a shit.

My clothes are always a mess. I fall over a lot ... fart at random ... and have no idea how you're supposed to apply eye-liner but there you go. I get by.

My spell at the Crumpled Clinic was caused by pressure. Pressure to achieve the impossible.

When I gave up trying to be perfect my health started to improve. Still got a fair way to go but at least I'm moving in the right direction.

"Why are you lying on your back in the middle of the lawn?" Jack asks, standing over me.

"I'm thinking." I whisper.

"Would you like a sun lounger ... be more comfortable." he asks.

"No thanks, I like looking at the cloud formations."

"Right."

"There's one over there looks just like Tony Blair." I tell him.

"Where?"

"There ... to the left of that one like a camel."

He flops down beside me and frowns as he studies the clouds whirling above us.

"It's nothing like Tony Blair ... more like Lionel Blair."

"I'm going to write to him anyway." I laugh.

"Who Lionel Blair ... whatever for ... dance lessons?"

"No idiot ... about my Crumpled Campaign."

"Do it then!" he laughs, rolling onto his back.

"I will ... I just need to think it through a bit."

"You do realise Mr Blair's no longer in charge?" Jack laughs.

"Don't care! In my book he should be!" I tell him.

This subject is a source of great amusement to Jack. My Crumpled Campaign. He has spent hours rolling with laughter at my agenda.

Well you know what they say ... he who laughs last and all that. Silly bugger!

"How far have you got with your campaign?"

"It's taking shape ... just need to tidy up some loose ends." I sigh.

"Tell me then."

"No ... you'll laugh again."

"I know, that's why I want you to tell me." he grins.

"Do I laugh at you when you think you've made a prototype for a new golf ball?"

"No."

"Well then ... don't mock."

"Yes dear."

"I've got as far as the Crumpled Cakes."

"Right."

"You know ... chocolate cakes especially made for people who feel crumpled."

"Okay."

"And Crumpled chocolate bars ... for really bad days."

"I'm with you so far." he nods.

"And the legislation of course."

"Eh?"

"Legislation...for days off work...Crumpled Days...for when life gets you down."

"And how do you think Tony will take all this?" he asks.

"Not sure ... this is a democracy after all ... we are allowed to make suggestions." I tell him.

"Old Tony will probably have a suggestion for you."

"I voted for him!" I protest.

"Yes and he's probably very grateful I'm sure."

"You won't laugh when I'm Cabinet Minister For Crumpled People."

"I think you'll find I will!" he roars, jumping to his feet.

"Cobblers!" I giggle.

"Yes dear."

Oh well. It gives me something to think about when I'm lying awake at night. That and the fact that you can no longer buy Spangles.

Why is that do you think? I used to love Spangles.

They had a unique flavour all of their own. Funny that.

Talking of funny ... Levy is grinning at me through the patio doors. When I say grinning, I really do mean grinning ...

What on earth is he doing ... daft dog?

"What's Levy up to?"

Jack is in the shed again, rooting around for some ancient golf club he can't find.

"Eh?"

"The dog ... come and see."

We both stare intently at the grinning dog. Standing stock still behind the glass. Daring us to come and give chase.

"What is he doing?" I ask again.

"He looks happy anyway." Jack smiles.

"He looks insane." I offer.

"Sounds about right."

"He's up to something. I can always tell."

"I'll go and see." Jack volunteers.

He strides off towards the house and I can hear the sounds of a scuffle, followed by Levy crashing through the back door and out into the garden.

"What is it?"

"Silly bugger's got a skull or something in his mouth." Jack laughs.

"A what?"

"I don't know, he won't let go of it ... looks like a skull of some description."

"He's been digging around in that compost heap all afternoon."

"Maybe it's human."

"Don't!" I squeal.

Jack makes a move towards the dog and at the whiff of a chase he's off, running for all he's worth.

Round and round the garden in a frenzy ... complete with the hideous grin.

Jack is nothing if not agile and finally corners The Joker with an impressive rugby tackle.

"Daft bugger ... it's a fox skull ... complete with teeth!" he laughs.

"Yuk!"

"Looks quite comical actually."

"Throw it away!"

"Spoilsport."

"Whatever will he dig up next?"

"Probably a mutant dumpling you've buried up there ... with eyes ... and a deformed head." Jack giggles.

"Fuck off!"

"Yes dear."

Chapter Four

... *Place Your Bets Please*

I can always tell when Pete's on the skids ... he rolls his own fags. And not very well I have to say.

He's sitting on the front step at the moment with what looks like a giant spliff dangling from his lips.

And when I say giant, I mean giant. It must be at least nine inches long with strands of Old Holburn sticking out from the sides.

Bless him. He tries. If that ruddy thing bursts into flames we'll have the fire brigade here again.

"Morning Pete ... you okay?"

"Fine thanks, just waiting for Gabriel to come back." he slurs, swigging a can of Magners Cider.

"Where's he gone?"

"To catch some toads up on the allotments."

"Whatever for?"

"We've got some serious betting going on later ... big money changing hands."

This should be fun! The pair of them have gone from collecting wood and delivering newspapers to the ancient art of toad racing!

Whatever next?

"Is that a new Olympic sport?" I laugh, heading up the path towards him.

"It should be ... some of those things can jump for England." he grins.

"I know. Levy loves this time of year, chasing the bloody things round the garden!" I grimace.

"Does he catch them?"

"Yes, all the time! Brings them into the house and drops them at my feet."

"They give off a vapour you know, he should be careful."

"I know but he doesn't care ... rolls them round his mouth like a marble."

"Then what?" Pete asks.

"Spit's them out ... soft-mouthed dog ... can carry anything without hurting it."

As if to demonstrate his skills, Levy gently picks up a snail, complete with shell, and catapults it against the wall of Pete's house.

It ricochets briefly before sliding ungraciously back down, landing in a crumpled heap on the flower border. No damage done. Just one extremely startled snail.

"So Pete, what's the toad racing all about?"

He smiles, an enormous sloppy grin and the mutant fag dangling from his lips falls into his lap.

"Your fag Pete" ...

"Pardon?"

"Your fag ... it's in your lap ... careful."

"Oh right." he beams, oblivious to the fact that he almost set fire to his fiddly bit's.

Desensitised is the word I'm looking for I think. His entire body numbed by alcohol. I've seen him fall off a set of ladders ... from a great height ... and just bounce back up again. He could be a stuntman with those skills.

Throw him off the top of a cliff and he wouldn't feel a thing.

And anyway, if they took him to hospital, he'd be as high as a kite on the painkillers. Yet another creature of cabbageness with all the prescribed medication he's on. He takes tablets to stop the shakes.

Tablets to stop his liver from shrivelling up. And extra strong painkillers for the hangovers.

And let's face it ... they must be pretty strong painkillers. Imagine what your head is like after just one night in the pub ... then multiply that by a million.

"Got quite a crowd coming later ... would you and Jack like to come along?" he asks.

"I'll see, Jack's got a lot on this week."

"You'd be more than welcome ... Gabriel's made a curry ... goat with sweet potatoes."

I won't even go there! Goat! My goodness, where on earth did he get the meat from?

There's a kiddies petting farm just up the road. No ... he wouldn't would he ... surely?

Slaughter an adorable pet?. Still, it could be worse.

I read somewhere once that travellers have a liking for squirrel stew.

Yuk! In Levy's case it would be called Cyril Casserole but I think even he'd draw the line at actually eating one.

"Here's the man!" Pete suddenly exclaims as Gabriel appears across the road.

He's carrying a large green bucket and a bottle of Newcastle Brown Ale.

Maybe he gets the toads drunk so that they're easier to catch.

"Any luck?" Pete asks him, peering into the bucket.

"Sure ... got about a dozen." Gabriel beams.

"Well done!"

"Nothing to it ... just blow a puff of smoke into their faces and they come quietly." he sighs.

I'm learning something new every day here! Imagine that. Blow smoke into a toads face and it surrenders. Christ!

Pete could have caught hundreds with that fag he's smoking. Wiped out an entire colony I should think. These two fascinate me they really do. Not a day goes by when I am not startled by their exploit's.

It beats living next door to an accountant I can tell you.

"I'll put them in the bath Pete." Gabriel says wandering off.

"Take my underpants out first then." Pete slurs.

"Sure ... sure" ... Gabriel smiles. His accent a soft Irish brogue.

Are you getting all this? This wonderful mental image of a bath full of dirty pants and toads?

Like I said, they fascinate me. Pete swapped his washing machine for a sandwich toaster ages ago.

Don't ask! I have no idea why. I have long since given up trying to fathom out how his addled brain works. He gets by ... sort of ... so who am I to question his reasoning?

"Better get a move on...the first race starts at six." he slurs, staggering off down the path.

"Okay Pete, might see you later."

He staggers off in the direction of the back garden, a veritable picture of well-groomed elegance.

A gold lurex shirt with shoulder pads ... psychedelic latex shorts and flip-flops with a daisy on the front.

Must be a summer sale on at Oxfam. I think Old Angel Gabriel has had quite an influence on Pete's dress sense since he arrived.

He seems to be veering more and more towards the hippy look lately.

Less formal than he used to be. A lot less formal. It's definitely an improvement on the army surplus coat and German fighter pilot helmet he wore last winter.

Are toads competitive do you think? I wouldn't have thought so myself but what do I know?

Can't imagine them getting all psyched up for the big race. Normally, they just sort of slob about don't they?

Big ... dopey ... laid-back creatures. We shall have to wait and see. Might be a few non-starters in this race I should think. As I head up the path, I can hear them both discussing the runners through the open bathroom window.

"Here's your winner Pete ... jumped out of the bucket twice." Gabriel laughs.

"He's a big bugger."

"And have you noticed ... he's only got one eye?" Gabriel points out.

"Probably been in a fight ... he'll do for me." Pete giggles.

***

49

The cars, complete with race goers ... began to arrive well before six. An assortment of clapped out bangers carrying ... well ... an assortment of clapped out bangers really. Extremely odd characters wearing all sorts of bizarre clothes. They say that like attracts like don't they?

One particularly festive fat man actually arrived in an ice-cream van, complete with jingle, and proceeded to hand out cornets to people passing by!

This came as a bit of a surprise to old Bolak who suddenly found herself the proud owner of a 99 with sprinkles. Made me laugh anyway.

Bolak's not an ice-cream sort of person and besides, vampires don't eat proper food do they?

She shoved it through the privet hedge at number nine across the way.

Probably full up after feasting on new-born babies during the night.

She's deteriorating rapidly that woman. More bonkers than ever. Last Monday I saw her talking to a wheelie-bin! I swear!

Jabbering away as if her life depended on it. Unless of course she's got some poor soul locked inside it. Nothing would surprise me with that one.

Mary tells me that Bolak's nephew has moved in to look after her. Bet the air fare from Transylvania cost a few bob.

Enough Bolaks anyway! Jack and I are here to enjoy ourselves and I don't think we'll be disappointed. Judging by this crowd, things are about to go bang.

Pete has set up an old pasting table in the back yard and it's piled high with booze. Mostly strong cider and cans of lager but still.

The curry's bubbling away on the oven and they've even invested in some plastic cutlery. I'm impressed! Who said the art of fine etiquette was dead?

"Did you slip something into my drink Cass or is this a weird dream?" Jack laughs.

"Stop it! It's not very often you get to witness a gathering like this."

"Glastonbury is probably the next best thing." he whispers.

"Only without the music."

"Have you clocked that geezer over there ... with one arm?" he nods, pointing to the kitchen.

I discreetly swivel round and scan the sea of faces crammed together in the tiny kitchen.

"Blimey ... wonder how he lost that?"

"In the war probably ... Vietnam I should think." Jack smiles.

I can see Jack's point. The one-armed bandit does indeed resemble one of those men you see on the back of a Harley Davidson.

Waist-length greasy hair, enormous beard and a tattooed neck.

He wouldn't really ride a Harley of course ... not with one arm.

"Now stay close to me Cass ... and keep your hand on my wallet." Jack grins.

"Jack!"

"Trust me ... I've just seen a woman putting Pete's alarm clock into her bag."

"Oh my life!"

"Have you got any gold fillings?"

"Stop it!"

"Keep your mouth closed or this lot will have them out in a jiffy!" he grins.

"You're scaring me now!"

"Good! Stay alert woman ... or you could end up in a trailer park in Texas!"

"Are you saying I look like trailer trash?"

"No ... you'd be the English equivalent ... caravan crap!"

It looks as if the first race is about to kick off so Jack and I weave our way through the crowd and make our way to the front.

Pete and Gabriel have constructed a sort of racetrack. A roll of plastic spread out along the lawn, running in a downward slope towards the yard.

They seem to be about to give starters orders with the toads lined up in readiness. I say lined up in the loosest possible terms.

Three are facing the wrong way and one appears to have keeled over and died.

Only One-Eyed Jack and a smaller one seem to be up for it. Chomping at the bit ... ready for the off.

"On your marks ... get set ... go!" Pete yells, falling over and the crowd roar in excitement.

I'm not sure the toads have a complete grasp of the English language as they remain rooted to the spot ... totally oblivious to the chaos around them.

The toad with one eye glares suspiciously at his rival on the left, then without any warning whatsoever, lunges forward and bites off one of its front legs.

Well! I don't know about you but I'd call that cheating. The crowd gasp in horror as the amputee keels over, his days at the racetrack over.

I think Jack was right. This is a bad dream. Maybe the fish we had for dinner was off.

We've got a man with one arm. A toad with one eye. And a toad minus a leg. Bizarre!

"Told you this could turn nasty, " Jack giggles, swigging on a bottle of beer.

"Shouldn't we do something ... I bet that bloody hurt ... having your leg bitten off!"

"What do you suggest ... making it a crutch?"

"I don't know you daft bugger ... maybe we could take it to the vet."

"Too late ... that cat from number five just ran off with it."

I do hope things improve or this could turn into a complete farce. What if all these punters demand a refund for the bets they've placed?

Jack and I saw several fifty-pound notes changing hands in the kitchen when we arrived. Gabriel appears to be in charge of the betting. He's got a wad of cash sticking out from his waistcoat pocket. A wad of cash and a carnation.

I saw him nick it out of Bolak's front garden earlier.

"Not to worry folks! The situations under control ... give us a second." Gabriel shouts.

Pete is on his hands and knees, gently begging the remaining entrants to get a move on. Sweat is seeping through the armpit's of his lurex shirt and I have to say he looks worried.

"We have a late entry!" Gabriel grins, gesturing to a figure at the back.

The crowd part and silence descends as the Vietnam Veteran suddenly moves menacingly towards the front.

He's carrying a cardboard box with air holes punctured in. What the fuck's he got in there? A rattlesnake? Oh my life!

"If this kicks off, I'll toss you back over the fence into our garden." Jack whispers.

"Cheers!"

"My pleasure."

"What about you?" I ask.

"I'll fight the geezer with the one arm ... be a fair match." he laughs.

"Prat!"

The geezer with the one arm appears to be called Vinny. It's plastered across the back of his leather jacket in metal studs.

Along with a transfer of a Kalashnikov rifle. Shit!

Vinny lowers his massive bulk onto the lawn and proceeds to open the box.

I have an awful feeling this won't be a Noel Edmond's sort of box.

We hold our breath as the lid is removed and gasp in unison as he takes out the biggest fuck-off toad I have ever seen in my life. He must have got that from Chernobyl! Only a nuclear disaster could produce such a beast. It must weigh as much as me!

If that thing comes near me I shall be forced to poke it with a large stick. Yuk!

"Ladies and gentlemen ... The Terminator!" Gabriel yells excitedly at the crowd.

Sounds about right. Terminator Toad. That bloody thing could eat the rest of the runners and still have room for a herd of gazelles.

"Blimey! It's a marine toad!" Jack whispers, taking another swig of his beer.

"How on earth do you know that?"

"Seen a programme about them on the Discovery channel." he boasts.

"Really?"

"Certain ... they can grow to the size of a large rat some of them."

This man never ceases to amaze me. His fountain of useless knowledge is unbelievable.

"And I thought you stayed up late at night to watch the porn channel." I grin.

"I do ... but you only ever get to see the first few minutes of those."

"That long eh?"

"Well ... maybe sixty seconds at a push." he boasts.

"Daft bugger!"

"I did last for four minutes one night but I had a head cold."

"Too much information thank you!" I laugh, ruffling his hair.

***

Poor old One-Eye Jack ... doesn't stand a chance against The Terminator.

There's always someone harder around the corner. You think you're the cock of The Cedars and along comes somebody even bigger and with more street cred.

I'm slightly miffed at this late entry. I've got a fiver riding on One-Eye Jack.

"Place your bets please!" Gabriel shouts to the stunned spectators.

The stampede that follows is laughable to say the least. A veritable crush of people all clamouring to place their money on the late entry.

I shall stick with the underdog ... or should that be underfrog? Who knows?

"Quiet please ... we're on the off!" he yells again, as the two toads are lined up at the start.

I can't bear to watch and close my eyes as Gabriel raises his hand in the air.

"On your marks ... get set ... go!"

The crowd cheer and I am forced to watch, caught up in the excitement of it all. T.T as I shall call him, takes the lead, lurching forward like a grotesque gargoyle, his eyes protruding with the effort.

Poor old Visibly Impaired remains behind briefly, probably shit-scared to get too close in case T.T gobbles him up. When this race is over, I shall make a run for it and put One-Eye Jack somewhere safe.

I wonder if there are any rescue centres for disabled toads?

"Come on Terminator!" Jack bawls into my ear, sending me deaf for a second.

"Come on Jack!" I bawl back.

"Eh?"

"One-Eye Jack ... the little guy." I tell him.

"Oh right."

***

After a slow start, the little guy seems to gird his loins and suddenly takes a leap onto the plastic sheeting. Not a giant leap I have to say but a leap all the same. T.T meanwhile is already half way down the track and heading for home. That was a fiver wasted. Jack won't mind ... I robbed it out of his wallet ... the one he asked me to keep a hand on.

"That bloody things been trained for this." I moan to anyone who will listen.

"I don't think there is such a thing as Toad Training Cass." Jack informs me.

"Well, he seems to know his way around a racecourse." I bite back.

"Cass ... it's a piece of plastic sheeting!" Jack grins.

"Yes, well."

"Now ... now ... don't be a bad loser." he laughs.

"I haven't lost yet!"

Although it's not looking good I have to say. T.T is almost at the finishing line and will be crossing the coloured tape at any minute I fear.

Pete is beside himself with excitement and makes the mistake of attempting a victory leap into the air. His drunken body is far too weak for this and he suddenly topples over, landing face first in the privet. Nothing new there then.

Except that the privet is bordering our garden and as he crashes through to the other side, Levy is alerted to an intruder and jumps the hedge in what can only be described as a magnificent athletic leap.

His entire body taut and straining with the effort. If I were watching this on TV I'd think it was the 4.30 at Aintree.

What follows next can only be described as a farce ... with my beloved boy as the main player.

Pete remains wedged in the hedge. Vinny is knocked onto his ample arse by people running to get away and as a finale, Levy snatches The Terminator and runs off onto the allotments.

Oh my life!

Pandemonium ... that would be an accurate word. Absolute, bloody pandemonium!

See, I'm used to Levy. I know he's quite harmless and would categorically trust him with my life

But these poor sods ... well ... can't say I blame them. The sight of a ninety-pound black beast, hurling himself over the hedge and running amok in a small garden must be terrifying.

Jack and I watch ... half in horror and half in amusement as several race goers skid unceremoniously down the plastic racetrack.

First past the post appears to be an extremely obese woman in a shell-suit, followed closely by a man in a trilby.

"Jack ... do something!" I bawl, terrified somebody will be killed in the fracas.

"Like what?" he laughs, his face crumpled with glee.

He's got a point I suppose. What do you do? Levy is half way up the M6 by now with The Terminator wedged firmly in his jaws. Pete's past caring and remains comatose in the hedge.

And Gabriel appears to find it all highly amusing anyway.

"That'll be a non-runner then. I declare the only remaining toad...the winner!"

Well I'll be buggered! Old One-Eye Jack did it after all! I knew he was worth investing that fiver in.

Wonder what the odds were? Could be in for a nice little earner here.

"There you go Cassie...that's twenty-five pounds you've won." Gabriel smiles, handing me a wad of crisp five pound notes.

"Thanks!" I beam, thrilled at my winnings.

"No...thank you...I'd have lost a fortune if The Terminator had won." he grins.

"Sorry about Levy ... he gets carried away." I grovel.

"No problem ... I owe him one." he laughs.

It takes a while before the chaos subsides and Jack and I watch fascinated as people pick themselves up and carry on as if nothing had happened.

The man in the trilby is demanding a stewards enquiry and even Pete fights his way out of the hedge and back to the booze table.

Gabriel decides to call it a day where racing is concerned and starts up a tune on his banjo.

Within minutes, people are jigging around the garden in various states of shock and undress.

Several have lost shoes in the stampede but it doesn't seem to deter them.

"You dancing?" Jack asks, heading for the lawn.

"You joking?" I laugh, not wishing to show them all up with my incredible dancing skills.

For a brief second, I think that the early evening sun is dispersing but on closer inspection realise the shadow is being cast by Vinny.

Oh fuck! I'd forgotten about him ... and his toad.

He appears to be heading towards Jack and I fear my head butting skills may be called for.

I've never seen Jack run away from anything in his life but in this case I feel he should make an exception.

I am just about to tell him so when Vinny catches up with him.

"Was that your dog pal?" he asks in a menacingly quiet voice.

"Yeah, sorry" ... Jack answers, looking him squarely in the eye.

"Never laughed so much in my life! Can I get you a beer?" he chuckles.

I fear I shall have to go home. A change of underwear may be required. Talk about a close call!

For a brief second there I thought it was all about to kick off and I'm certain that even with one arm, Vinny could take on all comers.

"Best party I've been to in ages!" Vinny chortles, still rocking with laughter.

"But what about your toad?" Jack asks him.

"He can look after himself. I've got three Rottweilers at home."

I really do have to go! My beloved boy running amok with a frog that can frighten a Rottweiler!

What if he swallows it and chokes to death? Oh my goodness!

I'm moving now as fast as my little legs will carry me. Heading for the allotments and lord only knows what.

I know he's up here somewhere. I can hear his tail swishing in the undergrowth. That tail is quite capable of knocking a pensioner over and when he's extremely excited it rotates at about a hundred revs a second.

True to form, I find the Toad Thief lying on his belly in the bushes.

The Terminator squatting directly opposite with a vicious glint in his eyes. It's a standoff and at this precise moment I'm not sure who I'd put my money on. Levy has the bulk and the strength of course but the toad has the experience. Living with three Rottweiler's must be a daily fight for survival.

"Leave it!" I bawl at him in the sternest tone I can manage.

He cares not a jot and edges closer to the toad with a devilish glint in his eye.

The prospect of munching on two pounds of toad too much to resist.

His enormous pink tongue lolloping out of the side of his mouth like a giant slice of honey-cured ham.

"Come on lad!" a gentle voice whispers over my shoulder and as ever, all is forgotten at the sound of His Masters Voice.

God that infuriates me! How does Jack do that?

"Come on Cass, the party's moving on to The Angel on the High Street."

He strides off with a disgustingly obedient labrador walking to heel by his side.

"What about the toad?" I yell, running after him.

"He'll never get in without a tie on." Jack grins.

***

Chapter Five

... One Cool Cat

This was inevitable I know but it doesn't make it any easier. Bilbo is dead.

No more prowling the lanes for him. No more attempts to rip my throat open!

No more frenzied fights from which he always emerged the victor.

Dead but not yet buried I'm afraid. Mary's in hospital, recovering from a cataract operation and when I broke the news to her she insisted that the burial be held off until she comes out.

Bless her! She loved that cat with a passion and I fear her life will be even emptier without him.

It's probably a blessing that she was away when he died. Considering the circumstances.

He was deaf you see. Obviously didn't hear it coming. The Co-op milk float that is. My only consolation is that it was all over in a second and I imagine death was instantaneous.

The milkman wasn't too pleased though. Several pints of semi-skimmed got broken on impact. And a dozen free range eggs.

The vet very kindly offered to keep Bilbo until Mary got home. She's due back tomorrow so I'm on my way to collect the ... erm ... deceased so to speak.

Trouble is, Jack's been called away to Kensington so I'm on the bus.

He left me the money for a cab but I spent it on some flowers for Mary.

Well, for Mary and the burial actually. She's bound to want to do things properly.

I do hope the bus back is empty. It's bloody hot today. Bilbo could start to decompose.

I've left Levy at home of course. He sulked, but one mention of the word vet and he ran and hid under the table.

I couldn't handle him ... and a long bus journey ... and a dead cat.

Here we go! Gird your loins girl and try not to cry again. Why do we do it eh?

Open up our homes and our hearts to creatures who go and die on us?

I'm no good at this. I cry at that RSPCA advert on television.

Beccy will understand. She's been working on reception for years and has seen me in floods of tears on numerous occasions. I even blub when other people's pets look sick in the surgery. Focus now! Get a grip woman!

"Morning Beccy ... I'm here to collect Bilbo." I tell her, hovering at the desk.

"Hello Cassie ... Levy okay?" she grins.

"Yes fine thanks."

"Mr Orchard managed to mend his glasses." she laughs.

"Oh thank goodness ... that dog's so clumsy." I nod.

"I'll go and get the cat." she smiles, disappearing into the back room.

How embarrassing! I was hoping they'd have forgotten about that incident.

Ruddy dog knocked the vet over and his glasses got broken in the fracas that followed. I was mortified and Jack offered to replace them but everyone was very kind. To his credit, Mr Orchard just sighed and even gave the boy a doggy treat as we left.

Jack said it was a cyanide pill but I beg to differ.

The vet loves Levy. And I think ... deep down ... Levy loves the vet as well.

I can hear giggling coming from the room at the back and marvel at how these girls keep smiling with all the traumas they witness every day.

I couldn't do it. One stiff spaniel and I'd be gone.

Beccy emerges finally, carrying a large cardboard carton and some paperwork.

"He's in here." she stutters, her face blotchy with embarrassment.

"You okay Beccy?" I ask, puzzled by her behaviour.

"Sorry ... we shouldn't laugh but" ... she giggles, her voice trailing off to nothing.

"That's okay ... I'm an incurable giggler myself ... what is it?"

"It's the cat ... he's ... take a look, " she titters, opening up the carton.

Oh my life! Now I see what all the hilarity was about. Bilbo appears to have been frozen. Stiff!

His face completely frozen into a horrendous petrified grin. With one ear pointing rigidly up to heaven.

Oh Christ! I know they said they'd keep him chilled for hygiene purposes but this is taking it a bit too far.

Some prat must have put him into the freezer by mistake!

"I'm sorry Cassie ... this is very unprofessional of me but" ... she laughs.

"No, honest ... it's okay ... I see what you mean." I giggle.

"The chiller unit is on the blink ... so sorry."

"Don't worry, I'll just have to thaw him out at home." I reassure her.

"Would you like to leave him with us. Until he's ... melted." she roars, collapsing with glee.

"No ... Mary's coming home tomorrow. I can sort this out. No worries."

"Sorry." she whispers, trying to regain her composure.

"Stop apologising ... it will be fine."

"Can you manage?" she asks handing me the box.

"Yes thanks, if you could just open the door for me please."

"Course ... mind how you go."

"Thanks Beccy."

"Bye."

Not only is Bilbo frozen but he weighs a ton now. I've carried frozen turkeys home at Christmas that have weighed less. Wish I'd kept that cab money now.

Now I'll have to wait probably an hour for the next bus. Oh shit! Hope he doesn't start to thaw out yet.

The bus will be awash with water. People will think I've wet myself if I leave a puddle on the floor. This just gets better and better. Hang on, here's a 29 ... that will do ... at least it takes me most of the way home.

Just one empty seat at the front. Have to pop the carton on the pushchair rack. Be out of the way there.

I slump down and try to regain my strength for the walk when I get off the bus.

It's quite a way but rather that than standing around waiting.

Calm down girl. Take a deep breath.

You can deal with this. By the time Mary arrives home tomorrow it will all be sorted. Quick burial and a sponge fancy and it will all be over.

She insisted that we have a bite to eat after.

I tried to dissuade her but she was having none of it. It was all I could do to talk her out of laying on a full funeral tea!

Boiled ham rolls and a sweet sherry and all that.

As the bus pulls up I struggle to remain upright with the weight of the carton and the cat.

Things are not helped by the driver who pulls off before I've even got both feet on the pavement. The age of chivalry is indeed long since dead!

Arsehole! I know you've got a timetable to stick to mate but if you hadn't spent ten minutes reading The Sun at the crossroads you'd be on time now.

Bilbo and I take our last walk together towards home. I say walk but it's more of a stagger really.

What must I look like? Drenched in sweat and weaving about like a drunken sailor?

It's the weight of the damn thing! Every time I think I've got it balanced I veer to the left.

Oh fuck it! This cat was a nightmare when he was alive ... now he's exactly that dead.

Sorry. Ma is always telling me not to speak ill of the dead. Like they care!

By the time I reach home I feel physically ill. What a wimp! My head is pounding ... my feet hurt and I have a blister on my hand from the handle on the carton. Oh ... and a nasty cut on my knee from the fall ... the second time ... I landed on the grass the first time.

Levy is intrigued by the carton and its contents, frantically racing round the house in anticipation of a new toy.

"You can't play with Bilbo ... he's dead ... and frozen." I tell him, putting the carton in the porch.

He's not impressed. I have seen him play with dead birds for hours. Gently nudging them up the bum with his nose in an effort to inject some life into the game.

"Now have some respect ... we've got a stiff in the house tonight." I tell him.

That's a thought. A whole twenty-four hours before the burial and that box is cardboard!

What if it gets soggy? What if the deceased drops to the floor when I pick it up.

Oh my life! How do I get myself into these situations?

Jack won't be back until late tonight and it's about 70 degrees out in the porch.

Better enlist the help of Pete. Never thought I'd hear myself say that.

Hey-Ho!

"It's Cassie...can you help please...I need you to make me a ... erm...coffin."

There is a pregnant pause as his soggy brain tries to digest this information.

"Is this a wind up?" he slurs, the familiar voice awash with whisky.

"Honest ... long story ... Bilbo's back from the vets and Mary wants to bury him tomorrow." I explain.

"Is he dead?"

"Course he's dead. Don't you remember the milkman ran over him?"

"Unigate?" he slurs."

"No! ... does it matter ... he's dead!" I bawl down the phone.

"That Unigate bloke's a menace ... always speeding he is." Pete adds.

"Anyway ... can you help?" I plead.

"No problem. How big a coffin do you need?"

For fucks sake! What does he think I'm burying?

"Look Pete ... listen carefully ... it's a cat ... average size ... I'll leave it with you."

"Okay Cass ... Gabriel and I will have a bash. I'll pop it round later."

"Cheers Pete. I appreciate it."

Now I have a migraine. Along with a blister and a cut on my knee. Better go and lie down for a while. Try to shake it off.

Got plenty of time before Jack is due home.

Sleep does not come easily as I toss and turn and fret about tomorrow. I do hope it all goes to plan for Mary's sake.

That cat has been her only companion for about ... let me think ... at least a hundred years. It seems like that anyway. Bilbo and his bed in the lavender bush.

His bad attitude and bad breath. His tendency to go for your throat if you disturbed his nap.

We shall miss the old man. So I imagine will the female moggies in this area. He's probably sired a million kittens over the years.

Mary would never have him neutered. She said it was nature's way.

Probably because she's a staunch Roman Catholic. God forbid that the Pope should get wind of the fact that her pussy had been interfered with ... if you get my drift.

***

"Cass ... have you upset the neighbours again ... there's a coffin on the front step?" It's Jack, finally home from work.

"It's for Mary" ... I waffle, still half asleep.

"You'll never get her into that, it's too small." he laughs walking away.

***

He was quite right. It is too small. Too small even for Bilbo. We've managed to get most of his body in but his front paws are sticking out of the lid.

Pete suggested we ... well ... sort of snap them to get them inside but I couldn't do it. How horrendous would that be? He's still sodding stiff that's why! You'd think he'd have thawed out by now after a whole night defrosting in the porch but no.

Stiff as a board! My life! Will this farce never end? Jack's been called out again to an emergency so it's just me ... an extremely sozzled Pete ...and one very cool cat. Literally!

Mary's back home. The ambulance bought her about half an hour ago. I rang to say we'd be over soon. In the meantime, Pete and I have to try to figure out how to make the deceased look dignified.

We stand in silence, gazing down at the macabre sight in front of us.

"Looks odd ... as if he's trying to claw his way out." Pete hiccups.

"That bugger probably will. He'll come back and haunt us for this!" I cry.

"We could put some socks on him. Tell Mary it's bandage. She'd never know."

"What an excellent idea. I've got some little ankle socks somewhere, we'll use those." I laugh, running off to find them.

Five minutes later we're at Mary's door. Complete with coffin ... flowers ...and a dead cat wearing lemon ankle socks.

Pete has made a special effort with his clothes and gone for a suitably dignified pair of black trousers and a black Ozzy Osbourne t-shirt. Thank god Mary's recovering from eye surgery. With a bit of luck she won't notice. To give you a rough idea of just how bad her eyesight is at the moment ... when I went to visit her a few days ago ... a nurse had left some of those cardboard pee-trays on the bedside locker.

Mary was wearing them on her feet. A fact that proved to be a source of great amusement to the other patients.

I swapped them for her slippers. When I left, she was doing the crossword with a thermometer.

She slowly makes her way towards the garden, with Pete and I following behind in silence.

Pete is carrying the coffin and I the flowers. Thankfully, it's not raining or this would turn into a real farce.

We hold our breath as she negotiates the steps down onto the lawn, both of us primed and ready to catch her should she fall.

"I thought here ... underneath the lavender bush." she smiles, her eyes filling with tears.

"Lovely spot Mary ... he'd like that." I tell her.

"I'll get the spade." Pete volunteers, lowering the coffin onto the lawn.

Poor old girl needs some support, so I edge closer and link arms with her just in case.

"Never mind Mary ... he had a wonderful life." I whisper, taking her hand.

"I can't believe he's gone." she sobs, her frail body shaking with emotion.

"I know ... I know."

"He was a tough old thing ... thought he'd outlive me." she wails.

"Well, I suppose in cat years he was about a hundred and seventy six." I smile.

She smiles back and I bite down hard on my lower lip as one solitary tear rolls down her cheek.

"The pain now is part of the happiness then" ... she whispers, "That's the deal."

Oh my life! That's it! I'm gone now ... floods of tears cascading down my face and onto my chin.

C.S. Lewis! I knew I recognised that quote. And he was so right! It is a deal! You have to take the pain on someone's passing ... sort of a trade-off for all the good times you shared when they were alive.

Yet another reason why Mary and I rub along so well, our mutual love of literature.

She may be fuddled and frail but the spark's still in there somewhere.

"Couldn't find a spade ... will this do?" Pete slurs, holding an ice-cream scoop in his hand.

"Yes fine Pete, just do what you can." I tell him, wiping several yards of snot off my nose.

We watch in reverence as he drops to his knees and begins scrabbling in the soft earth, creating quite a deep hole considering the sub-standard tool he's using.

Thankfully, it's a metal ice cream scoop.

A plastic one would be of no use whatsoever.

"That should do it." he suddenly announces, staggering to his feet.

"Thank you Pete ... very kind." Mary tells him.

"Let's lower him in shall we ... then Pete can cover him up" ... I smile at her.

"Best get it over with."

I have to say, it's at times like this that Pete shows what he's really made of. Within minutes he has Bilbo beneath the soil and the flowers placed gently onto the freshly dug earth.

Mary seems reluctant to move away so we stand in silence, waiting for her to make a move. The silence obviously proves too much for Pete, who suddenly clears his throat and decides to launch into the first few bars of Old Man River of all things. My life! Where did that come from?

"He just keeps rolling ... don't know where he's going ... keeps on flowing" ... Oh fuck! He's got the words all wrong but it's nice thought I suppose.

"Keep them dawgies rolling ... Rawhide!!!!"

Oh my life! He's changed course completely now! Where will he go to next I wonder?

Even Mary's beginning to look a tad bemused at this outburst, a faint smile playing on her lips.

"Thanks Pete...that was lovely." I lie, stopping him in mid flow before he goes completely mad.

"Yes thanks" ... Mary giggles, her mood lifted completely now.

Bless him! What would we do without that man?

Gentlemanly as ever, he softly takes Mary's arm and leads her back into the house.

His giant form shadowing her tiny frame as they shuffle along together. See, we get by!

It might seem like complete chaos at times but we get by.

"I'll be off now, Gabriel's doing a portrait at two" ... he informs us.

"Pardon?"

"Gabriel ... he's doing charcoal portrait's ... got some bloke coming for a sitting." Pete tells us.

"I didn't know he was an artist!" I exclaim, surprised by this new revelation.

"He's not ... he's done seven so far and they all look like Winston Churchill." he laughs.

"Oh dear."

"Would you like yours done Cass.?"

"No thanks ... I already bear a striking resemblance to Winston Churchill thank you." I giggle.

He lollops along the hallway and disappears out of the front door leaving Mary and I to tuck into the sponge fancies.

Several plates of sponge fancies actually. And an arctic roll.

69

"What's he doing in Oakham?" Mary suddenly asks me, mid-bite.

"Sorry?"

"Winston Churchill ... Pete said he was coming at two" ...

***

Chapter Six

... *Unidentified Flying Footwear*

Pa just rang from the hospital. Ma's been rushed into casualty and for the life of me I couldn't make out what he was saying. It was very garbled.

He sounded distraught! Oh my life!What on earth's wrong with her?

She was fine when I rang this morning. In the middle of a batch of lemon fairy cakes actually. They were supposed to be going to a fund raiser at the British Legion.

Please God don't let it be her heart. Let her survive until I get there. Please!

I'm running now which is unusual for me. Running so fast I shall probably end up in the Coronary Care Unit myself!

Don't let her die! I promise I'll stop taking the piss out of people God.

Just let her be okay!

These places are like meat markets. Hundreds of bodies lying around in various states' of undress.

Where is she? Oh my life! That bloke over there's got a can-opener sticking out of his chest!

That'll be a domestic. You can always tell.

"Tinned pears or peaches?"

"Haven't you got any mandarins?"

Not a good idea! Hassling a woman when she's hot in the kitchen. And holding a sharp object.

Where are they for goodness sake? Have I got the right hospital? I'm sure Pa said he was at The Royal Victoria.

Hard to tell what he was saying really, it sounded like he was cracking up.

I'd like to ask someone but there's a three-mile queue at the desk. What the fuck is going on?

Has there been a pile up on the M6? Never seen so many sick people in all my life. The neon waiting sign is flashing four hours!

God help you if you've had a stroke or some massive internal bleed.

Be dead before dark I should think.

"Cassie!"

"Pa! What on earth's happened? Where is she?" I wheeze, my lungs gasping for air.

"She's over in that cubicle. Sorry if I frightened you." he laughs.

"Don't be silly, what is it?

"I ... oh dear" ... he waffles, quite obviously finding it hard to put into words.

"Oh no! Pa ... don't!" I scream, fearing the worst.

"Cassie calm down! She'll be fine." he suddenly blurts out, taking my hand.

"What is it then?"

"She ... er ... sorry ... she got hit by a flying welly!" he roars, bursting into a fit of giggles.

"Eh?"

"A welly...at the fund raiser...they had a welly wanging contest and she got in the way."

"My life!"

"Sorry ... I know it's not funny." he chortles, his face red with the effort.

"Pa!"

"Clonked her right on the bonce!" he titters, incapable with laughter now.

"Stop it!" I laugh, giving him a hug.

"The Tug-O-War Team carried her off the field." he adds as an afterthought.

I slump down onto one of the vinyl chairs and try to regain my composure. My heart is pounding ... ditto my head ... and my kidneys appear to have jumped up into my throat. For a brief second then, I thought she was gone, and the all-consuming panic that engulfed me was quite shocking.

Thank goodness she's okay. Well...sort of. Better to be hit by a welly than a total cardiac arrest.

"Can I see her?" I ask, smiling at his bemused expression.

"Sure, straight through here, come with me." he grins, gesturing to a row of cubicles.

I follow, taking several deep breaths in the process. Don't want Ma to see me in this state.

"She's a bit bruised but she'll be fine." he tells me, pulling back the curtains to reveal a rather startled old man having his piles swabbed.

By an equally startled charge nurse I have to say.

"Sorry!" Pa blushes, closing the curtain again.

"Pa!"

"So sorry." he stutters.

"Which cubicle is she in Pa?" I ask him, exasperated.

"Sorry ... they all look the same don't they?" he wails.

We are confronted by a sea of identical cubicles and I see no other way for it than to improvise.

"Ma!!!!!" I yell at the top of my voice, knowing she will respond to her child in distress.

"Is that you Cassie?" a tiny voice answers from within the cubicle to my left.

"Thank goodness!" My tactic worked.

"Here she is." Pa beams, pulling back yet another curtain to reveal Ma flat out on the bed.

She is indeed bruised. A corker of a bruise stretching from her forehead right down her cheek to the bottom of her chin. A bright purple bruise which I imagine will look worse by tomorrow.

For some strange reason, the welly is sitting on a chair by the bedside. Come to bring grapes probably.

"Ma ... are you okay?" I cry, throwing myself on the bed.

"Stop fussing Cassie ... your father made them bring me ... you know how he panics!"

"Head injuries are nasty Ma ... you have to get checked out."

"Out cold she was." Pa informs me, fiddling with the radio headset on the wall.

"I was not!" she yells, " Just stunned for a moment!"

"I bet you were ... being smacked in the head with that thing." I sympathise.

"HE bought that along!" she barks, " How embarrassing!"

"I thought they'd need to see what caused the injury." Pa mutters, tuning into Radio 4.

"Yes well ... fetch my clothes Cassie ... I'm getting out of here!" she yells.

"Ma, you can't ... they might want to keep an eye on you." I plead.

"Your father can keep an eye on me!" she roars indignantly.

I have long since learnt that it's impossible to get Ma to do anything she doesn't want to do.

Years of experience have taught me to keep quiet and just go with the flow. Fighting against her inevitably means a futile battle, with everybody involved exhausted from the effort.

"Find my underclothes Cassie!" she yells, getting hysterical.

"Okay Ma, calm down!"

"Lying here with all my privates exposed ... it's not nice!"

"Ma" ...

"Why they deemed it necessary to remove my pants ... well really!" she snaps excitedly.

"They have to give you a thorough going over Ma." I whisper, trying to reason with her.

"It was a bang on the head ... not a dropped uterus!" she bawls back.

Told you didn't I? This could turn nasty at any minute. God help any doctor who sees fit to take on Ma.

She is indeed a very private person ... especially where her privates are concerned. It's a generational thing ... women of Ma's age ... a generation raised on the motto Keep Your Hand On Your Halfpenny, which roughly translated means never expose your snatch to a stranger. Something along those lines anyway.

Women of Ma's age keep everything wrapped under several layers of Damart.

No lycra thongs on her washing line I can tell you. Just plain, white, pure cotton ... with especially reinforced gussets.

"I'm just going to take a look at your x-ray then we'll have a chat." a voice suddenly pipes up from behind me.

A doctor ... and a friendly one at that ... emerges from outside the curtain, holding a set of x-rays in one hand and a ham roll in the other.

"Yes well ... I have to get home ... if you could hurry it up." Ma glares at him.

"No problem, be back in a jiff." he smiles, biting hungrily into the roll.

He disappears again and Ma sighs, exasperated with all the fuss.

I follow him discreetly, hoping to have a quiet word and hurry things along. When I catch up with him he's surrounded by medical students, all staring intently at Ma's x-ray, illuminated now on the machine high up on the wall. I sneak up behind them and watch, fascinated, as he describes the injury and the necessity to x-ray the chest area for trauma injuries. From the fall apparently.

Welly wangs onto head ... Ma falls over ... x-ray required, bearing in mind her age and the force of the impact.

Sounds reasonable enough to me. Bruising extensive on right shoulder.

No fractures. Chest cavity clear. Hang on! What the fuck's that? Great bigmass on the left side!

Oh my life! It's a tumour! Am I the only one to have noticed it? Oh Ma!

"Look!" I bawl hysterically at the startled group, pushing myself forward.

"What's that?"

A kindly looking Chinese student ... a young girl of about twenty ... looks at me sympathetically ...

"That's the heart" ... she smiles, believing I have wandered down from the psychiatric ward.

"Oh right ... well done ... carry on!" I waffle, trying to melt back into the group.

Phew! That's a relief! Thought I'd spotted something sinister then. With an air of total disregard, I waft along the corridor, hoping nobody has called security.

Ma is still lying agitated on the bed.

Pa meanwhile continues to listen to Radio 4.

"Everything looks okay Ma, you'll be home soon." I tell her.

"Did you find my pants!" she bawls, losing the plot ... she's never at her best while knickerless.

"Sorry, no ... I was looking at your x-rays." I stutter.

"Dum...de...dum...de...dum...de...dum." Pa sings, tuning into the Archers.

This is not looking good. I fear that blood will be shed very soon if she's forced to remain confined to this cubicle.

Ma is a no-nonsense ... no-fuss ... I can cope kind of woman. The fact that she has just been rendered unconscious by a low-flying welly is of no consequence to her.

Crikey ... the Luftwaffe tried to dive-bomb her in the war and they came unstuck as well!

Take more than an item of footwear to finish Ma off.

"Best if we keep you in overnight ... just to make sure" ... a voice says.

The doctor's back ... minus the ham roll. He's got a pork pie in his hand instead now.

"Only for observation. Head traumas can be unpredictable." he grins.

Ma can be unpredictable as well ... a fact he is about to find out I fear.

"Have you got my pants!! she roars at him, taking him completely by surprise.

"Ma!"

"I ... erm ... no" ... he stammers, shoving the pork pie into his pocket.

"Well somebody has!" she rants, losing the plot completely.

"I'll ask the nurse." he grovels apologetically, disappearing through the curtain again.

"Ma! He's doing his best. Stop fretting about your pants. We'll find them."

"Fa...le...la...le...la...le...la" Pa croons, blissfully unaware of the fracas going on around him.

A fist fight is avoided by a young student nurse, who suddenly pops her head through the curtain and hands me Ma's pants ... along with the rest of her clothes ... in a green plastic bag.

"There you go ... we'll be taking you to Perranporth in a minute." she smiles.

"Eh?"

Without any explanation, she disappears again, leaving us puzzling over her last statement.

"That's in Cornwall isn't it?" Ma trembles, even more agitated now.

"No idea ... what on earth did she mean?"

"They're not transferring me to the coast. Pass me my things Cassandra ... I'm off!"

"This is ridiculous!" I cry, almost hysterical myself.

"I know there's a bed shortage but ... who'll look after your father?" she cries, leaping off the bed.

"Calm down! I'll go and find out what's going on."

Before I can do just that, a porter arrives with a wheelchair and a copy of Razzle in his top pocket.

Ma is caught unawares, struggling to get back into her pants as he casually whips the curtain aside.

"Oops ... sorry Madam ... Perranporth Ward?" he trills.

Mystery solved! Maybe this wing has all its wards named after Cornish resorts.

For a second there, I had visions of Ma being forcibly strapped inside an ambulance, heading up the M5.

"Come on Ma ... let's get you settled." I tell her, gently guiding her into the wheelchair.

Her rage has diminished somewhat now and been replaced with shame.

In over fifty years, Pa has been the only man allowed the privilege of seeing Ma's pants. Until now! She is mortified and it shows.

It could take a while before she recovers from this. I follow as the porter wheels her slowly towards the lift. He is doing his best to make conversation but she's having none of it.

In Ma's day, if a bloke saw your knickers you were considered engaged. She is livid I know, but keeping it under the surface for now!

"Pa!" I bellow, trying to attract his attention. He's well away now, somewhere in Ambridge.

"Sorry Cass ... where's your mother?"

"On her way to Perranporth!" I tell him, grabbing his hand and dragging him along behind me.

The ward appears to be quite busy with an assortment of medics and nurses rushing around attending to the patients. Every bed is occupied.

By women and men!

A mixed ward! Ma will not be pleased with this!

The omens are not looking good as the porter deposit's her at the only empty bed ... right next to the exit doors. Now you and I both know it's an old wives tale. . . . but to someone of Ma's age, being placed in the last bed in the ward means you're next out.

Feet first in a wooden box. Oh dear!

To compound our problems, the old guy in the next bed appears to have lost the ability to dress himself properly.

His todger lolloping carelessly through the open fly in his pyjama trousers.

My life! This will finish Ma off! What with the porter ... and her pants ... and now this!

I smile nervously at him, hoping to diffuse the situation. He responds by giving me the V sign.

Pa looks mortified on our behalf.

78

The two women in his life being flashed at in public. To his credit, he takes the situation in hand and does the first thing that comes into his head. With one swift movement, he deftly leans over and covers the beast with his flat cap. Well done Pa!

I wouldn't even have thought of that!

"You'd better throw that cap in the bin when you get home!" Ma tells him, glaring at The Flasher.

"Poor old sod ... he can't help it." Pa smiles, "Probably all on his own in this world."

"I'm not surprised if he goes around dangling that in people's faces." Ma snorts.

Can this get any worse I ask myself? I can't leave her here overnight. What if Floppydick decides to get frisky during the night?

Goodness me ... she'd swing him round by the balls! Really she would!

Ma doesn't do rude. Her manners are impeccable. Her table napkins crisp. This is not a woman to trifle with. And certainly not a woman to shake your trouser snake at.

"Got any smokes?" Old Todger Ted suddenly beams at me.

"Sorry, not with me I'm afraid." I tell him gently.

"How about a Guinness?" he tries again in a lovely lilting Irish brogue.

"Er ... no" ...

"Any biscuit's in that bag?"

"No ... sorry."

"Feck off then!" he bawls, giving me yet another V sign.

You have to laugh don't you? Even Pa sees the funny side of this bizarre situation and covers his face with his hands in despair.

I have a feeling this is going to be an eventful night.

"That does it!" Ma suddenly announces, throwing back the bed covers, "I'm off!"

"Ma, you can't!"

"Just watch me!" she roars, struggling to get back into her pleated skirt.

"What about your head?" Pa tries to reason with her.

"It's still attached to my neck as far as I know!" she bellows, slipping into her shoes.

This is a no win situation. Ma is in her seventies. Been there ... done that ... bought the t-shirt.

If you've ever jostled with a pensioner in an early morning bus queue, you'll get the idea.

Pa and I watch helplessly as she strides off down the ward ...

"I'm going to find matron!" she announces to anyone who will listen.

"She'll have a job ... there are no matrons any more." I giggle to Pa.

The fracas has attracted the attention of one of the nurses, who waddles across to see what's going on.

I say waddle in the kindest possible way. She has the look of a nurse who survives on burgers and boxes of Quality Street donated by grateful patients.

"Is everything alright?" she asks, shoving a toffee penny into her mouth.

"Ma wants to sign herself out." I tell her, gesturing to my mother who is now disappearing out of sight. Heading for home no doubt.

"She can't do that!" she remonstrates, biting on a coconut creme.

"I think you'll find she can!" I laugh.

"Well, be it on her own head then!" she snaps, opening a hazelnut whirl.

I think this is where I came in! Indeed it was on her own head.

The welly that is. Now she's legging it up the motorway as fast as her little legs will carry her. Determined to escape this madhouse.

And The Paddy with the penis. Oh my life! Where's he gone to now? He was here a minute ago. God forbid that he's taken a shine to Ma and followed her!

"Where's that old guy gone?" I ask the nurse, pointing to the empty bed.

"Oh ... Patrick's always wandering off. He'll be making his way down to The Red Fox." she sighs, chocolate dribbling out of the side of her mouth.

"Sorry?"

"The pub on The Green ... he often pops out for a pint. I'll organise a search party" ... she smiles, heading to the office.

No wonder the NHS is going down the tubes! Matron would never have allowed this!

Patrick in the pub ... still wearing his pyjamas ... and with his todger hanging out! God forbid!

Ma's got the right idea I think. This is a madhouse.

"Better go catch up with Ma" ... I sigh, exhausted by all this drama.

"She'll be home by now ... whisking custard for the trifle." Pa smiles.

"Course! It's Sunday tomorrow. I forgot."

We make our way through the maze of corridors, scanning every face in the hope of finding Ma.

She's long gone and will no doubt have arrived home ... made the custard ... and washed the net curtains by the time we get back.

As we amble across The Green, a familiar figure catches my eye.

Patrick, still wearing his pyjamas, and sitting in the sun outside the Red Fox. A pint of Guinness in one hand and a roll-up in the other.

He is also wearing Pa's cap.

"Patrick ... they're sending out a search party for you!" I giggle, always amused by the bizarre.

"Sure ... I'm not lost!" he grins back, draining the pint in his glass and heading for the bar.

Chapter Seven

... *The Suicidal Scotsman*

It was very kind of Tom to do this for us and I truly am grateful but I do have my doubts. He pitched up last weekend with an envelope ...

Go away for the weekend folks he said. I'll pay. Be a nice treat for you both. And I'm sure it will be but you know what I'm like. I'm happy at home. I actually like the day to day routine and the familiarity.

Since I became a Crumpled Cousin, I feel safe there. I am quite content to spend my days wrestling with a mutant black labrador and practising my dance routines in the dining room.

Too late now. It's all booked and paid for. Can't back out now. Tom's paid a small fortune for this and it would be extremely rude of me to decline such a generous offer.

First-class train tickets...two nights in a four-star hotel...and a bottle of champagne in the room on arrival apparently.

Bless that boy! I must have done something right as a mother ... somewhere along the line anyway. Can't think of anything off hand but there you go.

He's even offered to move into our house, with Hannah for the weekend. To look after Levy.

There are several tons of steak in the freezer ... two-dozen pints of milk ... and an assortment of doggy treats.

Tom and Hannah have said they'll eat out.

I know he'll be fine. They're both as dotty as we are about dogs. But I worry. That boy loves a bedtime story and I'm not sure Tom will indulge him to those extremes.

I've left a copy of Spot Goes To The Circus by the dog's bed just in case.

The trains due at any minute and Jack is keeping a firm hand on my jumper. I do tend to get drawn to railway lines.

Funny how the track sort of pulls you towards it. No wonder so many people fall under the 4.15 express from Fife.

Haven't been on a train for years. Jack tells me it's all changed now.

The man with the black face, shovelling coal at the front, has long since gone.

I suspect he was taking the piss but I'll let it go for now.

He's just been and bought me twenty quids worth of magazines from W.H. Smith so I can¹t complain. It's a five hour journey apparently and he doesn't want me to get bored and start fiddling with the emergency cord.

He got me a sandwich as well...and a bag of pick & mix. Bless him. I shall never go hungry with Jack around.

Hope he got some of those wriggly worms. Don't you just love wrapping them round your teeth and pulling on them until they snap? The wriggly worms that is ... not your teeth.

"Stand back Cass ... here it comes." he tells me excitedly, gripping my arm.

The last time I went on a train ... which was when I was a child I think ... it sort of chugged into the station with a jolly Fat Controller at the front.

This monster roars past us, exceeding speeds of possibly a hundred and fifty miles an hour, sparks flying from the track as it grinds to a halt.

Tom has reserved our seats so there's no need to rush. Thinks of everything that lad does.

We make our way to the front and as ever, Jack insists on carrying all the luggage ... and my lunch ... leaving me to struggle with the pick & mix.

Good job he's got the build as he is forced to physically lift me onto the train because I'm scared of the gap. That awful gaping hole under the carriage. A person could fall into that and never be seen alive again. We discussed my fears on the way here in the Taxi, and Yusuf the driver agreed with me as well. He even offered to give Jack a hand but he said he'd manage.

"Over here Cass." Jack directs me, stashing the luggage in one of the racks.

"Lovely!" I grin at him, flopping down onto a seat by the window.

He sit's next to me and taking a pen from his pocket, starts to scribble on a scrap of paper.

"What are you doing?"

"Making you a name-tag ... just in case." he laughs.

"Hilarious."

"Don't want you wandering off again. Come here, let's pin it onto your coat."

"Stop it!"

"I'm serious! Remember Brighton? Three hours searching for you in the funfair."

"I was fine! Just looking at some of the side-shows!" I protest.

"What ... John Merrick ... that sort of thing?"

"Actually, I thought it was a bearded lady but it was one of those funny mirror things." I tell him, pulling a face.

"Anyway ... if you do get lost ... look for a policeman ... big feet ... funny hat." he laughs.

"Yes dear."

Why he worries so much about me I'll never know. I'm fast approaching fifty for Gods' sake!

Granted, I do tend to wander off and have a habit of talking to strangers but still. It's nice to know he still cares.

He demonstrates this by searching through the pick & mix for me.

"Wriggly worm?" he grins, handing me a giant one, all of six inches long.

What more could a woman ask for? Magazines ... a ham and pickle sarnie and a wriggly worm.

We are just about to settle back and have a wriggly-worm eating contest, when the peace is shattered by the arrival of two elderly women, crashing through the carriage doors and flopping down onto the seats opposite. Within seconds, the table is awash with thermos flasks and Tupperware boxes and an assortment of boiled sweets.

"Told you not to queue up for them donuts Doris ... we nearly missed the train."

"Get away! Wouldn't be a holiday without some custard donuts Blanche."

Blanche and Doris. Obviously well-travelled women. They have the look of women who have scrutinised every bed and breakfast on the South Coast.

"Hello ladies ... can I give you a hand with those bags?" Jack asks, leaping to his feet.

"Thanks lad ... just shove them out of the way over there if you could." Blanche grins.

"Plymouth?" Doris asks, offering me a boiled sweet.

"Yes, just for the weekend." I nod, helping myself to a barley sugar.

"Dirty or clean?" she roars, her head rolling backwards, exposing a half-eaten lemon drop.

"Clean!" I protest, laughing along with her.

"Dirty I hope!" Jack grins, sitting back down again.

Doris continues to chuckle to herself as the train pulls out of the station.

Within minutes, we have left the confines of the city and are making our way towards the coast. The grimy industrial unit's exchanged for green fields and rolling hills. Within half an hour, Doris and Blanche have told us their life history and chomped their way through several packets of sandwiches and a large box of custard donuts.

Blanche had her eye on my last wriggly worm but I managed to shove it down my throat before she grabbed it.

They are staying at Sea Breezes ... a bed and breakfast which they've visited before.

Best sausages this side of the Pennines Blanche informs us. And proper pillows apparently.

I have no idea what an improper pillow is but suspect they mean the feathered variety.

"You should visit the Ho while you're there." Doris informs Jack across the table.

"I'm not sure Cassie would like that!" he laughs, his interpretation going right over her head.

Blanche is fast asleep, quite exhausted after completing a particularly taxing puzzle in her Word Search book.

That and the effort of digesting five custard donuts.

"Never been inside that Marriot Hotel." Doris whispers to me, trying not to wake Blanche.

"It looks lovely in the brochure ... I'm looking forward to it." I tell her.

"Bet they've got real milk in the rooms ... not that UHT stuff we get at Sea Breezes." she grimaces.

"I'm sure."

"And those little bars of soap all individually wrapped." she gushes excitedly.

"I expect so."

"I knew somebody once who got a shower gel ... and a free loofah!" she trills.

Bless her! Funny how elderly people are impressed by the tiniest details isn't it? Ma and Pa for instance, they spent the night in a B&B in Barmouth once and were ecstatic to find a free packet of shortbread biscuit's on the tea tray in their hotel room.

I suppose it's the little things that count. The tiny gestures of goodwill.

With me, as long as there are no pubic hairs in the shower tray, I'm happy.

By the time the train pulls into Plymouth station I feel as if I've known these two all my life.

I shall miss Doris and her loose false teeth. And Blanche with her heaving bosom. Good job there was a table to rest them on.

My life! She'd never have survived a five hour train journey with all that weight dragging her down. Joy oh joy! To reach an age when you don't give a shit about your boobs nose diving south. To abandon all the niceties of struggling into a garment that strangulates your chest and bruises your shoulders. I relish the thought of the days to come when I too will abandon my bra and swap if for a thermal vest.

They do pants as well! Huge, voluminous pants that you could carry a kilo of sprouts in.

And bloomers! Even better! Lilac coloured bloomers with elastic at the knee.

I shall be able to shoplift with abandon and pretend I have Alzheimer's when questioned.

"Sorry your worship ... it's all very vague ... who am I ... where am I?"

Are you getting my drift? I shall get Jack a pair of long johns and we can hit Waitrose together.

Doris is forced to wake Blanche ... and her bosoms ... as the train slides into the station. She is startled and seems unaware of where she is ...

"You've got dribble down your chin, " Doris tells her, getting to her feet.

"Sorry, it's my gums ... they've shrunk." she tells us sleepily.

Something else to look forward to in my old age. Shrunken gums! Along with drooping tit's and curvature of the spine!

Great! No wonder tiny babies are shit-scared of their Granny's!

Must be like having Quasimodo pick you up and bounce you on their knee.

We leave our new friends at the station entrance. Jack offering to get them a taxi and they having none of it, insisting that a car will arrive soon to take them to Sea Breezes.

We make our way outside and breathe in the crisp, salty air. A refreshing change after the stuffiness of the train.

"Come on Cass ... here's a taxi rank." Jack says, heading for an empty cab.

"Marriot Hotel please mate" ... he tells the driver, as we collapse onto the back seat.

87

"You sure pal?" the driver asks in a somewhat bemused tone.

"Yes ... the Marriot please." Jack says again.

"Okay then ... if you insist." he sighs, pulling away.

We are a bit puzzled by this and assume he's having a bad day. Until he pulls up again roughly sixty seconds later outside the hotel. How silly!

It was literally around the corner! Within spitting distance I think is the correct expression. Talk about prats! No wonder he looked at us as if we'd just landed!

"That'll be five-pounds fifty." he smirks, "Sorry mate, standard tariff!"

I'm all for head butting him there and then but Jack simply smiles sweetly and hands over the dosh.

We fall out of the taxi in fits of giggles with the driver shaking his head in despair.

"Bet he wishes all his fares were like that." Jack laughs.

"What a pair of pillocks!" I giggle, following him into reception.

For a split second, I suspect that we are in the wrong hotel as the reception area appears to be heaving with cartoon characters.

Yogi Bear ... Donald Duck ... and several Minnie Mouse's lounging around on sofa's, drinking coffee. I shouldn't have eaten that ham and pickle sarnie. I appear to be hallucinating now.

"What's all this about then?" a bemused Jack asks the girl on reception.

"Theme park convention." she grins, " This lot will be off to Euro Disney next month."

"Oh right."

"They have to be trained you see, " she continues "In the art of mingling."

Mingling! Fuck me ... not exactly rocket science is it? You just amble through the crowds waving at anyone under ten I imagine. Whatever next?

"We've got a room booked ... Mr and Mrs Ryder." Jack tells her.

"Yes, we've been expecting you. Room 431. Take the lift to the fourth floor ... over there." she points.

"Thanks."

"You're welcome. Enjoy your stay!"

We make our way to the lift. Stepping over a rather relaxed Goofy who is lying on the floor by the bar.

This is the problem you see. Having worked in the hotel trade for years, I am familiar with the corporate jolly where the guests are given a free bar. Tell them it's free and they go doolally ... drinking everything in sight until they quite literally fall over.

And to be perfectly honest, who can blame them? This lot deserve a stiff drink ... being incarcerated in an assortment of frankly quite ridiculous suit's for hours on end. I imagine they work up quite a thirst inside there.

Room 431 is all the brochure promised and more. Luxurious decor with fabulous views over the bay.

Spotlessly clean throughout and a positive plethora of freebies in the sumptuous bathroom. Doris would be ecstatic!

"This is fantastic Jack!" I grin, gazing out of the window.

"Wonderful!" he agrees, flopping down onto the king-size bed.

"Look ... champagne and a fruit basket!

"And real milk on the tea-tray." I laugh.

"That's class!"

What a delightful hotel. If only Doris and Blanche could get a glimpse of all this. I might just parcel up all the freebies and send them over to Sea Breezes. That would make their day I bet.

I shall keep the champagne though. It's a bottle of Moet. Even I'm not that generous.

"Lunch?" Jack smiles, flicking through the menu on the bedside table.

"Lovely!"

"A La Carte or Brasserie?" he asks.

"Don't care as long as they serve chips."

"They do children's portions ... fish fingers ... chicken nuggets" ... he laughs.

"No thanks! Those nugget things are stuffed with sawdust." I tell him.

"Eh?"

"Sawdust and wood shavings. I saw it on TV honest!"

"Wood shavings?"

"Yes! And giblets ... stuff that you find shoved up a chicken's bum."

"I'll stick to the fish I think." he grimaces.

"Fine if you want mercury poisoning." I giggle.

"Eh?"

"It was on Panorama ... I think ... or was that something to do with the fillings in your teeth?"

"Cass ... you really should get out more" ...

And get out more we do. The next two days spent blissfully ambling around the town and along the extensive docks, with Jack holding on to me for dear life as we negotiate the rugged coastal paths.

I've seen that 999 programme and have no desire to be filmed being winched to safety by an RAF helicopter.

Plymouth really is a lovely place with so much history to explore and after exhausting ourselves on the last day, we trundle back to the hotel for food and much-needed sleep.

"Night Cass ... get some sleep, we've got a train to catch in the morning."

"Night."

"Did you get all the gifts you wanted to buy?" he yawns, drifting off to sleep.

"Think so ... got Ma and Pa the whisky ... and a sugar dummy for Levy" ...

"He'll like that."

"Oh and that rubber bone thing."

"Good" ...

"And that tea-towel with a ship on" ...

"For the dog?"

"No silly, for Mary."

"Oh right."

"Jack! I forgot about Hannah!"

"She won't mind ... get her some chocolates at the station" ... he yawns.

"No! She doesn't eat chocolates. I'll pop down to reception. Look in that little shop" ... I cry, jumping out of bed.

"Cass ... it's late. Leave it until morning."

"Back in a jiff!"

"Cass??"

It's only when I get into the lift, that I realise I'm still wearing my pyjamas and slippers.

A Winnie the Pooh matching set. Not to worry, it's late and I'll blend in nicely with all those theme park workers.

Probably think I'm one of them and drag me into the bar. Christ! When we went down for breakfast this morning Jack had to queue for a full English along with Daffy Duck and Yogi Bear!

Wish I'd bought the camcorder with me ... his face was a picture.

Looks very serene at this time of night. Lots of subtle lighting and an air of calm about the place.

Even the night-porters awake! Sitting in his little office going over some paperwork.

I'm impressed. I wonder if he could help?

"Excuse me ... I know it's late but I need to buy a gift for someone." I whisper.

His face says it all as he looks me up and down ... taking in the ridiculous pyjamas and slippers.

"Of course madam ... what sort of gift were you looking for?" he asks.

"Erm ... not sure ... it's for my daughter-in-law" ...

"Well, we're a bit limited at this time of night but I'll take a look out the back" ... he sighs. Wandering off towards the back office.

Now that's service for you! Fancy! It's past midnight and he's doing his best. Bless him.

"Would any of these be of any use madam?" he asks, plonking a box onto the desk.

"I really do appreciate this ... thank you." I smile.

"Let me see ... how about a sewing kit?" he smiles, searching through the box.

"Erm ... no ... I don't think so" ... I whisper.

"Some shampoo?" he tries again.

"Thanks but no ... really."..

"Here you go ... a Marriot shower cap" ... he beams, handing me the tiny packet.

"Oh right ... well thanks ... you've been a great help." I stammer, desperate to get away.

Hannah will be thrilled! I shall have to wait until tomorrow and see if there's a Sock Shop on the station.

There usually is isn't there? I shall get her some ... well ... socks ... I suppose.

I'm just about to climb back into the lift when all hell breaks loose. Out of the darkness of the bar, Tweety Pie emerges, running for all he's worth, his cheeks flapping with exertion.

"Quick somebody help! It¹s Porky Pig ... he's up on the roof!"

For some strange reason ... and I have no idea how my warped mind works on this ... but I suddenly think of that expression ... you know ... and pigs might fly. Don't ask! You know I'm not well.

"Eh? ... which roof?" the night-porter yells across the foyer.

"The hotel roof you idiot!" Tweety yells back, "Quick ... he's threatening to jump!"

Oh my life! Poor bloke! What shall we do?

"Don't panic! Don't panic!" I yell, doing my impression of that bloke out of Dads Army.

I wish Tilly were here. She'd know what to do. I'm not very good with suicidal people.

Especially one's dressed as Porky Pig. How can you possibly have a serious conversation with someone dressed as a pig?

"I'll call the police!" the night-porter shouts, picking up the phone.

"I'll call his wife!" Tweety Pie shouts back.

Who the fuck shall I call ... Ghostbusters? I really am useless in situations like this. Calm down!

Everybody stay calm!

"Police are on their way ... and a doctor ... can you wait for them ... show them the way?" the porter begs me.

"Yes of course ... you go on" ... I tell him, praying he gets to the roof in time.

"Tell them to take the fire stairs, it's quicker!" he bawls, disappearing into the darkness.

Okay fine ... let's take stock shall we? It's after midnight. I'm in a hotel foyer dressed in Winnie The Pooh pyjamas.

Porky Pig is on the roof threatening to jump and the police are on their way. And a doctor apparently. I do hope he's a psychiatrist.

Be no good sending a kidney specialist out on a call like this would it?

Oh shit! I could be curled up in bed now with Jack.

Instead, I'm on the lookout for the emergency services. The police will be a doddle to spot ... those hats a dead giveaway.

But the doctor could be a very different kettle of fish.

Unless he's wearing a white coat and a stethoscope of course.

"His wife says he's been depressed for ages ... since he lost his job!" Tweety Pie pipes up.

"How awful!"

"Bit of a comedown I suppose. He used to be an airline pilot." Tweety tells me.

"Oh my life!"

"Got the sack ... left under a bit of a cloud" ... he whispers.

"Poor bloke!"

"Better go and see if I can help." he sighs, waddling off towards the staircase.

Oh my goodness! Pilot to Porky Pig all in one foul swoop. How mortified must that guy be?

Wonder what he did to get the sack? None of my business really but it makes you wonder.

It would have to be something pretty serious I should think for an airline to sack a pilot.

Maybe he crashed. You can't get more serious than that can you?

Oh ... the police are here! That was quick. Blue lights and everything. I'm impressed.

"Is this a wind up?" a rather surly officer asks approaching me.

"No ... he's up on the roof ... really!" I tell him, looking very credible in my pyjamas.

"Porky Pig?" he asks again, still looking dubious.

"Yes ... truly ... he was a pilot ... now he's ... erm ... a pig" ... I stammer.

"Are you taking the piss?" his companion growls at me, quite rudely I feel.

"Look! Go and see. He'll be splattered all across the car park if you hang around here!" I growl back.

They hover distractedly, not knowing whether to believe me or not and the situation is only saved by the arrival of the doctor.

An extremely fresh-faced young girl who has apparently just graduated from the Fisher Price Medical School. She looks terrified and it shows!

"Suicidal Scotsman?" she shouts, wafting through reception.

"He's on the roof!" I yell, the situation becoming more desperate by the second.

"I don't carry tranquillisers." she quivers, close to tears.

"What about a parachute?" I bark back. I'm losing the plot myself now.

"Come on miss ... we'll come up with you." Officer Dibble says, taking control, and all three hurry away towards the stairs.

I am left standing alone in the foyer feeling shell-shocked and rather silly.

Bet this one will go down a bomb at the station.

No point me going back to bed yet. I'd never sleep thinking of poor Porky. I could be lying in bed and he could sail past the bloody window!

How guilty would I feel then? Might as well hang around for a bit ... at least see that he's okay. See, if this were home ... in Oakham ... I could offer some advice. Get Tilly to set up some therapy sessions for him. He could join our group.

Alan would like that. Be somebody else in fancy dress for him to relate to. But it's not.

It's Plymouth and I have no idea what the resources are in this area for the mentally ill.

Besides, the doctor said Suicidal Scotsman.

He's travelled a fair way to top himself.

"Be down in a minute. The coppers dragged him off the ledge!" the porter gasps.

He's looking quite ashen I have to say. Probably shock. Either that or the prospect of scraping Porky's bit's off the car park.

"Thank goodness!" I shudder.

"I had a feeling he was a jumper. Wanted a room on a high floor when he checked in" ... he tells me.

"Really?"

"You can always tell. They get that look about um."

"Oh well ... at least he's okay. Here they come. Taking him to the station I expect."

I watch helplessly as Porky Pig is bundled into the back of the police car, his enlarged head straining against the confines of the car roof.

The doctor can't wait to get away and roars off into the darkness without a backward glance. Tweety Pie and I are left shivering on the front steps,

95

waving dejectedly to an incredibly unhappy looking pig.

"Think I'll go back to insurance. You know where you are with insurance" ... he sighs.

"Goodnight."

"Night."

I make my way back upstairs, pyjamas flapping against my legs. Jack is still fast asleep and moans softly as I crawl into bed beside him.

"Cass you're freezing! Where have you been?" he groans, snuggling under the duvet.

"Outside with Tweety Pie ... the police took Porky Pig away" ...

"I won't ask." he sighs, drifting back to sleep.

"Best not."

Chapter Eight

... *Situation Very Vacant*

I think I can safely say that I am unemployable now. It's a fact!

After two years of Trifledom, it's very unlikely that any employer would see fit to put my name on the payroll. They get twitchy you see.

The mere whiff of a history of mental illness and you won't see their arses for dust.

Can't say I blame them. I wouldn't employ me either.

I truly would love to contribute. To society and Jack's bank balance ... but doing what?

Tilly is doing her best ... struggling to arm us with the defence mechanisms we'll need when we are let loose.

Not literally of course ... I may be crumpled but I'm not ready for a secure unit yet.

Preparing for pressure I think she calls it. Arming yourself against taking on too much. Learning to say no.

We are getting there. As a group, I feel we have taken great steps since our first session. Alan has popped his cherry!

And Alicia's given up wearing surgical stockings so that's a bonus. And me?

I now know that mental illness is just that ... an illness ... like any other. You may not be able to see it but that doesn't mean it doesn't exist.

Today's session is supposed to be a guide to finding employment. Tilly just asked us what sort of job we'd like.

Where do you start?

Alicia has her notebook out again. I have made it my mission in life to rob that and read it.

Does that woman never do anything before writing it down? Fancy a fuck? ... just check my book!

How awful to lead such a neat and ordered existence. It would drive me mad. She has the look of a woman who colour co-ordinates her bra drawer.

"Alicia ... any ideas?" Tilly asks, sitting down.

"Several options actually, but one in particular appeals" ...

"And what would that be?" Tilly asks.

"Well, in another life ... I'd love to have been a lady-in-waiting ... to the Queen Mother" ... she gushes.

Fuck me! It would have to be in another life ... she's dead you silly tart!

"Cucumber sandwiches and an afternoon tea tray, " she sighs, her piggy little eyes glazing over.

Oh get real you silly mare! Trust Alicia to choose a job that involves doing as little as possible.

If I were in charge at the Job Centre I'd send you for a position as a cleaner. Cleaning the bogs at The Pig & Whistle.

Nice little reality check that would be!

"I feel I'd fit in nicely in the Royal Household" ... she continues at full throttle.

Here we go! Her Royal Humpback! Stop her Tilly before I have to step in and smack her one.

"Okay fine, let's move on shall we? Alan ... how about you?"

Alan looks a tad distracted today or should I say slightly more distracted than normal.

He's wearing one green sock and one purple one and has his jumper on inside out.

"Always wanted me own van, " he suddenly blurts out.

"What ... to use for deliveries or something?" Tilly asks, leaning forward.

"No silly! Ice-cream van ... with the chimes on the top!" he frowns.

"Oh right I see!" she smiles.

"I'm good on ice-creams ... could go on Mastermind with ice-creams." he tells us proudly.

I'm not sure there is an ice-cream section on Mastermind. That would be a new category!

Alan ... your starter for ten is a Cornish Cornet.

"For goodness sake ... that's not a real job ... stupid boy!" Arsehole Face suddenly hisses at him.

Here we go! It's kicking off again! Why does she find it necessary to put this lad down at every opportunity?

He's trying for fuck's sake! There's more involved in selling ice-cream than cutting up cucumber sarnies you bitter old bitch!

"Try telling that to Ben & Jerry!" I snap back at her, daring her to continue.

"Who?" she snaps, glaring at me.

"Ben & Jerry ... billionaires from selling ice-cream" ... I inform her.

"Never heard of them!" she snorts, looking down her nose at me again.

"You haven't lived love ... you should try a bowlful of Chubby Hubby some time!"

"I'd prefer it if you didn't call me love." she glares, shuffling uncomfortably in her chair.

"What shall I call you then ... fuck face?" I rant.

"Cassie!" Tilly yells, stepping in once again to prevent a fist fight.

We remain deadlocked. Glaring at each other across the room. You'd think Alicia would have learned by now.

That lad has enough problems in his life without that bitch picking on him.

Vulnerable you see.

Alan might just as well have Kick Me stamped on his arse. He has the look of a loser and people like Alicia seem to take great pleasure in doing just that.

Well I've got news for you love ... not on my watch!!

"You were saying Alan ... do go on" ... Tilly whispers softly.

"Course, people don't realise there's a lot involved." he grins, looking shyly over at Alicia.

"Absolutely!" Tilly says encouragingly, hoping he'll open up more.

"Be trouble if you got your sprinkles mixed up with your chopped nuts." he says.

"Erm ... quite" ...

"Some kids are allergic to nuts ... swell up like a balloon they do."

"Really?" Tilly asks looking interested.

"Swell up and die ... one kid was twice the size ... seen it on Real Rescues."

"Oh dear" ...

"You only get thirty seconds with that elastic shock" ... he beams, his eyes lighting up.

And who says television isn't educational? Bless him! I think he actually means anaphylactic shock but there you go ... close enough. It's nice to see him so animated about something.

Until a few minutes ago he was looking quite depressed ... poor sod.

"And you Cassie?" Tilly asks me, trying to divert from the subject of exploding children.

Yet again, I am caught on the hop, having given the subject no thought whatsoever. My head has been all over the place this week and it shows.

I am forced to improvise as usual ...

"I'd like to work at Cadburys." I lie, playing for time.

"Oh that would be wonderful!" Tilly laughs, "Think of all that chocolate."

"Exactly ... I could cope with that." I smile.

"I believe you are allowed to eat it while you work." she giggles.

"Imagine ... a dozen bars of Dairy Milk for dinner." I laugh.

"Your teeth would fall out." Alicia suddenly snorts, looking at me with contempt.

"That's okay, I could suck the chocolate ... through a straw if necessary!" I bite back.

I do wish Alicia would get a life! She takes everything SO seriously, including herself.

A simple hypothetical exercise like this and she has to get all morbid and intense. If truth be known I would hate to work in a chocolate factory.

They say the smell's enough to put you off chocolate for life.

I'd make an exception if it were Mars though. Not that the situation's ever likely to arise. I'm not sure I'd ever be allowed to operate machinery.

"Okay ... let's move on shall we?" Tilly giggles, "I'd like you all to come out into the grounds" ...

We follow like sheep, all three of us puzzled at this new concept. Never been into the grounds before.

Perhaps Tilly's going to line us all up against the wall and shoot us.

"Today, we are going to do something symbolic." she says, leading us into the courtyard.

"Eh?" Alan grunts looking perplexed.

"Symbolic Alan ... a sort of a gesture." she explains.

He looks quite worried now. Alan's not one for gestures.

"We are going to let off some balloons...I want you to imagine that they carry all your problems" ... Tilly sings in that lovely reassuring tone.

I get it! What a wonderful idea. This girl is nothing if not innovative in her thinking.

"Just let the balloons drift off into the sky ... taking all your cares along with them" ...

"How absurd!" Alicia whispers between gritted teeth.

"How wonderful!" I grin, goading her into a frenzy.

"Will they have our name and address on?" Alan suddenly pipes up.

"Erm ... no Alan ... why?" Tilly asks.

"In case people find um" ... he whispers.

"No Alan ... no name tags." Tilly sighs.

"It's just a fun thing to do Alan that's all." I tell him, hoping to ease his fears.

101

"Oh right" ...

"If you wait there, I'll go and fetch the balloons ... they're helium ones so they'll soar!" Tilly giggles.

She skips off in the direction of the unit and we wait expectantly for her return. Alicia is still sulking but Alan looks quite excited now.

I can tell this by the fact that he's fiddling with his privates again.

He always does that when he's excited.

"Here you go!" Tilly grins, handing us each a balloon.

And what beautiful balloons! Great big psychedelic ones with coloured ribbons tied on the end.

"Now take a few minutes ... think of all the little niggling problems in your life ... then let go" ... she whispers.

I don't really have any problems at the moment. Nothing major anyway. Firmer breasts and a lottery win might help but nothing serious.

"I forgot my balloon ... back in a jiff" ... Tilly giggles, skipping off again, leaving us to our own devices.

Which was a mistake I feel. You know what it's like. Leave the classroom and the kids go wild.

I have no idea what goes on in my head but without hesitating, I quickly unravel the ribbon on my balloon and inhale the helium within.

A trick I perfected years ago when Tom was a toddler.

"Hey Alan ... give it a go!" I squeak at him in my best Minnie Mouse voice.

He seems startled for a second, then decides to join in the fun and unravels his too, inhaling deeply.

"Hi-ho ... hi-ho ... it's off to work we go!" he giggles, his voice a quivering falsetto.

"Come on Grumpy ... live a little!" I squeak at Alicia, inhaling yet again.

"With a shovel and a pick ... !" Alan sings, jigging around the courtyard like a loon.

"You two are unbalanced!" Grumpy barks, storming off to tell teacher no doubt ... her ample arse quivering in indignation.

Told you! That woman has no sense of the ridiculous whatsoever! I meanwhile am an expert in all things ridiculous. This is ridiculous ... but it's fun! Alan's previous sadness dispelled within seconds and all for the sake of a balloon. I shall have an incredibly sore throat later but hey-ho!

The joy on that lad's face is priceless.

"Da - da - da - da - da - da -da ... Muppet show tonight!" he bawls like a strangled frog, his voice rising with every gasp.

Give it some welly lad! I have lost the plot completely now and join him as he launches himself off the steps into a frenzied foot-stomp ... his gangly legs lashing out in all directions We are so caught up in the moment, that we both fail to notice that Grumpy is back ... with Tilly.

"See what I mean Tilly ... tell them!" Grumpy snaps, waving her arms in disgust.

I think Tilly would if she could but she seems to be experiencing difficulty speaking at the moment.

Her face a picture of disbelief and amusement. Can't say I blame her ... I'm no dancer at the best of times and must look a right prat ... doing my impression of that little, fat Swedish chef ...with Alan impersonating Kermit.

"When you're quite ready" ... she finally giggles, flopping down onto the garden wall.

Kermit stops mid-stomp and looks suitably remorseful. Shame! He was having so much fun.

I feel it's up to me to apologise ... I started this after all.

"Sorry Tilly ... I got carried away." I tell her, putting on my most pathetic expression.

"No problem ... you were obviously having fun." she smiles, "Shall we release the balloons?"

Grumpy doesn't want to play any more. She's throwing her toys out of the pram in temper.

"Told you this was ridiculous!" she barks, throwing her balloon into the rose bushes nearby.

It splatters against the thorns and slowly hisses to a halt. Tilly does nothing, refusing to rise to the bait and be drawn into yet another argument.

"Okay Alan, would you like to release your balloon?" she smiles.

"Yeah!" he grins, excitedly launching it into the air.

"Well done!"

"My turn now!" I squeak, releasing mine into the wind.

Both balloons soar skywards, the ribbons fluttering in the breeze. We gaze upwards, craning our necks until they disappear out of sight.

I really do feel better for that.

"Thanks Tilly, that was a lovely idea." I tell her.

"You're welcome."

"Tracey wanted balloons at the wedding ... on all the tables ... too expensive though" ... Alan sighs.

Oh no ... here we go again!

"Leave it with me Alan ... I ... erm ... know somebody in the balloon trade." I lie.

"Cheers Cassie!"

"No problem."

Tilly is shaking her head again. What with the wedding cake and now several hundred balloons.

This wedding is costing Jack a fortune.

"Any particular colour Alan?" I ask as we make our way out, "You know, to match your outfit's?"

"Nah ... anything will do ... we haven't decided on outfit's yet."

"Oh right."

"I'll probably wear my Captain Kirk suit" ...

***

CAKE CRISIS II

Soak 10 kilos of mixed fruit in hot water.
Add zest of 24 lemons.
Gently fold in 72 packets of sponge mix.
Find shovel in shed.
Light oven on Gas mark 4.
Light fag.
Lie down in dark room.
Have nightmare about being chased by giant cake.
Tweet Jamie Oliver.

Chapter Nine

... *Lenny The Leg*

Gabriel's gone. Well, for the time being anyway. Jack saw him hitch-hiking on the Oakham Road early on Friday morning. Ambling along without a care.

All his worldly goods stuffed into a bedroll on his back. Pete says he's on his way to a horse fair in Somerset. Be back in a week or so he says. We shall see.

I have to say, my original doubts about him have proved unfounded. Granted, he's a geezer and one who ducks and dives his way through life, but he's a gentle soul and seems to have been a genuine friend to Pete.

They have spent the last few months drinking their way through the entire contents of several breweries but despite that, I can honestly say they've never been a problem. The odd rowdy night when they've had a session out in the garden but nothing serious.

Rather that, than Fiona ... She of The Fuckwit Face ... our neighbour on the other side.

Fiona and Henry. Says it all really doesn't it?

Designer people with designer friends. Tossers is a more accurate description I feel. Sorry, but I speak as I find and I find them both infuriating! They're in Bermuda at the moment.

Scuba diving with dolphins or something. Let us pray that Fiona's aqua lung works.

Their house is locked up and empty for the duration I think. I have no idea how long it takes to put a snorkel on a dolphin.

I expect they'll be gone for a while. It's the circuit you see.

The Raaaarrrrly Route as I call it. A social whirl of jaunts abroad to meet up with like-minded over privileged pillocks.

Caymen Islands in the spring ... Rock in Cornwall in the summer and Kloisters in winter. Suffice to say, a weekend in Blackpool is not on their agenda.

I have nothing whatsoever against people with squillions in the bank. Good luck to them.

What I do object to, is people like Fiona who are minted and malicious. Every time she opens her exquisitely glossed lips, a veritable cesspool of crap spouts forth.

She seems to have an opinion on everything, from the scurge of the unemployed to the demise of the Royal Opera House. Twat!

Family Fortunes you see. Not the Vernon Kay variety ... but a substantial trust fund set up by Daddy.

I got all this info from a snippet in the local rag. Henry was pictured opening up his new offices in the city. He's a trader apparently.

Not your average market trader ... nothing Del Boy about our Henry.

Henry trades in shares and ... bulls and ... bears whatever they are.

And Fiona? The Daddy in question made his fortune from a diamond mine in South Africa.

Now there's a surprise! Squillions earned from the sweat off the backs of several hundred slaves no doubt.

Suffice to say, Fiona and I will never agree ... on anything ... and that's fine by me.

One of my greatest pleasures in life is jigging around the garden, hair in rollers, singing My Old Man's A Dustman.

Just to wind her up.

We think they've put old Crawford into a cattery. Haven't seen him around for a while so they must have done.

No doubt it will be a very chic cattery with smoked salmon served on a silver platter every night. And some poor YTS kid at hand to wipe his ample arse for him.

I could never pack Levy off to a kennels. Goodness me ... it would break my heart. Plus the fact that no kennels in this county would take him on.

The insurance premiums would be too high.

I thought they might have asked me to keep an eye on the house but they didn't. No surprises there then.

Fiona thinks I'm a ... what's the word ... oh yes ... cretin ... think that's it anyway.

I looked it up in the dictionary and it means simple I think. Sounds about right! Whatever!

Fuckwit's opinions are of no consequence to me. I don't talk to pork.

Give me Pete any day ... with all his problems. At least you know where you are with Pete.

He's in the kitchen at the moment. I can hear him clearing away the empties from last night.

I must say, he's doing his bit for the environment with all the bottles he recycles. The Council could install a bottle bank outside his house.

"Morning Pete ... how are you today ... missing Gabriel I bet." I shout across the hedge.

He surfaces, looking ever the picture of sartorial elegance, wearing just his underpants and a soppy grin.

"Morning Cassie ... you okay?" he yawns, tripping over the watering can.

"Oops!" I laugh.

"No problem" ... he sighs, struggling to his feet.

"Have you heard from Gabriel?"

"No ... he keeps on the move." he informs me dejectedly.

I bet he does! On his toes is the correct expression I think. From the police and various other security forces.

"Never mind. If you ever fancy a chat, you know where I am." I offer.

"Thanks Cassie but I've got Lenny here for a few weeks." he informs me.

I really am afraid to ask! Lenny who for goodness sake? Henry? Kravitz? Who knows?

"He's working at the school ... Oakham Juniors." he continues.

"Oh ... a teacher?" I sigh, relieved at this information.

"No ... lollipop man." he smiles.

Well there you go! He's working anyway and I have to say I feel lollipop men ... and women ... are vastly under rated and under paid.

Would you do that job? Dicing with death on the roads every morning? Me either!

"That's a dangerous occupation." I add.

"Absolutely ... especially with his leg." he yawns, scratching casually at his dangly bit's.

Oh fuck! Here we go again! What leg?

"His leg?"

"Mm ... great big deformed thing it is, " he whispers, "Some botched surgery years ago."

Oh my life! Deformed? I shall be afraid to look!

"Oh dear ... that sounds awful."

"He copes with it ... just means he has problems with his trousers."

I really don't want to go there but you have to don't you? Can't ignore a human being in distress.

"Trousers?" I ask again, fearing the worst.

"Yeah ... needs the left leg bigger than the right see ... cos of the swelling."

Let's take stock shall we? Pete has a new lodger called Lenny. Lenny had surgery which went badly wrong and now his left leg is deformed ... and swollen ... and his trousers don't fit.

"I imagine that could be difficult." I tell him sympathetically.

"Course ... his ... erm ... left bollocks bigger as well ... on that side." Pete says.

My life! Will this never end? Unbalanced bollocks as well! Poor bloke.

"Goodness!" I blush.

"Would you like to meet him? He's in the kitchen icing some fondant fancies."

I'm not sure I'm up to this. Where do you look? Now that Pete's filled me in on the gory details, I shall have a job to keep my eyes above waist level.

"Erm ... yes ... if you like." I dither, making my way to the side gate.

Did he say icing some fondant fancies? My life ... is Lenny gay as well? This gets more complicated by the minute.

"Lenny! Cassie's here to meet you!" Pete bawls into the kitchen.

"Be right out!" a cheery voice calls back, followed by the sound of the oven door closing.

"Chelsea buns." Pete informs me, as if it's the most natural thing in the world to say.

I'll give him his due. He does seem to give shelter to people who can cook. Gabriel was a dab hand at goat curry and apple pies.

"Cassie...I've heard a lot about you!" Lenny cries, limping in from the kitchen.

"Ditto!" I tell him, shaking his outstretched hand.

"Pete tells me you're barmy." he giggles, lowering his enormous frame onto the sofa.

"Cheers!" I laugh along with him.

"In the nicest possible way of course." he laughs.

"Have a seat Cassie. The buns will be ready soon." Pete says, ambling off into the kitchen.

"All the finest ingredients." Lenny boasts, "No synthetic rubbish in my cakes."

"Sounds delicious." I dribble, salivating already.

"Used to be my trade you see ... before the op." he sighs, his eyes misting over.

"Chef?"

"No my dear...a Master Baker...trained with some of the top patisserie people in London."

"Wow really?"

"Oh yes ... my blueberry muffins were the talk of the town in those days."

"I'm a terrible cook!" I laugh, sitting down on the easy chair opposite.

"Yes, so Pete tells me." he giggles, "I gather you have problems with your dumplings?"

I'm not sure which way this conversation is going but I like Lenny. He has that rare quality of being open and refreshingly honest.

He also has the kindest eyes I have ever seen ... great big pools of pale blue, sparkling in the centre of his chubby face. Granted, he's got one enormous bollock as well but there you go.

Hopefully, the bollock and I will never be introduced.

"Just check on the oven" ... he suddenly announces, struggling to his feet ... his ample stomach wobbling with the effort.

Must have been a good cook. He seems to have eaten most of the pastries he baked. I watch, fascinated as he wobbles off into the kitchen. His left leg dragging slightly behind the right.

Poor bugger. Must be an effort carrying that around all day.

It really is quite a noticeable deformity.

At least three times the size of the other. I do hope that ratio doesn't apply to the bollock. He'll be needing a truss if it does.

"Fondant fancy?" he suddenly asks, reappearing with a tray full of cakes.

"Oh yes please!"

"Homemade icing ... I don't touch the shop stuff." he tells me with pride.

"I'm impressed!" I tell him, biting into the delicious soft sponge.

He disappears yet again and I am left munching on very possibly the best fondant fancy I have ever tasted.

Delicious doesn't come into it. These fancies are fantastic! You have to admire a guy with a disability ... and a giant gonad ... who can cook like this.

"This is fantastic!" I shout through the kitchen door.

"Wait till you try my profiteroles!" Lenny calls back excitedly.

"And his Viennese whirls" ... Pete joins in.

I think I may just have died and gone to heaven! An artist such as this living right next door.

Maybe he could give me a few lessons. Maybe after thirty years I could actually produce something edible for Jack. That would be a first.

I take the opportunity to watch them both as they meander around the kitchen. Pete opening a tin of Pal for Budd and Lenny adding elaborate decorations to the fancies. Budd always lies faithfully at Pete's feet.

Those adorable eyes scrutinising his every move. It's quite true what they say about a dog. Their love is unconditional. All they ask is that we feed them and love them and we get so much in return.

In my case, it's severe bruising and the odd broken nose but there you go.

Lenny reminds me of someone and I can't quite put my finger on it. He has one of those familiar faces that you think you've seen before. I'm sure we haven't. I would remember that leg.

Portly. That's the word Ma would use ... portly. I think it's a polite word for fat but he is extremely round shall we say.

Round and jolly with a smiley face and laughing eyes. And that hairstyle.

The one middle-aged men adopt when they're going bald. Sort of Bobby Charlton style with a bit combed over the top. Bless him.

"There you go ... take some home for later." he smiles, handing me a plate full of fancies.

"That's very kind" ...

"Not at all. Call round tomorrow and you can have some of my Eccles cakes."

Christ! I shall be thirty stone in a few weeks. It's like living next door to Greggs! At least I won't have to worry if Pete's eating enough.

He'll look like the Pilsbury Dough Boy soon.

"I shall have to sit for a bit ... gives me jip after a while" ... he tells me, massaging his leg.

"Sorry ... it must be painful." I empathise.

"Not really, just heavy." he sighs, leaning back in his chair.

"We weighed it the other night." Pete yells, still in the kitchen.

"Oh really?" I stammer, unsure as to how to respond.

"Couple of stone it was ... bit tricky to get an accurate reading." Pete informs me.

"Suffice to say, it's a bit of a problem." Lenny sighs.

"Pete tells me it was the surgery."

"Cocked it up big style" ... Pete bawls from the kitchen.

"Shunt. They put a shunt in my groin to drain the fluid and it went wrong."

"My life!"

"Blew up like a balloon. Never been the same since." Lenny sighs.

"Crikey!"

"Still ... can't complain ... still got all my own teeth." he says in all earnestness.

That's one way of looking at it I suppose, although I'm not altogether certain I'd be so magnanimous if I were left with an exploding leg and a ... well ... a ballooning bollock.

"Lost my job at the hotel of course ... couldn't get used to it ... kept falling over, " Lenny laughs.

"My goodness!" I giggle nervously.

"Bit dangerous in a kitchen. Falling over." he grins.

"Yes quite."

"Just filling in time now. Crossing the kiddies over" ...

"I think that's an admirable job, " I tell him"Think of all those little people relying on you."

"Buggers drive me mad!" he laughs, "They call me Lenny The Leg!"

***

"Jack ... are you asleep?" I whisper.

"Yes"

"Perhaps I could ask Lenny to help me with the wedding cake ... for Alan" ...

"Good idea." he smiles, turning over to face me.

"Why are you awake anyway?" I ask.

"Trying to work out where I put that golf club." he sighs.

"The driver?"

"Yes."

"Titanium with the reinforced shaft?"

"Yes ... why ... have you seen it?" he asks, suddenly interested.

"No." I lie.

"Cass!"

"Sorry."

"What have you done with it?" he sighs.

"You know that fence post that kept falling over ...?"

"Yes."

"I used it to hammer that back into the soil. It's a bit bent." I grovel.

"Well it would be ... night Cass."

"It's under the compost heap."

Chapter Ten

... Orville & I

Yet another summer approaching and activity on the pond is hotting up. We seem to have an abundance of wildlife at the moment, including an enormous water rat who I have nicknamed Mac.

I think it's a water rat anyway. It's definitely a rat and he lives in the water so it makes sense.

Great big bloody thing he is. Frightened me to death when I first saw him scurrying along the bank.

Levy spotted him first and gave chase, thinking it was a cat. He seemed quite startled when Mac dived into the water and disappeared. He followed of course but Gilbert's on patrol at the moment and chased him out of the water.

Even Levy knows when to admit defeat.

Gilbert is fiercely protective of Gertie and her brood and quite rightly so. Just three goslings this year. Maybe Gertie's becoming less fertile with age.

I can remember one particular year when she gave birth to nine.

Perhaps her fallopian tubes are blocked.

I absolutely love this time of year. The pond is awash with babies of all descriptions. Moorhens ... ducklings ... goslings ... and even the odd seagull en route to Eastbourne.

Our grocery bill rockets during these months with several trays of bread every week to pay for.

I wish I could spice up their diet but have no idea what treats to buy for baby birds. I tried them on Trill once but they weren't impressed.

Gertie's goslings are as adorable as ever. Three delightful bundles of yellow and grey down ... sploshing along in the water after Gertie.

I have nicknamed them Flip ... Flap ... and Flop and am keeping everything crossed for their survival. Neville has been a star as ever. Spending hours on watch, hiding in the bushes in case any hungry cats are roaming about. Bless that man! I'd like to give him a big hug for his efforts but it wouldn't be appropriate. He lives alone and wears a flat cap.

Another scorching hot day. Levy's out in the garden ... applying his factor 15. Can't be too careful can you? I read somewhere once that pigs are prone to sunburn! Brings a whole new meaning to the expression roast pork!

Just pop across to see Mary while he's busy.

He's got some magazines and a cold drink so he'll be fine. Crikey! It must be hot ... even Mary's opened her windows ... a rarity I have to say.

The fact that she appears to be drying a pair of voluminous bloomers across the windowsill is neither here nor there.

"Morning Mary ... what a scorcher!" I yell, letting myself in.

"I was just about to ring you Cassie ... Bilbo's back!" she calls from the kitchen.

Oh my life! A reincarnated cat? Looks as if the dementia's moving on at a fair pace.

"Eh?"

"Come through ... he's in here." she giggles excitedly.

I'm almost afraid to look but curiosity gets the better of me and I slowly edge my way into the room. I always was a wuzzy where ghosts are concerned.

"Look Cassie! He came back ... told you he wasn't dead!" she cries, pointing to a spot under the kitchen table.

I peer closer and take a sharp intake of breath as two enormous cats eyes glint at me from the darkness. Fuck me! The bugger's back to haunt me for putting ankle socks on him.

"Oh Christ!" is all I can manage ... my legs buckling with the shock.

"Gave me a bit of a turn as well when he popped through the cat flap!" she laughs.

No ... it can't be! Get a grip girl! Bilbo was dead ... we buried him ... under the lavender bush.

"He's even got a nice new collar on." she smiles, opening a tin of best salmon.

Now I KNOW it's not Bilbo! Bilbo would never be seen dead in a collar. That cat was too street wise for accessories.

"Collar?"

"Yes ... lovely sparkly thing with little diamonds on."

Conclusive proof! As if Bilbo would ever wear diamonds! I think not!

"Let's take a look at him shall we?" I smile, crawling underneath the table on all fours.

The Reincarnated Cat and I stare at each other suspiciously. He has the advantage of being able to see in the dark and looks me up and down with disdain.

I try not to make any sudden movements in case he lunges at my throat.

Years of handling Bilbo taught me that much.

He has quite gentle eyes actually. And an almost kindly face. And possibly the biggest body I have ever seen! How on earth he ever got through that cat flap I'll never know. If this cat is a reincarnation I bet he was a club bouncer in a former life. Is it the Hindu religion who believe in reincarnation? Saw it on television I think ... or was that Pingu? ... who knows?

"Come on lad ... dinner time!" Mary sings, placing a dish of red salmon onto the floor.

I beat a hasty retreat for fear of being trampled in the stampede and watch, fascinated, as the cat slinks past me and straight to the dish.

His body taught and muscular. His fur a beautiful shade of Persian blue.

This is one posh cat I have to say. A potential champion I should think.

I bet his owners are distraught. Probably have a police helicopter scouring the woods as we speak.

"Mary ... he's lovely ... but" ... I try to tell her as gently as possible.

"I know ... he's put a bit of weight on" ... she stops me in mid-flow.

Put a bit of weight on? My life! Changed his breed ... and his colour ... and had a cornea transplant as well by the look of it!

Bilbo had shocking green eyes. This cats' are a deep amber colour!

Be pointless me even attempting to get through to her. Besides which, I haven't seen her so animated for a long time. What the heck!

If she wants to believe this is Bilbo then let her. He'll probably be gone again by tomorrow. No harm done. In her present state, she'll forget he was ever here anyway.

"He's enjoying that salmon." I smile, defeated.

"Of course he is! Always was his favourite, " she beams, opening another tin.

Charlie! I shall call him Charlie ... The Reincarnated Cat! It seems appropriate somehow.

See ... this proves my theory regarding cat flaps. I have always suspected that they are an open invitation to gate crashers. If your average moggy can squeeze through, then so can a variety of intruders. Small dogs ... giant mice ... and even reincarnated cats.

"Better go Mary ... I'll pop in again later." I tell her.

"You be careful out there...had a funny bloke at the door earlier" ... she says.

"In what way Mary?" I ask her, alarmed that she may have opened the door to a stranger.

"Ugly bugger ... big nose ... and one of those funny hats!" she snorts.

"Hat?"

"You know ... leather trousers!" she says.

"A biker you mean ... with a crash helmet?"

"No ... silly sod ... apple strudel!" she yells, exasperated.

Oh my life! Where is this conversation going I ask myself? I shall have to pursue it ... lord knows who she's been opening the door to.

"Mary, you've lost me. Can we start again?" I plead.

"Look ... one of those funny hats ... with a feather in!" she snaps, losing the plot.

Bingo! A trilby! One of those silly Tyrolean titfers with a daft little feather on the side.

"Oh right! Got you! What did he want?"

"A smacked arse ... cheeky bugger ... said I needed some work done on the roof!"

"Cheek! I hope you told him where to go."

"I certainly did. On his bike I think ... saw him wobble away across the roundabout" ...

"A builder ... on a bike ... what about his tools?" I laugh.

"Never trust a man with a feather in his hat." Mary sings.

"I'll remember that."

"And never sleep with a man with nostril hair!" she warns me in all seriousness.

"Erm ... right." I giggle.

"My mother gave me that bit of advice." she rambles, stroking Charlie.

"Really?"

"Oh yes ... that and a packet of Palmolive soap." she tells me distractedly.

Bless that woman! Such pearls of wisdom and it's not even midday yet. She has a point about the nostril hair. I couldn't ... could you?

I have no idea what the Palmolive is about. Mary was raised on some isolated farm back in Ireland. Maybe Palmolive was a luxury. Actually, I think anything was a luxury for Mary and her nine brothers and sisters! Space being the operative word I should think.

Imagine ten kids ... two adults ... and a variety of livestock ... all crammed in together. No wonder she left and came to England!

"And on that note ... I'll be off Mary" ... I laugh.

"Thanks for popping in Cass ... you're a good soul." she whispers.

"Can I get you anything from the shops later?"

"Some fish heads from the market please ... for Bilbo."

Fish heads! Oh dear ... don't think old Charlie will appreciate that. Looks more like a Cordon Bleu cat to me.

Probably raised on slivers of cod roe and caviar.

"See you later Mary" ...

As I close the front door, Mary is sitting at the kitchen table ... with Charlie purring at her feet.

She's mooching around in her knitting bag ... probably about to start work on a cardigan for him.

I don't know why she bothers. Bilbo never wore that hat she knitted for him.

***

I knew I shouldn't have left that dog on his own. He gets bored easily and now look! Daft sod's got himself wedged inside the water barrel. It's empty thank goodness. We only keep it in case of a drought and that's highly unlikely in this country. He either got bored or he's practising his barrel rolling skills. By the look of the lawn I'd say the latter. Look at the state of this place. Great big chunks of turf scattered all across the path and two terracotta pots smashed.

"Levy! Get out of there!" I bawl, chasing him ... mid-roll ... down the garden.

His weight means that he gains momentum on the slope and he suddenly screeches to a halt by the fence. If I didn't know better I'd swear he's grinning.

Honestly! Great big sloppy grin with his tongue lolloping out of his mouth.

"Come on ... daft sod ... let's go for a walk" ...

He is at my side in an instant ... all thoughts of barrel rolling gone. Mainly because I'm secreting a large packet of bacon flavoured doggy treats about my person. This lad can sniff out bacon from a distance of roughly three miles. Our early morning walks are quite often interrupted by his quest for a rasher of smoked back. He has been known to stop ... mid-stride ... right in the middle of a main road and raise his nose in the air, breathing in the bacon as we call it.

"Morning Cassie. Beautiful day!"

"Hi Pete ... Hi Lenny!"

They are sitting on the low stone wall that surrounds Pete's front garden. Pete holding the obligatory can of Strongbow while Lenny dangles his bloated leg carelessly over the side.

They both appear to be dressed for the weather and are even wearing sunglasses. That's a first!

"Nice glasses! I must get myself a new pair. Sat on mine." I tell them.

"I'll get you a pair of these. Syd sells them up at the market." Pete informs me.

"Thanks! What make are they?" I ask, just out of curiosity.

"Mike." Pete says, taking his off and offering them to me.

"Eh?"

"Mike ones! Syd says they're all the rage." Lenny pipes up.

For a split second, I think he means Nike but nothing is ever that simple. They are indeed Mike glasses! There it is, emblazoned across the bridge, Mike!

You have to laugh don't you?

"Lovely!" I lie, desperate to get away before he insists on giving them to me.

Now, I'm not a designer person as you know but even I draw the line at wearing Mike glasses with a rip off tick on the side. People would take the piss!

"Just off to feed the goslings." I tell them, backing away.

"I'll be in the market Friday. I'll get you a pair." Pete smiles.

"Thanks."

"They do them in pink if you prefer." Lenny offers.

"No ... honest ... black will be fine" ... I grimace, "How much?"

"Ninety-nine pence."

"Lovely! Get Jack a pair as well would you?" I giggle, knowing full well he'll be mortified.

"Consider it done!" Pete slurs opening another can.

I can't help but take a glance back at them as I turn the corner. Tweedledum and Tweedledee ... sitting on the wall in their Mike sunglasses.

If they're still there when I get back I'll take a few snapshots with my Olympiss camera.

***

It's exceptionally quiet on the pond. Must be the heat. Maybe all the babies are taking an afternoon snooze.

Even Gilbert appears to be missing and he's normally on patrol twenty-four hours a day. Neville's over there under the beech tree ... I'll amble over and have a chat ...

"Stay there Cassie!" he suddenly yells as I open the gate into the enclosure,

"Stay there!"

Oh dear. That sounded quite urgent. I wonder what's wrong?

"Sorry?" I call back.

"Don't come over ... wait there!" he shouts, gesturing for me to move back.

I do as I am told and stand stock still with Levy, rooted to the spot. The silence is quite spooky and I fear the worst as Neville approaches, his head lowered ... his expression sombre.

"Sorry Cassie ... there's no easy way to say this ... it's Gertie" ...

"What is it?" my voice rises in panic.

"She's out there ... on the water ... I think she's dead." he whispers gently.

"No!!"

"Sorry ... I was just about to wade in and fetch her out." he whispers.

"Oh Neville ... what about the babies?" I wail.

"Don't get upset Cassie ... we'll do what we can."

I follow his gaze and squint against the glare of the sun at the shimmering water. There she is.

Floating serenely ... carried along on the breeze ... her once magnificent head bowed in submission.

She must be dead. Gertie would never leave her babies alone.

"Oh Neville, this is dreadful!" I cry, hot, salty tears gushing down my cheeks.

"Come on Cassie ... sit on the bench while I go and get her." he tells me gently, leading me towards the seat.

I watch, horrified, as he wades purposefully through the water, gently making his way towards the dead goose.

The pond is only waist-high at its peak and he strides out, reaching the corpse in seconds. Neville is a big guy and gently scoops her up into his arms as if he were cradling a small child.

I can't bear to watch and burying my face into Levy's fur, sob like an idiot.

Oh Gertie! What on earth will those babies do now?

"Bloody cruel old Mother Nature!" he sighs, bringing Gertie back to the bank.

"What is it?" I wail, losing the plot completely at the sad sight before me.

"Looks as if something's had a go at her neck. Lost a lot of blood I think."

"Oh my goodness!" I sob.

"It'll be a fox, mark my words. A cat couldn't inflict this much damage."

"Bastard!" I weep overwhelmed with anger.

"Exactly. Nothing we can do now except bury the old girl." he sighs, laying her down on the bank.

I'm not up to this. I can't cope with animal deaths. It's just so bloody sad and so unfair!

Here she was ... minding her own business ... bringing up her brood ... and now this.

"Neville ... I can't" ... I stammer, breaking down again.

"You go home Cassie. I'll deal with this" ...

"Are you sure?"

"Go on. I'll make sure she has a decent send off." he sighs.

Levy and I make our way home in a totally dazed state. He always senses when I'm upset and nuzzles my hand as we slowly amble back along Park Ridge. His incredibly soulful eyes watching my face and taking in every sob.

Pete and Lenny have disappeared from the wall and I'm thankful for that. I'm never at my best during times of bereavement. I cried for hours once when I accidentally poured Domestos onto a frog lurking in the drain.

It died an agonising death and I witnessed every bloody second.

Took me weeks to get over that I can tell you. I must tell Jack. He was very fond of old Gertie.

"It's me ... I ... oh Jack!" I sob, unable to get the words out.

"Cass! What is it?" his voice full of concern.

"It's ... oh ... it was awful ... oh Jack!" I sob.

"What? Cass ... slow down ... what is it ... is it Tom?" he asks.

"No ... Tom's fine ... it's Gertie ... broken neck ... Neville" ... I blabber.

"Neville rang her neck?" he shouts incredulously.

"No! Neville thinks a fox attacked her." I weep.

"Oh Cass ... I'm sorry ... will you be okay?"

"Sorry ... she just looked so sad ... and the babies ... what shall we do?"

"Don't worry. We'll sort something out. Go and make a cuppa. I'll be back soon"

"Okay"

"Don't cry Cass ... I hate to see you cry" ... he says gently.

"Sorry ... you know me and animals."

"I know Cass ... I know ... now go get that cuppa" ...

We shall have to sort something out. Can't let Flip ... Flap ... and Flop die as well. I shall have to become their foster mom.

I can do that. Just make sure they're fed and kept safe. Neville will help. And Jack too.

By the time Jack arrives home, I have regained a little of my composure and managed to rustle up some incredibly soggy scrambled eggs and a salad for tea.

My face has taken on its usual mutant proportions after a crisis.

Hugely swollen nose and piggy little eyes along with roughly two yards of snot dangling from my inflamed nose.

"Cass ... you daft bugger ... come here." he whispers, wrapping his arms around me.

"Jack, she looked so sad ... and ... pitiful." I sob.

"Never mind. She did a marvellous job with those babies."

"Yes but what now?"

"Nature will take its course I suppose. They'll manage."

"I was thinking. Maybe I could foster them. You know ... like people do with kittens" ...

"Bit of a difference Cass. Goslings need a pond to swim on." he smiles.

"And a mother who can teach them how to fly ... I'm a bit like Orville in that department." I sob.

"Absolutely."

"It's not going to work is it?" I moan dejectedly.

"They'll survive. Nature has a way of working things out." he reassures me.

"In the meantime, I shall keep an eye out for that fox. Scumbag!" I snap.

"He's a marked man." he winces, biting on a piece of eggshell.

"Too right!"

"Leave these scrambled eggs out for him. That should finish him off!"

"Would you like some home-made rice pudding?" I ask.

"No thanks."

Chapter Eleven

... A Severe Case Of Foot & Mouth

Jack was right about this. He tried to talk me out of it but I'm a stubborn little bugger and as usual refused to budge.

Wish I'd have listened to him now. He did try to warn me. Oh well!

I'm here now so I might as well make the best of a bad lot and get on with it. I'm actually going for an interview! For a job! Whey-hey!

How about that for progress? Jack says it's too early yet and I should chill out for a little longer. Get my head together and all that. Yeah right!

Like my head is ever going to be totally together! Bless him!

It's not exactly rocket science anyway. Just a few hours a week in the library at Oakham University.

I have no qualifications whatsoever ... just an all-consuming passion for books. That should help surely?

The prospect of spending my days browsing through acres of literature was just too good to miss. So here I am. Granted, I look nothing like a librarian. I don't own a twin-set or a string of pearls but I have made an effort ... of sorts.

I've combed my hair and even applied some lipstick ... badly but there you go. And I've dyed my summer sandals.

Nice sombre shade of black as opposed to their original pastel blue colour.

Shaving the old legs was a bit of a nightmare but I don't think they'll notice the plasters.

I shall tell them I have a skin disease ... that should get the sympathy vote.

This university campus is amazing. It's almost like a little city within itself. It has a bank and a book shop and lots of other amenities.

I passed a very impressive swimming pool back there.

Actually, I passed it three times. Along with five circuit's round the science block.

Suffice to say, I'm lost. Nothing new there then! I imagine you'd need a degree to find your way to the lecture rooms in this place.

The heat's not helping. It must be eighty in the shade and I'm beginning to wilt now.

The interview is scheduled for one-thirty but it's only midday.

I was panicking and thought I'd set out early just in case. Considering the university is only a ten minute walk from home, I feel I misjudged that one.

Should have worn a hat. I had sunstroke once and it's not a pleasant experience. Don't think turning up in a Russian style Cossack hat would have impressed them though do you? I don't do hats and Ma bought me the bloody thing last winter. She seemed to think it was ideal for walking Levy in the woods.

He took an instant dislike to it so I sometimes put it on just to wind him up.

Jack says I only need to grow my moustache a bit longer and I can get a job as a woodsman.

Phew! This is getting uncomfortable now. I can feel sweat trickling down my back and my blouse is sticking to me in all the wrong places.

How attractive is that? Arriving for an interview drenched in sweat!

They'll think I have a body odour problem. As well as the skin disease.

I shall have to find somewhere shady to sit down for a while. I can't decide if this is sunstroke or hysteria.

Next time I'll listen to Jack when he tries to tell me something.

"Excuse me ... can you tell me, is there a coffee bar or something around here?"

"Vas?"

"Eh?"

Just my luck! Thousands of students on this campus and I have to pick the Bosnian bloke to ask.

"Erm ... drink ...?" I ask again, hoping he'll understand.

"Vant with me ... beer?" he slobbers, his eyes glinting with lust.

"Certainly not!" I tell him indignantly, "I need a drink ... thirsty ... erm ... Coke?" I rasp, definitely hysterical now.

"Vant cock?" he grins, his ugly face leering even closer to mine.

Oh my life! Now I'm scared! What is it with these cretins? Do I look as if I cruise university campus's looking for sex?

Jack has instructed me on exactly what to do in situations like this.

Go for the bollocks basically. And if that fails ... shout as loudly as you can.

Which is all well and good in theory but in reality it's a bit more complex than that. Besides which, this guy is a big bugger.

I don't think I could reach his bollocks. Even standing on a step ladder.

"Go away!" I bawl at the top of my voice, shattering several windows in the process. Polite but firm. That's the way to do it.

Look him in the eye and don't show any fear. They know when you're afraid.

Your pupils dilate and you sweat apparently. Which means I'm fucked at the moment cos I'm drenched in the stuff. He's not moving and seems excited by my response.

He has that jittery look ... and a quite obvious erection within his track suit bottoms.

"Fuck off!" I yell ... with menace this time and I have to say, he seems to get the message.

He shuffles off into the distance, taking his erection with him thank goodness. Well really!

That young man needs treatment of some sort. Castration would be appropriate I feel.

He's also urgently in need of an eye test. See what happens when you wear a skirt?

Expose your ankles and some men just lose the plot. I shall be glad to get back into my jeans.

There ... he's gone now. Just sit down on this wall and get myself together. Deep breaths girl.

They'll expect you to be calm for this position. Librarians are not prone to hysteria. They glide effortlessly down the aisles, dispensing knowledge to all those seeking it. Cool and collected ... that's the way.

Oh fuck! The dye on my sandals has run! Must be the heat. My toes are a filthy black colour and my heels! This is dreadful!

I have the look of a bag-lady about me now. Sweaty armpit's ... fuzzy hair and filthy feet. My life! Can this get any worse? I shall have to go home again.

Take a hot shower and lie down in a dark room. I'd never get back in time. Then it would look as if I've chickened out. I can't. Tilly was so excited when I told her about this.

Probably because if I did get the job, it would mean she'd never have to see me again.

Get a grip girl! You can do this. You've faced far worse in your life. You're the woman who walked through the village with your skirt tucked into your knickers ... the result of a hurried change of clothes while shopping for jeans. You can do this! Think! Try to reverse the situation.

Tissues. I have some in my pocket. Wipe it off. Clean up the feet and carry on as normal.

There you go! Problem solved. Except I have no water. You need moisture to clean off dirt.

Have to spit on the tissue. Get some scrubbing action going. There you go. No spit. I'm so ruddy hot and bothered my saliva's dried up.

It's making me gag just attempting it. There's a girl over there giving me funny looks. Probably thinks I've got TB.

Fucking hell! Ruddy dye's all over my mouth now! I have morphed into a Black and White Minstrel. I can't do this! I need Jack! He'd know what to do. Roll around on the grass laughing probably, but still.

Jack is a cool customer and can be relied on totally in a crisis. I, on the other hand am a wimp. If everything doesn't go to plan, I fall to pieces. I have to do this.

If only to prove to Tilly ... and Jack ... that I'm capable of doing something.

I shall wing it. Breeze in there and pretend I'm on top form. Psychologically, I shall have an advantage as they will be far too busy concentrating on what appears to be a severe case of foot and mouth.

If I do get the job, no doubt we will all laugh about this during tea-breaks in future.

Or maybe not. Whatever, plod on girl. Give it your best.

"Sorry, can you direct me to the English faculty?" I bravely ask a startled looking young girl.

"Erm ... sure ... over there on the right" ... she points.

"Thanks. I'm here for an interview." I grin, falling into step by her side.

"Your lips are black, " she informs me, staring intently at my mouth.

"I know. Dye off my sandals." I tell her trying to appear cool.

"And your teeth" ... she giggles, staring into my gaping gob.

I have gone past caring now. You know when you just get to that stage where you really don't give a fuck? Well, I have reached that point.

And beyond. She veers to the left and disappears into one of the buildings.

Obviously not wishing to be seen out with a bag lady ... with rotten teeth.

Block E. The library section. Room 7. Here we go. Get in there and show them what you're made of. If nothing comes of all this at least it will have been a learning curve.

I will have learnt that you should never dye your sandals black.

"Cassie Ryder. I have an interview at one-thirty. Bit early I'm afraid." I grin at the girl on the desk.

She is quite obviously mesmerised by my mouth and stares closely at it while trying not to laugh.

"Can I get you anything while you wait?" she asks, adjusting her glasses.

Such as? A hot bath? Some extensive dental work?

"Thanks ... I'm fine." I tell her, lying through my blackened teeth.

"Take a seat over there. I'll tell the board that you're here" ...

The board! What's all that about then? It's a part-time post in the library. Not a doctorate.

This is not looking good. I expected a quick chat with some old biddy in a tweed skirt. Got that wrong didn't I?

I watch as she whispers into the phone and then gets to her feet.

"This way ... they have a slot." she smiles, ushering me through a door into the inner sanctum.

An impressive board room of some description with oak panelled walls and several armchairs scattered at angles around it. If I didn't know better, I would almost expect Michael Caine to be lounging in one of them. I would be Rita of course.

Intimidated. Overwhelmed. And common of course.

"Please, take a seat." a kindly voice whispers, calling me towards the far end of the room.

And a shower ... the voice is probably dying to add. The lighting is quite harsh and I fear that my filthy feet are about to be exposed.

131

Three board members then. Two male ... one gender unknown. I think it's a woman but it's difficult to tell. She has a herringbone jacket and a crew cut. Could be a tranny ... who knows?

"Just relax. We try to make these as informal as possible." she tells me, not bothering to look up.

I sit as instructed and tuck the offensive feet underneath the chair. The mouth is beyond saving.

I'm here now ... just have to grin and bear it. Or rather bear it but don't grin. Remember the teeth?

"We'll fire off a few questions. Just answer as you see fit." Lily Savage snaps.

"Right, got that." I smile awkwardly.

"What was the last thing you read?" Lily asks.

"Woman's Own." I babble, mouth engaging before brain.

"Any societies?" she continues, still not looking me in the eye.

"RSPCA ... RSPB ... erm ... YMCA" ... I giggle, losing the plot.

This is not going well. The two men appear to have lost the will to live and shuffle their papers nervously as Lily fires off her list of totally inane questions. Societies! What's all that about then?

Maybe she means The Masons or something. I should have worn my trousers then I could have rolled up one leg and given her a secret handshake or something.

"Bennett or Binchy?" she barks, twirling her moustache.

"Bennett ... if you mean Alan ... you know ... Talking Heads and all that." I groan.

"I was thinking more of his theatre work. Kafkas Dick perhaps?" she spit's.

"Eh?"

"Stage play. Never mind." she sighs impatiently, rolling her eyes towards heaven.

Did I hear that right? Kafkas Dick! What the fuck is that? Oh bollocks! Jack was right ...

I'm not ready for this yet. Should stick to my own ... go work in a cake shop or something.

I'm good on cakes. There are no pretentions where ring donuts are concerned. Oh cack!

"I see you attended King Edward's." she drawls, flicking through my notes.

"That's the grammar school ... not the spud" ... I titter, past caring now.

"Quite."

"I have O Level English Lit ... and Language." I boast.

"And a diploma in metalwork." I grin, going in for the kill.

"We'll give you a call shall we?" Lily barks, dismissing me in an instant.

I take it that means this interview is over then. How rude!

It's taken me weeks to prepare for this and I've got sunstroke wandering around the campus. Thanks a lot pal!

I may not look like suitable librarian material but a fair chance would have been nice.

"Right. Thanks for your time anyway." I smile manically, getting to my feet.

The fact that I forget my feet are wrapped around the chair legs is bought home to me as I try to stand and topple unceremoniously forward, crashing heavily onto the oak table ... my head landing roughly three inches away from Lily's outstretched hand.

"Goodness! Are you alright?" she asks, helping me up.

"Fine! Never better!" I giggle, my face crimson with embarrassment.

"Cheerio then!" she trills looking stunned.

"Bye!" I wave cheerily, limping off into the sunset.

I can feel their eyes boring holes in my back as I waft out of the room, casually glancing at the rows of books lining the walls.

Stick your job missus! We would never have got on anyway.

She has the look of a woman who wears corduroy trousers at the weekends and very possibly smokes a pipe.

133

Academics see! It's another world and one for which I'm not quite ready yet.

I consider myself to be reasonably articulate and well-read but you quite obviously need a Master's degree in Nuclear Physics to dispense books here.

Hey-ho! Something else will turn up soon.

Maybe I could get a job in a newsagents. Start off selling magazines and work my way up.

Oh fuck it! All this fuss for ten hours a week! I'd much rather be at home with Levy anyway. He takes me for what I am ... warts and all ... which is what I love about animals.

They don't care if your Latin is weak. As long as you can open a tin you're fine.

As I shuffle past reception, another candidate is waiting to enter the lions' den. She'll get the job.

You can tell can't you? A thirty-something wearing a suit. And carrying a very battered copy of Ibsen. Nice move love!

You'll fit in perfectly in there. I wish I'd thought of that.

Could have bought along one of my Bunty annuals.

Jack says it's their loss anyway. He was waiting for me when I got back. Bless that man.

"So you're not very up on old Kafkas Dick then?" he laughs, pouring the tea.

"Never heard of him ... or his dick!" I wail.

"I should hope not woman!"

"Does that mean I'm thick?" I ask plaintively, looking for sympathy.

"Yes!" he laughs.

"I've got nice tit's though!" I tell him.

"Undoubtedly."

"I could do Readers Wives! Those awful women in those magazines!" I laugh.

"What ... Gloria from Greater Manchester ... into S&M and all that?" He asks.

"In my case that would be sausage and mash."

"Cass ... your sausage and mash is dreadful!"

"Forget that then."

"Chocolate Hob Nob?" he asks, passing me the plate.
"Are we back to dirty magazines again?"
"Never read them." he lies.
"Liar!"
"I just look at the pictures."
"Jack!!"
"Silly tart!"

Chapter Twelve

... Open Wide

Ma has a dental appointment today and I have to go along with her. Not that she's scared or anything. Good God no! That's never gonna happen!

Ma's not scared of anything. It's just that during her last appointment a few weeks ago, the dentist saw fit to give her a new set of dentures which can only be described as well ... horses teeth really.

I have taken to calling her Shergar and she is not amused.

Ma is extremely particular about her appearance and hasn't really been out of the house since the new noshers were installed. She has taken to shopping at the all-night Asda in case anyone recognises her.

Pa is knackered. He's not up to pushing a trolley at two in the morning.

I told her at the time to go back and insist something be done but she's very pliable where professionals are concerned is Ma.

She trusts them you see. Implicitly. If anyone in a white coat tells Ma anything she'll swear it's gospel. Even the ice-cream man.

The ruddy teeth were quite obviously made for someone else. A six-foot builder probably.

There's been a clerical error somewhere and it's got to the point now where Ma is beginning to lose weight! Chewing is impossible as she can barely close her mouth.

Pa put his foot down, quite forcefully for Pa and she's agreed to go back.

I have bought a brown paper bag with me to pop over her head until we get there.

"Come on Ma. I'll come in with you and explain." I tell her.

"Your father was going to do that but he's indisposed!" she yells from the kitchen.

"What's wrong now?" I ask intrigued.

"Go and take a look! Just take a look!" she screams, verging on the hysterical.

Pa is sitting in his easy-chair in the lounge. His hands soaking in a plastic bowl ... steam rising from the soapy water within.

"You alright Pa?"

"Fine. She's in a flap. I've made a bit of a mess of my hands, " he sighs.

"Sorry?"

"My hands. Bert at the Legion gave me some stuff for that rash ... between my fingers."

"And?"

"Said to soak them for an hour. Now look!" he cries, raising his hands out of the water.

Bert has indeed given him some stuff! I have no idea what that stuff is but it appears to have turned Pa's hands a delicate shade of chestnut brown.

From a distance, it looks as if he's wearing gloves.

"Pa! What on earth is it?" I laugh.

"Iodine. Bert swears by it, " he tells me forlornly, "cleared up his athletes foot."

"Oh crikey!" I giggle.

"It won't come off!" he giggles too, joining in the fun.

"It will eventually Pa. Just keep them in water until we get back."

"Come on Cassandra! We'll be late!" Ma barks, slamming out of the front door.

I follow ... at a distance. In that mood, she could take my head off easily with those teeth.

Mr Crump ... The Cavity King! He has lots of letters after his name but none of them remotely connected to dentistry I shouldn't think. He's a nice old guy and I'm sure he means well but things have moved on in the world of dentistry and Mr Crump hasn't. Ma and Pa have been on his list since the

137

sixties and I swear some of the equipment he uses dates back to the Victorian era.

This place scares the shit out of me but they keep coming back for more. Every six months for a check-up and every couple of years for new dentures. Ma lost all her teeth during pregnancy.

Conjures up a lovely mental image don't you think? Some malicious midwife punching her in the mouth to calm her down! No ... seriously ... it was something to do with the calcium levels in her body. So it's all my fault really I suppose.

"Good morning. Can I help?" Jessie on the desk shouts. Jessie is eighty two and deaf.

"Ma's got somebody else's teeth!" I yell at her in order to make myself heard.

"Oh dear. So has Mr Walton ... how odd!" she yells back.

Things are falling into place now. Mr Walton ... whoever he is ... is obviously walking around wearing my mother's teeth!

Silly old bat probably mixed the bags up since she also acts as Mr Crump's dental assistant. What a nightmare! This is the last straw. I shall register them both with my dentist after this.

"Can we see Mr Crump?" I bawl into her left ear as she leans over the desk.

"Yes, go on through. He's having a coffee."

A coffee and a fag no doubt. Mr Crump is the only dentist I know who actually smokes while he's working! A Benson & Hedges dangling from his lips as he leans over his patients.

It's not hygienic is it?

"Come on Cassandra. You're making a show of me!" Ma hisses, heading for the surgery door.

Making a show of her! She's the one racing in the 2.30 at Haydock! I follow as she strides purposefully into the surgery ... the teeth entering the room at least thirty seconds before her head.

"Mr Crump! These teeth are all wrong!" she snaps, opening her mouth to its full capacity.

"Oh my goodness! They do seem a trifle large." he nods sympathetically.

A trifle large! Where were you when they were installed pal? In another room?

Silly sod!

"Take a seat and I'll have a look." he waffles, lighting up another cigarette.

"My gums are sore. I've had nothing solid for a week!" Ma moans.

"Oh dear!"

"Chicken soup and semolina." she continues, on a roll now.

"Problems chewing?" he asks distractedly, peering into the gaping chasm before him.

Problems chewing! Poor bugger can't close her mouth, let alone chew!

"Terrible. I've got a whole box of Thorntons toffee unopened at home."

"I see the problem. These teeth belong to Mr Walton!" he smiles, flicking ash into the sink.

"Who the hell's Mr Walton?" I butt in, exasperated at his lack of professionalism.

"Retired bus inspector. Oakham Park Road" ... he tells us.

"Didn't he used to do the Outer Circle route?" Ma pipes up in all innocence.

"I believe so. Until he got moved onto the Ring and Ride" ... Crump nods.

For fucks sake! Never mind bus timetables! Get those teeth sorted before she dies of malnutrition you incompetent old fart!

"So presumably, if Ma's got his dentures ... he'll have hers." I snap, giving him one of my looks.

"Quite right. He was in here earlier. Left them behind for some adjustment."

"Oh thank goodness! Can we sort this out now so that I can eat tonight?" Ma pleads.

139

"Of course my dear. I'll get Jessie to give them a scrub for you."

Whoa! Stop right there! I draw the line at letting Ma put some old blokes dentures into her gob.

"Mr Crump! Can't we order a new set. I mean ... the others have been in Mr Walton's mouth." I grimace.

"Don't worry my dear. He only wears them on a Sunday." Crump assures me.

"Eh?"

"His son takes him out for lunch. On Sundays" ... he tells me.

"Oh that's nice." Ma says, nodding her head in approval, "I wonder where they go?"

"Black Bear I think." the dentist from hell informs us.

"They do a nice roast there." she tells me, "four different choices of meat I think."

Excuse me? Have I received a bang on the head within the last half hour or so? Here we are, discussing the niceties of Sunday lunch at the Black Bear, while my mother is about to have recycled dentures inserted into her mouth! Heaven forbid!

"Anyway! Can we get back to the teeth. I'm not happy about this Ma." I yell.

"Stop fussing Cassandra. Mr Crump knows what he's doing." she hisses at me.

"Yeah right! If he did he wouldn't have given you the wrong set in the first place!" I yell back indignantly.

I give up! Ma is not a woman to wrestle with. Especially in a confined space. I concede defeat and opt for a more tactful approach instead.

"The least you could do is sterilise the bloody things!" I bawl at Mr Crump.

"Of course. Take a seat in the waiting room and I'll be with you shortly."

"Thank you so much Mr Crump. I'm very grateful." Ma gushes glaring at me.

Fine! Slap some skanky dentures into your mouth! See if I care! Don't come crying to me if you get gingivitis!

"Come along Cassandra. Let Mr Crump get on with his work." Ma snaps.

Jessie is still at the desk. Plucking stray hairs from her upper lip. Delightful!

We sit. Ma browsing through an ancient copy of Womans Realm while I desperately try to wipe out the mental image of Mr Walton chewing on his Sunday roast.

See what I mean ... about Ma being pliable where professionals are concerned?

Just because he's medical ... of sorts ... she happily goes along with anything he says. I swear if he told her to stand on her hands during her next appointment she would. Generational you see. Ma's generation don't argue. Not with people who have letters after their name. Doctors ... dentists ... chiropodists ... they know best.

They are trained you see ... or so she's fond of telling me. I suspect Mr Crump got his diploma from some dodgy correspondence college in Mexico.

"Mr Crumps ready for you now." Jessie smiles, waving over at Ma.

I keep out of it and watch as she scurries off back into the surgery.

Bless her! Anything rather than create a fuss.

Ma doesn't do fuss. She puts up and shuts up. Those bloody teeth must have been agony for weeks and there she is sucking soup through a straw! Unbelievable!

She emerges minutes later, grinning from ear to ear. Her new ... or nearly new teeth ... glinting in the harsh light of the waiting room.

She'll be able to eat steak tonight. And crunchy carrots.

"There you go Cassie ... good as new!" she beams, exposing her gum line.

"Lovely Ma!"

"He's wonderful for his age, and considering his sights going." Jessie smiles at us.

Sights going? Oh my life! Should this man be allowed to practise I ask myself?

"Still plays squash every weekend as well." she gushes, her face glowing with pride.

Squash? How the fuck does he see the ball? The mind boggles it really does.

"Come along Cassandra, let¹s get home" ... Ma barks heading for the door.

"Coming Ma."

"See you in six months!" Jessie yells, startling an elderly man standing by the desk.

I have my suspicions regarding Mr Crump. He only ever seems to treat pensioners. People in their twilight years so to speak.

And he only deals in cash which I find a tad disconcerting as well.

Methinks he's actually a denture maker with delusions. I bet he's never done a filling in his life.

There are no diplomas on his surgery walls and a distinct lack of dental equipment.

But he has the white coat you see. Nuff said.

***

"Seems to me that you have two options Pa" ...

"What are those?"

"Either wear gloves or keep your hands in your pockets."

"It's too hot for gloves."

"Keep your hands in your pockets then."

"People might think I'm a bit odd" ...

"In what way?"

"You know ... a bloke with his hands in his pockets" ...

"What ... like pocket billiards?"

"Exactly!"

"Wear your new cardigan then. The purple one with the pockets in."

"Your Mother won't like it. She hates that cardigan."

"Why?"
"She says I look like a plum in it."
"Rather a plum than a pervert Pa" ...
"Good point" ...

Chapter Thirteen

... Wiggy

I swear that dog's been here before. In another life I mean. Bugger!

He has this uncanny knack of getting himself into bother and then bolting when it kicks off. I suspect he was a hyperactive child in a former life. And as with any other doting mother ... my boy can do no wrong. Bless him!

He's just accidentally flipped a bench over. Trying to scrabble underneath for the remainder of a cheese cob.

He's so big you see, and clumsy...and totally oblivious to the chaos he causes.

Now I have to try and turn the bench back over and it's bloody heavy! He's disappeared of course. I saw his arse disappear into the woods seconds ago.

Strictly speaking, we are both banned from these woods. Jack says it's too dangerous ... a woman on her own in such a secluded place ... but we often sneak up here and spend a few hours chasing each other through the trees.

I'm not scared anyway. Not while I have Levy with me.

It would be an incredibly foolish flasher who dares to whip his willy out in front of that boy.

Jack got me a mobile a few years back...for emergencies. I can't find the bloody thing now and have no idea where I've left it.

Never got the hang of it anyway. All those buttons and codes and people ringing you when you're trying to get some peace. I have no desire to be contacted when I'm out thank you!

The phone at home is bad enough. I actually saw a tiny child last week, chattering away on a mobile. Couldn't have been more than five or six! How stupid is that?

For the life of me...I cannot think of any situation that would require a five year old to need a mobile!

If they're not at home or in bed then surely they're at school?

Where on earth would a five year old be that would require them to use a mobile? A nightclub? Restaurant? To call for a cab after a night out?

How ridiculous! I had a mobile when I was five ... my gob! If ever I was in distress I'd use it to shout Ma who was never more than a few feet away.

Now I have to find that dog. It's getting late and Jack will be home soon. I know he's in here somewhere. Hiding probably.

Yet another one of his favourite games ... hide and seek. He hides and I seek normally. No good me trying to hide. He's gun dog stock remember and could sniff me out from ten miles away.

"Levy!" I bawl at the top of my voice, hoping he'll respond for once.

Nothing! A big fat zilch as usual. He gets distracted easily you see. Short attention span and all that.

Probably way up high in a tree somewhere, chasing a Cyril. Or a pervert.

"Chocolate buttons!" I call again, using an old trick that normally brings him to heel.

True to form ... his enormous bulk skids out of the trees and lands unceremoniously at my feet.

"Good lad!"

Never fails. His eyes sparkling with excitement. His humungous tail swishing in anticipation.

"Come on ... let's go." I tell him, handing him the packet as we make our way towards the lane.

I had no idea it was so late. Time flies when you're rolling around in the bracken with half a ton of labrador.

I have squirrel shit on my boots and several muddy paw prints on my jacket. Let's hope there are no small children around.

They'll think I'm that witch out of Harry Potter.

I really do love this place. You can walk for hours and never see another soul and on certain days the sun seems to dance along the top of the trees, creating wonderful psychedelic patterns on the leaves.

Best of all, I love the tranquillity. No noise ... no people ... no phones.

Perfect!

Levy loves it because of the numerous animal scents and scraps of food left by picnickers. So far today he's found a cheese roll ... two digestive biscuit's and a carton of semi-skimmed milk.

He is walking in front of me as usual. His wonderful gait lolling from side to side. His head high, nostrils sucking in the afternoon air for anything edible.

God, I do love that lad! Sometimes, I just get overwhelmed by his sheer magnificence and have to bite down hard on my lip to stop the tears from flowing. Daft isn't it? Does this face care? There is SO much going on inside his handsome head and it fascinates me. What does he think about I wonder? Squirrels and sex mainly but I'd love to know.

Without any warning whatsoever he suddenly stops dead in his tracks, every muscle in his taut body straining with the effort. His eyes darting around the shadows in the trees, searching for something.

The hair on his back raised and angry. This is not good. I have seen the signs before and it usually means danger of some description. He did exactly the same a few weeks ago in the garden only then it was a hedgehog hiding under a pot. I stand stock still behind him, my heart racing and every inch of me wishing I'd kept that mobile handy.

Stay calm girl. It's probably just a mouse or something. Or a murderer! Oh my life! Jack was right! This place is too secluded for a woman on her own. Help!

He's on alert now. Oh fuck it! A stage further on from the danger signals. A low, menacing rumble coming from somewhere deep within his belly.

Gumbling we call it. A cross between a growl and a grumble.

Now I am scared! I slip his lead on and hold him to heel. If somebody is out there, he'll have to take us both on together! I would fight to the death for this lad and he for me ... I have no doubt of that.

Jack says in a situation like this, I should leg it and run for all I'm worth to get help. I don't think so! A seventy year old with a withered leg could out run me.

"Steady lad!" I whisper, stroking his humungous head in an effort to calm him down.

The words are no sooner out of my mouth than he takes off ... with me hanging on for grim death ... in the direction of the copse.

A circle of elms with a grassy area in the middle. Families use it for picnics and local teenagers for...well...shagging I suppose you could call it.

In the summer months the place is knee deep in condoms!

How irresponsible is that? Levy picked one up once and I was forced to wrestle him to the ground to retrieve it!

With me doing my impression of a water skier on dry land, we hurtle along, exceeding speeds of possibly thirty miles an hour until he reaches the edge of the copse and suddenly stops dead.

I am shaken ... literally ... and gasp for air as my lungs threaten to explode at any minute.

The silence within the wood is deafening now, except for my wheezing chest and ... a sort of low pitched moaning ... coming from that direction over there.

Oh my goodness! What if it's someone lying injured. A park keeper having a heart attack? Or a rambler having a fit?

I'm no good at First Aid. Do you pump the chest first or blow up their nostrils?

Levy seems winded as well and takes a few seconds to get his breath. His mouth hanging open, inhaling great gulps of crisp, cold air.

His chest rising and falling with the effort. My chest is rising and falling too but with fright. We are even deeper in the woods now than we were before.

It will be pitch black soon and Jack will have a search party out. I expect an RAF helicopter to hover overhead at any minute.

It takes a while for my eyes to adjust to the darkness but I can just about make out a car of some description. It's parked at the side of the copse with no lights on and no driver as far as I can see.

What a ridiculous place to abandon a car! Idiot! Unless he's come here to top himself!

Oh my life! Could be fixing a hosepipe to the exhaust right now! I shall have to go and investigate. Can't just walk away and let him die. Oh shit!

With Levy still on the lead, I slowly scramble through the bushes and edge closer to get a better look.

My SAS training comes in useful here as we navigate our way silently through the undergrowth. When I say SAS, I mean Silly Arsehole Society of course, not the armed forces.

We are no more than ten feet away from the passenger side when a head pops up quite unexpectedly, causing me to jump out of my skin. Firstly, because I wasn't expecting it and secondly because the head in question belongs to Alicia!

My life! What on earth is she doing out here in the woods at this time of day?

Birdwatching perhaps? Collecting conkers? I doubt it!

I'd recognise that sour face anywhere. And the Save The Whale sticker on the windscreen.

Curiouser and curiouser! I'm intrigued now! Alicia alone in the woods? Surely not?

Alicia's a lady with a linen hankie tucked into her knickers. She's not a squirrel shit type of person. And definitely not a woman to be out after dark.

Although I personally feel she looks at her best under subdued lighting.

Whatever ... it is Alicia ... I'm certain of that. And now her heads disappeared again! What is going on? Maybe she's tired. Popped in here for a little rest on her way home from Buckingham Palace perhaps?

She should be careful ... this place is dodgy after dark.

Now I don't know what to do. If I walk off and something happens to her I'll never forgive myself. I can't stand the woman but wouldn't wish her any harm.

Maybe if I just stroll past casually like. Pretend I'm looking for bluebells or something. Hang on ... more movement ... looks like a ... goodness ... it's a man! A bloke ... sitting up now in the driver's seat! Well I never!

Alicia! You tart!

Joy oh joy! Alicia has a life after all! And quite a murky one by the look of it. Why would any couple choose to park up in a dark wood? Oh! My life!

I'll leave it to your imagination!

Bet he's married! A dirty tart to boot! Unless they get their kicks by doing it outdoors. Some people do apparently. Something else I've learnt from watching the Discovery Channel. Oh well, whatever floats your boat and all that. I'll leave them to it. None of my business really and I have no desire to get a reputation for being a peeping tom. Better make a move.

Sadly, Levy thinks differently and without any warning leaps forward and makes a beeline for the car, his legs striding out purposefully through the undergrowth. Must have food in that car.

Maybe they've been having a picnic.

"Come back!" I yell at the top of my voice, but sadly to no avail as he charges off ahead of me.

In a few giant strides, he's at the car and has his huge head shoved curiously through the open passenger window.

His gorilla sized nose sniffing the interior for signs of food. Alicia is taken totally by surprise and screams as his slobbery chops slap against her face.

To be fair, I'd probably scream as well under the circumstances.

Imagine that lunging at you out of the darkness of a wood!

The guy in the driver's seat seems petrified and remains frozen to the spot ... the colour draining from his face. Probably thinks he's in the middle of the remake of Hound Of The Baskervilles.

"Levy! Get down!" I gasp, reaching the car and jerking him away by the collar.

For a second, I feel as if I'm in a time warp as no-one moves or utters one single word. They'll be in shock.

I've seen that expression before when this daft bugger has leapt out unexpectedly at some poor unsuspecting soul.

"Sorry ... I really am ... so sorry" ... I waffle breathlessly.

"And so you damn well should be! Get that beast away from this car!" the guy yells.

Beast? Excuse me? Did you say beast? I'm sorry ... I call him all sorts myself but never beast.

"Look ... I've said I'm sorry. He was just being playful!" I yell back.

"Damn dogs! Shouldn't be allowed in this wood!" he snarls, shaking his fist at me.

Two mistakes there I feel. The first being to suggest that dogs be banned from the wood and secondly to shake a fist at me. Strike three pal and you're out!

"Don't be so ridiculous! This is a public wood ... for people ... not perverts!" I bawl back at him.

"You trollop!" he barks, shoving his head closer to the window, "Clear off!"

Eh? Did I hear that right? Trollop! What sort of an expression is that? I'm useless at sex mate ... there's no way I'd ever make a living as a trollop.

Cheeky bastard!

"You two should find somewhere more private for your humping!" I tell them.

"I shall have you arrested young woman!" he yells back.

"For what you muppet? Walking in the woods?" I shall have you arrested for shagging in public!" I snarl.

"We were not!" he rages back.

"Oh ... so you always drive without your trousers on do you?" I giggle.

A fact that had escaped my notice until he wriggled about in his seat! Cheeky bugger ... yelling at me and he's out here with his balls blowing in the wind!

Alicia is obviously mortified. I can tell this by the fact she's got a copy of The Daily Express wrapped around her face now.

Trying to hide but not succeeding I'm afraid. Too late love! Your secret is out ... literally!

"I suggest you clear off before I call the police. Indecent exposure's a serious offence." I tell him.

"William ... can we just go please!" Alicia mumbles from somewhere under the newspaper.

"Yes William ... take your ... erm ... willy and just go please" ... I laugh.

"You are a very rude young woman!" Willy Wonka stutters, pulling up his pants.

"And you are a very dirty old man!" I shout at the top of my voice.

"William!" Alicia screams, burying her head in her hands.

Oh how the mighty are fallen! To think she's spent the last two years sniping and gloating over Alan and I during our therapy sessions.

She obviously needs therapy of a different sort for sexual dysfunction.

Fancy shagging in the woods where children come to play!

"Get away from the car!" Willy bawls as Levy attempts to put his head through the window again.

"I wouldn't do that if I were you. He doesn't take kindly to people shouting."

151

"Off! Go on ... off with you!" he rants, taking no notice of my warning.

Mistake number three I feel! To raise your voice ... and your hand ... to my dog. I'm a very tolerant person but even I have my limit's.

Well ... okay ... I'm not a tolerant person but still.

I am just about to reach across and whack old William in the kisser when Levy lunges forward.

There is a tussle and I fear the worst but within seconds he's off and charging away into the woods.

"My hairpiece!" William cries to Alicia, "He's got my new hairpiece!"

Oh my life! I wondered what he'd got in his gob. Willy's Wig. Oh dear! What can I say? Except tough shit really. Serves you right for being rude and well bald really.

"Drive on William! We'll get another!" Alicia whimpers, shrinking visibly before my eyes.

"But it cost a fortune! Willy wails.

"Now William!"

"Alright darling ... alright" ... he whimpers, starting the engine.

And drive on they do. At speed and with great determination to escape.

Alicia and Wiggy ... driving off into the sunset together. Pillocks! I swear to God, that bitch will never look down her nose at me again. All those airs and graces and patronising looks!

Which is fine if you have the morals to go with it but really! Pulling his plonka in public ... with a kiddies play park just across the way!

***

I'm in deep shit now! It's dark and Jack is at the window looking worried. He's holding his mobile. Bet he's calling out Air Sea Rescue. Wait till I tell him what I know!

"Cass! Where on earth have you been? I was getting worried!"

"Sorry ... been in the woods ... got a bit sidetracked" ...

"I thought we'd discussed this Cass. It's dangerous up there." he sighs.

"Sorry."

"What's the dog got on his head?"

"A hairpiece. He snatched it off William in the woods. His trousers were around his ankles."

"What!!"

"It's okay. Listen, William was with Alicia ... they were you know ... shagging!"

"Never!" I can tell he's interested now.

"True!"

"Why would anyone choose a ginger hairpiece?" he suddenly asks, looking perplexed.

"Eh?"

"Ginger ... look it's a ginger one. Why choose that colour when you could have black ... or grey" ...

Valid point."

"Or chestnut brown even. Blimey ... gingers not exactly unobtrusive is it?" he laughs.

"Anyway. They were definitely at it. Alicia had the face of a freshly fucked woman." I tell him.

"Where do you get these expressions from?" he roars, shaking with mirth.

"Listen, I know about these things. Women do get that look. After sex" ...

"She was probably just startled ... by that hairpiece." Jack laughs.

***

Chapter Fourteen

... *Lob The Builder*

The builder on the bike is back. I've been watching him for the past ten minutes out of the window. Good job Jack's binoculars were at hand.

He's over at number seven, lurking in the front garden and still wearing that ridiculous hat! Builder my arse!

I know several legitimate builders and none of them would be seen dead in a hat like that. Wonder what he's up to? Probably casing the joint for a burglary. Or peeping into windows. He'll have a shock if he shoves his nose into number thirty, they have a German Shepherd called Rocky.

He's coming this way now. How he ever manages to get anywhere on that ruddy bike amazes me. It's ancient and far too small for his enormous frame.

I've seen him around quite a bit lately and it fascinates me how he stays upright. Maybe he used to work in a circus as a trick cyclist.

Here we go! He's coming up the drive. Well I shan't be using your services pal.

I couldn't possibly trust anyone in a hat like that.

"Can I help you?" I ask, opening the front door and catching him unawares.

"Those roof tiles are a bit old. I can sort them out if you like" ... he smirks.

"Sorry, that roof was retiled less than a year ago. Nice try pal!"

"Come off it!" he grins, his face flushed with perspiration.

Excuse me? Come off it? Come off what exactly? This is about to kick off big time.

"Look pal! Like I said, nice try but my husbands an engineer thanks."

He looks momentarily stunned then suddenly removes his stupid hat and runs his fat fingers around the brim. I can see why he wears it now.

He's almost bald except for a swathe of grey, greasy hair combed over the top of his scalp. He also appears to have a chronic dandruff problem as a positive hailstorm of it cascades down onto his shoulders.

"Have you got any electrical jobs? I'm good with washing machines." he informs me.

"Nope!" I snap wishing he'd just disappear.

"How about plumbing then. Need any taps fixing?"

What is this? From builder to sparky to plumber in ten seconds! Desperate more like.

"You're beginning to annoy me now! Watch my lips ... no thank you!" I shout at him.

"Auntie said I'd have trouble with you." he suddenly mutters under his breath.

"Auntie! And who would that be?" I bite.

"Mrs Bolak. I'm Lobonovich ... her nephew" ...

Hello! The lights are on but nobody's at home. I should have known ... he looks like a Lob.

"Yes well, your Auntie was right. I don't take kindly to strangers on my doorstep thank you."

"She says you're a bit funny." he bites back, fiddling nervously with his hat.

Okay! Here we go! I'm in my own house minding my own business and this twat pitches up.

"Funny? She says I'm a bit funny? And that from a woman who sleeps in a coffin!" I yell.

"That's a lie!" he remonstrates, "Just because we come from the Eastern Block."

"Here's twenty-pence!" I shout, delving into my pocket, "Go phone someone who gives a fuck!"

I get the distinct impression that Lob has never been confronted by a mouthy female before.

155

Maybe all the women in the Eastern Block are subservient and silent. Get real pal! This is the twenty-first century and we answer back.

"In my country, we all do jobs for each other. That's how we earn a living." he smirks.

"Yes well in this country, we all go out to work ... and get a proper job!"

"I have a job ... keeping watch over Auntie." he smirks again.

"I don't think you're doing a very good job of it. She just flew past on her broomstick!" I laugh.

"I could put a curse on you." he suddenly grins quite menacingly.

"Yes and I could put my hand on you ... right across your fat face!" I rant.

We reach a deadlock with him glaring at me and I clenching my fists in anticipation of a fight.

He really is an ugly bugger! Inside and out! The podgy face and sweaty forehead. Two piggy eyes ... far too close together for my liking. And the eyebrows! You could grow cabbages in them.

Combine all that with the dirty anorak and crimplene trousers and you must be getting my drift.

Realistically, I'd say he's about fifty but he looks much older. And I always thought vampires stayed eternally young!

"I could mow that lawn for you." he persists, sneakily edging his foot inside the door.

"I could break your leg. If you don't remove that foot!" I shout.

"You are a very strong woman." he leers.

"Yes, and my husband's a lot stronger. Massive bloke. Metal plate in his head." I lie.

Yet another pause as his brain kicks into gear and tries to register what I've just said.

Jack doesn't really have a metal plate in his head but he is strong ... and mightily intolerant of anyone who upsets his wife.

Especially rude, creepy, Eastern Block blokes who jam their size eleven feet into the doorway. I am becoming bored with this now. I have a wedding cake to make and my legs to shave.

"I think you'd better go. I have things to do." I tell him, closing the door on his foot.

"Shall I call back later? When you're not so busy?" he leers, forcing the foot further inside.

Right! That does it! I can take so much but he's gone too far now!

"Levy!" I bawl, opening the lounge door to the dog, ..." TELETUBBY!!!"

Now I know this won't make any sense to most of you but you have to understand that Levy is no ordinary dog. For some strange reason, he positively detests Teletubbys on television and goes round and round in an agitated state whenever they come on.

Anyway, Lob does bear a striking resemblance to Tinky Winky.

This fact is bought home to me as Levy lunges at the intruder, knocking him flat onto his back on the drive.

"Jesus!" is all he can manage as he finds himself straddled by ninety-pounds of excited dog.

I am tempted to leave him there until Jack arrives home but think better of it.

I have no idea if Old Lob is carrying any diseases. Levy only has jabs for distemper and parvo.

Lob has the look of a man who carries a virus. And possibly a fatal one at that.

"Come here lad!" I whisper, praying he'll do as he's told and amazingly enough he does!

"Auntie won't like this!" Lob rants, picking himself up off the gravel.

"Oh go stick your head up a dead bears bum!" I rant, slamming the door in his face.

Damn cheek! Trying to force his way in here! And those armpit's! Phew! Talk about turgid!

What if he tries that on with some poor old dear living on her own? I'd better ring Mary. I shall be keeping an eye on that one. And so will Levy.

Told you that family were barmy!

Bet he's flown over from Transylvania with a blood transfusion for Bolak. She's been looking a bit pale lately. Although vampires do don't they?

Levy has calmed down a tad. He's humping one of the cushions off the sofa. Must remember to pop that into the wash later. Somebody should pop old Lob into the wash. Bet he has a crust on his pants. Sorry! That was vile. But probably true.

What the hell is he doing now? My life! Lob's still on the drive. Sitting on the wall.

"I told you to go away ... go on ... do one!" I yell at him, flinging the front door open again.

"And what if I don't?" he sneers, kicking his heels against the stonework.

"Then I shall have to shoot you ... with my ... erm ... shotgun. It's in the pantry" ... I lie.

Could be a bit of a problem here. I have a plastic water pistol that I use to water the plants but nothing capable of causing any serious damage.

He seems uncertain for a second then decides against it and moves away.

Slowly and with menace.

"I could treat these plants. With some chemicals. I'm good with chemicals." he grins.

Good with chemicals? What would that be then? Formaldehyde? Arsenic? Embalming fluid?

"Then go boil your head in sulphuric acid!" I shout, slamming the front door yet again.

I'm all of a dither now. He's spooky that guy. Reminds me of that Bates bloke ... Norman. The one who kept his mother in a rocking chair by the window.

What a horrible man! Strikes me he's been inhaling some of those chemicals and it's addled his brain.

Anyway, he's gone now thank God. Jack will be furious when I tell him. Maybe better not.

I don't want any fisticuffs on the drive. Old Lob could fly into the bedroom window and suck all his blood out in the middle of the night. I shall keep a clove of garlic under the pillow just in case.

Right. Wedding cake. Just the fourth attempt. It's costing Jack a fortune in ingredients and time is running out. At a push I could ask Lenny to help but I really would like to do this one myself. I've bought the figures for on the top tier. At least, I did buy them but Levy ate the groom's head.

Looks like he's deformed. I can buy another one. Just add it to the list. Along with several hundred balloons.

Have to pop to the shop. I'm out of mixed peel and eggs ... and flour ... and sultanas.

***

"Hello Mary ... Cassie here."

"Sorry no she's not" ... her fuddled brain responds.

"Eh?"

"Can I help?" Mary asks.

"Mary! It's Cassie.!"

"Hello Cassie. Somebody's looking for you."

"No ... Mary ... listen. Don't answer the door to that guy in the funny hat."

"Who ... the postman?" She's off on one again!

"No! The builder ... on the bike!" I tell her.

"Has he got my post then?"

"Oh my life!" I wail exasperated.

"I thought it was late. I'm expecting a letter off Michael." she laughs.

"That's nice."

"Can I give her a message?" she asks kindly.

"Who???"

"Cassie."

"No thanks."

159

"Bye!"

***

CAKE CRISIS IV

Prepare mixture for microwave cake in blender.
Scrape mixture off ceiling and walls.
Ring Argos and order new microwave.
Feed leftover mixture to birds in garden.
Bury dead pigeon under patio.
E-mail Anthony Worrall Thompson.

***

Chapter Fifteen

King Dong & The Dahlias

Mary's out in the front garden putting in some bedding plants. Pete just rang to say she's using a giant dildo to dig holes in the soil! Hello! Here we go again! Poor Pete sounded a bit embarrassed and I can't say I blame him. Where on earth did she get that from? I shall have to go across and sort this out. Can't have her making a show of herself. If she were thinking straight she'd be mortified! She's been deteriorating rapidly for a while and it breaks my heart to witness the speed of her decline.

Better go and see what's going on. Take her a trowel instead.

Bless her! Down on her hands and knees planting some dahlias. Not bad for an old girl of ninety-three.

A game old girl as well judging by the look of that vibrator! Goodness me!

It's positively huge! Big black thing with ... well ... an attachment on the end! I must be terribly naïve. Who designs these things?

And worse still ... who buys them?

"Morning Mary! Dahlias eh? Be lovely." I tell her, kneeling down by her side.

"Helen at the florist got them in for me." she smiles.

"She has some beautiful plants. Bet they'll last for ages." I nod.

"Might plant some runner beans alongside. You can't beat fresh greens" ... she says, thrusting the vibrator into the soil.

That's an interesting mix! Runner beans and dahlias! I swear the new medication she's on is making her even more fuddled. Cabbageness you see.

Who knows what these prescribed chemicals do to your brain?

Her aches and pains seem to have diminished but her minds messy.

She seems to have periods of clarity when she's focused and the old Mary that we all know and love and then on other days, she'll troll around with a tea cosy on her head and insist on calling me Pat.

"Is that new?" I ask, pointing to the dildo.

"Marvellous gadget. Ordered it out of that catalogue that came through the door last month." she tells me.

"Oh right" ... I giggle.

"Only cost me ten pounds. It's got a switch on here ... look!"

And indeed it does have a switch! And several different movements apparently. Oh my life!

Bloody things whizzing round now like a rampant black pudding!.

"Mary! Better switch it off eh? Save the batteries." I giggle, gently taking it out of her hand.

What do you do? Bet the poor old sod thought it was a gardening catalogue. I shall have to get rid of the bloody thing. Discreetly bury it somewhere.

Can't put it in the dustbin ... what if the bin men see it?

Goodness! They'll think I'm a nympho!

"Shall we go indoors Mary? It's getting a bit chilly out here."

"If you like. I'll put those carrots in tomorrow" ... she sighs, getting to her feet.

See what I mean? A few seconds ago it was runner beans ... now it's carrots. I'm at a loss as to how to help. I'm out of my depth and reluctant to suggest Social Services to the family. Make that call and there's no going back.

Time to ring Michael, her eldest, and have a quiet word I think.

Michael lives in Oxford. He's an oncologist at The Radcliffe. Michael is also due for retirement himself soon so no spring chicken as you can see.

He's Mary's eldest. The eldest of seven! Her brood are scattered across the globe and it's a testament to her skills as a parent that they're all incredibly well-educated and working in successful fields.

Catherine is a teacher in Paris. Ditto Philip in Brussels.

Siobhan lives in Dublin and works as a midwife.

Then there's Kenny ... he's an optician in Florida of all places. David's an accountant in Cambridge.

And finally, Joseph, the youngest. He runs a hotel in St Brelade's Bay. And delightful kids they are too.

She could have upped sticks and gone to live with any one of them but chooses to remain in her own home and I can't say I blame her. The house is full of wonderful memories and now, in her dotage, she clings to those memories as a way of holding on to the past.

Mounted photos and portraits of her brood cover the walls inside.

At the last count, she was the proud grandmother to eighteen and great-grandmother to five! What a marvellous achievement!

I have dropped several heavy hints to Tom and Hannah regarding my longing for a grandchild but no joy so far. Mind you. Would you willingly subject a baby to me as it's grandmother?

"Bilbo's asleep on the bed upstairs" ... she whispers, tip-toeing through the hall.

Still around then? Charlie The Reincarnated Cat. Not surprising really considering she's feeding him a diet of best salmon and full cream milk.

We did try him with the fish-heads but he spat them out in disgust. Yet more confirmation that this is definitely not Bilbo! Bilbo loved the odd fish-head ... and dead mouse ... and splattered rat!

I still have the rampant vibrator in my back pocket and feel quite guilty at having to ... well ... steal it really. I have no choice in this.

If I leave it here, she'll be out there on sunny days churning up the garden with it ...and causing no end of distress to the neighbours! And this is my dilemma you see. Mary is proud and strong and fiercely independent. She is also going ga-ga and I'm torn as to what to do for the best.

If I grass her up to Social Services, they'll cart her off for all sorts of vile tests and if I keep quiet, chances are she'll end up splattered across the bumper of a lorry like some grotesque mascot.

Last Monday it was the M42. Two extremely pleasant patrol officers found her ambling along the Southbound carriageway at three in the afternoon.

She was heading in the direction of Rhyl but swore she was on track for Tesco.

Lord knows I do try but it's getting to the stage where she needs round the clock care and I can't do that. The responsibility is overwhelming and recently I've been lying awake at night praying that she doesn't wander onto the fast lane wearing one of her flannelette nighties and obligatory hairnet.

"Fancy a cuppa?" I ask, as she flops down into the armchair, overcome with tiredness.

In seconds, she's fast asleep, head lolling backwards on a cushion. Bella will be here soon. I shall have to make sure she doesn't wake her up.

Not that Bella makes a lot of noise. Bella barely moves.

For a carer she certainly has the knack of skiving down to a fine art. Bella originates from Barbados and longs to go back.

Mary and I wish she would too! The woman is a nightmare

How she ever wangled her way into a job caring for the elderly I will never know. Bella doesn't care ... at all ... not about Mary anyway.

She flounces and pouts and goes into a strop whenever Mary asks her to do anything that remotely involves the word work.

On really bad days, she makes that awful sucking noise through her front teeth which I have to say, I find quite offensive. I have promised Mary that

I'll smash those front teeth down her fat throat if she does it again. And I will!

How disrespectful is that? To curse and cuss an elderly lady? An old lady who until quite recently was a pillar of this community. Bloody Bella!

Several hundred pounds a month she gets paid and yet in the last six months, I don't think she's actually done more than ten minutes work in total.

She arrives, late ... then proceeds to make herself a cup of powdered soup which she drinks while watching the television. If pushed, she might run a cloth over the kitchen work tops or rinse a few cups and that's it!

Mary and I have given up suggesting she tackle jobs such as ironing or hoovering. Lazy cow!

To be fair, I don't think her size helps. At a rough guess I'd say she weighs about twenty stone and that's a conservative guess. She has those knees...you know ... those grossly inflated rubbery knees with several folds of fat quivering above the line of her hold-up stockings. And the arms too.

Bingo-wings I think they're called. Vast folds of fat shuddering downwards from her armpit's.

I suspect her breasts alone weigh about six-stone. And I thought I had problems buying bras! I don't think Bella actually wears a bra as her nipples are roughly in line with her knee-caps.

Which is fine. I don't have a problem with big people. Just lazy ... rude ... disrespectful people and Bella falls into that category I'm afraid.

I have bent over backwards to make allowances for her appalling behaviour and have reached the conclusion that Bella's a ...what's the word ...oh yes ... arsehole!

Here she comes now ... waddling up the path, a look of agitation and annoyance on her fat face.

Yet another case of mistaken profession. Bella would be better suited as a traffic warden. I feel sure that if she got hit by a bus, the bus would sustain the greater damage. I shall suggest that career move to her next time she whinges on about how hard she has to work. What bollocks! If this is what caring for the elderly is all about then I'll give it a miss thanks.

In the unlikely event that I should reach Mary's age, I'll go and live in Sweden where they practise euthanasia.

She'll be mightily miffed that I'm here again. If I weren't, I'm sure she'd let herself in and climb into bed for a couple of hours sleep. She has the look of a woman who enjoys her sleep.

That skanky look that comes from climbing out of bed and going to work in your jogging bottoms and Bob Marley t-shirt.

She doesn't bother with the regulation overall issued by the agency. No point really as she never does anything that could remotely involve the word work or dirt.

"Morning Bella!" I grin, opening the front door.

"Bitch melted me extensions!" she bawls, yanking off her baseball cap to reveal what can only be described as a positive tangle of knotted hair and bits of glue.

"Oh dear" ... I sympathise, trying not to laugh.

"Can't stay long. Gotta get back." she rants, crashing through to the kitchen.

Here we go again! Every week she has a crisis of some kind which invariably means her leaving early to sort it out.

This really isn't good enough. Mary is actually paying for this service and it strikes me she's being well and truly shafted. By Bella and the agency that employs her.

"Keep the noise down Bella, Mary's asleep in the lounge, " I whisper, following her into the kitchen. She ignores me and proceeds to make her customary cup of soup, slamming the kettle onto the work surface and noisily throwing some plates into the sink.

"Not my problem! I here to do a job!" she yells, giving me a dirty look.

"That'll be a first then!" I bite back, throwing her an even dirtier look.

"Old woman!" she barks with contempt, " My boy got more brain and he only five!"

Enough already! This is about to kick off. It's been brewing for a while now.

"Whoa! Stop right there! How dare you talk about Mary like that!" I yell, moving closer.

She seems startled for a second and swirls around, her eyes blazing, to confront me.

"It nothing to do with you!" she snaps, pushing past me into the sitting room.

I follow, her ample arse wobbling in indignation as she slumps down onto the sofa and grabs the remote control. I stand defiantly in front of her, blocking her view of the screen.

"Bella, we appear to have a problem here." I tell her in a controlled voice.

She glares angrily back and makes that awful sucking noise with her teeth.

That being her first mistake I feel.

"Mary is very old and very frail and I will not tolerate you talking about her like that" ... I tell her.

More sucking of the teeth and a distinct rolling of the eyes towards heaven.

"Either you learn some respect or" ...

"Or what?" she sneers, turning up the volume on the set.

"Or I shall have to fire you!" I shout above the din.

"You can't do that!" she laughs, throwing her beaded head back.

"Oh really? I think you'll find I can. Now fuck off!" I laugh back.

Funnily enough, she stops laughing and a strange gurgling noise appears to emanate from her throat.

Either she's having a cardiac arrest or she's about to implode with anger. I'm not fussed either way.

How dare she! God only knows what she gets up to in other houses where the residents are alone.

If this does turn nasty I shall beat her about the head with the dildo in my pocket. That should calm her down a bit.

"Biaaatch!" she screams at me, raising her obese body out of the chair.

"Bothered!" I smile back as she struggles to get to her fat feet.

I stand rooted to the spot as she wafts past and makes her way into the kitchen again.

Her cup of soup stone cold and congealed no doubt. Grabbing her bag off the table, she slams down the hallway and out of the front door.

The glass panel shuddering as it bangs shut.

Oh dear! I've done it now! She'll go back to the agency and report me no doubt. I shall end up in court when she sues me for compensation.

Could be talking half a million squid I should think.

Like I said ... bothered! Mary is the important issue here and somebody has to stand up for her rights. Besides, they can sue the arse off me if they like. I've only got sixty-nine pence in the bank.

Thankfully, Mary has slept through the fracas. Her hearing is going as well as everything else.

I creep into the lounge and sit down softly on the footstool beside her. Watching as her eyelids flicker with the remnants of a dream no doubt.

She won't miss Bella. Let's be honest here ... I don't think she even knows who Bella is. Just some stranger who pops in to watch TV three times a week.

She's waking now ... slowly coming back to reality after her dream.

"Bella's gone Mary" ... I tell her, adjusting the cushion behind her head.

Her face takes a while to register what I've said and for a minute she looks quite sad.

"Was it the thyroid?" she asks, catching me unawares.

"Sorry?"

"The thyroid ... she's been in and out of hospital for years with that bloody thing."

"Who has Mary?" I ask getting even more confused.

"Her ... who you just said ... with the fibroid" ... she tells me adamantly.

"Fibroid?"

"You're losing your marbles Cassie! You said she was dead ... Stella!" she shouts at me.

"No Mary. I said Bella not Stella" ... I laugh.

"That's the one. Stella with the fibroid. Big as a rugby ball it was. God rest her soul." she sighs sadly.

No point me trying to clarify all this. She'll have forgotten the conversation in a few minutes.

At ninety-three, she's not doing bad all things considered but it's so sad. Not for her. For those of us watching this gradual decline. She's cartwheeling into a chasm of confusion and I'm powerless to help.

It's selfish of me I know, but I just want to hang onto the old Mary. The Mary who led us all in a conga around the lanes at the Golden Jubilee party.

The Mary who could recite Wordsworth off by heart without hesitation.

The Mary who recognised me as Cassie and not the Co-op milkman.

"Would you like some lunch?" I ask, glancing at the clock on the mantelpiece.

"No thanks love, I just had something" ... she yawns sleepily.

"What was that then Mary?"

"I had a sandwich." she insists.

"Really?" I persist, knowing she hasn't eaten since breakfast.

"Tuna and treacle." she tells me, licking her lips.

Not one of her best concoctions granted but not the worst either. On Tuesday, I let myself in to find her devouring a plate of sausages sprinkled with Smarties.

What do you do?

Except smile and try to make sure she gets plenty of fluids with her medication.

"I'll leave you to have a rest then. See you later." I whisper, picking up my keys.

"Okay ... We'll order some flowers tomorrow shall we?"

"Flowers?"

"For Stella. Find out when the funeral is will you?"

"Of course. Have a nap now ... be back later" ...

I'm floundering with all this. I'm not trained for it and have no idea if this is the pattern of events with dementia. I really will have to call Michael.

He'll know what to do. Mary herself said quite recently she was racing towards the Final Frontier and it looks as if she was right.

I close the door quietly behind me and on my way down the path remove the tin of Smedleys carrots she's planted upside down in the flowerbed.

***

"Cassie! Why is there a big black dildo on top of the fridge?" Jack asks.

"Sorry. I took it off Mary. Forgot I'd put it up there."

"What was Mary doing with it?" he laughs.

"Bedding in her dahlias."

"Sounds about right."

"Poor old soul. I'm worried about her Jack" ...

"I know pet but there's not a lot we can do."

"She actually ordered that through the post!"

"I hope it came in a plain brown wrapper." he smiles, examining the object in question.

"Horrible isn't it?" I shudder.

"Bit on the small side." he laughs, twirling it around.

"Yeah right!"

"Says King Dong on the side! They actually name these things?" he laughs.

"What would yours be called then?" I giggle.

"Oh I don't know. Something along the lines of ... Good God!"

"Right."

"Or maybe ... Get That Thing Away From Me!"

"Enough!"

"Or ... How Does He Fit It In His Trousers ... that sort of thing" ...

"Idiot!"

Chapter Sixteen

... Roll Up! Roll Up!

Yet another summer coming to an end and August almost over. I love this time of year not only because of the warm balmy evenings but August heralds the Oakham Carnival ... possibly the highlight of my social calender.

Shows you how much I get out doesn't it? Can I help it? I love this village and the people in it and the carnival brings everybody together for a whole day of fun and candy floss and the obligatory fight when the pubs close.

Everybody in the village turns out for it and it's lovely to see the old familiar faces, browsing around the stalls, munching on toffee-apples.

I volunteered to make the toffee-apples a few years back but oddly enough my offer was declined. Funny that! Jack and I strolled along the High Street late last night and it was awash with volunteers ... setting up stalls and fixing strands of coloured lights to the lamp posts.

There's even a bouncy castle this year. I shall have to keep Mary away or she'll be somersaulting into space.

We are taking her with us of course. In years gone by, she'd have been in there, baking cakes and organising the tombola stall but not any more.

I helped her to pick out an outfit last night and after much deliberation she settled on a pretty floral pink dress with matching straw hat.

An improvement on the swimming costume and cardigan she intended to wear.

Pete and Lenny are in the Tug-O-War team from the Pig & Whistle. That should be interesting.

Pete will be hammered by midday and lord knows how Lenny's leg will hold up under the strain.

Unless they use it as an anchor of course. Could be onto a winner if they do.

Levy has been up since five ... he always gets excited on Carnival day.

Last year, he won two goldfish and a stuffed bear.

Sadly, he ate all three but there you go.

"Are you okay in the back there?" I ask Mary as she settles into the back of the car.

"Fine thanks."

"Would you like some music on Mary?" Jack smiles, glancing in the rear view mirror.

"That would be lovely!" she beams, gently stroking Levy's head.

"Here you go! Matt Munro ... one of your favourites!" I laugh, slipping in the CD.

Jack's face says it all as Matt's soothing voice drifts around the car interior. Jack is not a Matt fan but will tolerate him on short trips with Mary.

Bless her! She does love her music and Matt is one of her favourites.

"Cass! This is embarrassing!" he laughs, turning off the drive.

"Why?"

"A hot sunny day ... windows down ... sunroof open ...and Matt Munro blaring out!"

"Snob!" I giggle.

"I'm losing my street cred with this!" he grins as we head for the village.

"I never had any!" I tell him, turning up the volume.

Mary remains oblivious in the back seat ... humming along gently to that lovely Softly track. One of her favourites.

"Cass ... don't look now but there's a coach load of pensioners behind" ... Jack tells me.

"So?"

"I think they're following us! It's this ruddy CD!" he laughs.

"Don't be ridiculous! They're probably on their way to the Carnival." I giggle.

"Look! They're all waving at us now" ... Jack wails.

"Stop it!"

"We could get lumbered with that lot. You can take them to the toilet!" he roars.

"Enough!"

"Have to form a crocodile. See none of them get lost" ...

"Jack! I shall need the toilet in a minute."

"I could do with a visit." Mary suddenly pipes up from the back seat.

"Nearly there Mary. Can you hang on?" I ask.

"Course. Is it much further?" she whispers, shoving her head out of the open window.

"No. Be there in a few minutes."

"Can't see the sea yet" ... she says in all innocence.

"Oh blimey!" I whisper, nudging Jack.

"Just don't let her wander off." he smiles, turning into the car park.

Good job we started out early. There are crowds of people milling about already and only a few spaces left in the car park.

We normally walk but with Mary it would have taken us two days.

"Come on then ladies! Let's hit the fair!" Jack laughs, helping Mary out of the car.

"I'll buy you a stick of rock Jack." she giggles, still thinking we're in Blackpool.

"Lovely!"

"I must send Edith a postcard." she smiles, searching in her bag for a pen.

Oh dear! Edith has been dead for two years. They used to go to the library together every Tuesday. Levy is anxious to get to the candy floss and sit's at my feet, tail swishing in anticipation.

"Okay Mary." I reassure her, "We'll get one later."

Walking is going to be a bit of a problem. Especially with these crowds. I'd hate Mary to get trampled on in the rush.

Jack senses my concern and as ever has the situation in hand.

"How about a ride in one of those Mary?" he smiles, pointing to a line of wheelchairs.

"Lovely! Give my legs a rest." she sighs.

"Sorted!" Jack grins, grabbing a chair and gently easing her into it.

You have to hand it to the organisers. They've thought of everything and quite right too.

There are even half a dozen pushchairs for tired little toddlers. And a man with a first aid kit and a determined expression sitting outside the butchers.

Bless him! These kind souls give up their free time at events such as this to care for the fainting and the footsore. I shall take him a hot dog later.

"Where to first ladies?" Jack asks, easing the wheelchair through the throng.

"The Tower!" Mary cries excitedly, "They have tea-dances in the afternoon."

We both smile and head off in the direction of The Tower, which is approximately two hundred and fifty miles away on the Lancashire coast I think. She'll forget about it in a minute.

By the time we reach the High Street she's in her element ... giggling at the sight of a clown making balloon animals for a crowd of children.

And laughing out loud at a group of Boy Scouts hurtling up and down on the bouncy castle.

Levy is off and running, making his way to the face-painting stall. Last year they made him up as a lion and he spent the day frightening several small children to death. Let's hope they do something a bit gentler this year. A monkey perhaps. That would be appropriate.

"Oh look! There's Pete ... and Lenny!" I cry.

They are lying on the grass outside the pub along with several other blokes, all looking the worse for wear.

If my watch is right it's just after ten. Must be hung over from last night.

Pete appears to be wearing a pair of leather shorts. Another Oxfam sale no doubt. Lenny has taken a safer option and gone for a pair of denim dungarees. Nice and baggy. Give The Leg room to move. I don't suppose he gets the chance to wear shorts. Not with the big bollock.

Goodness me ... imagine that bulging out of one side! Heaven forbid!

"Cassie! Over here! Can I get you a drink?" Pete hiccups, staggering to his feet.

"Bit early for me thanks Pete."

"Are they open already?" Jack smiles.

"No ... Tommo's got a boot full in his car ... round the back." he grins, pointing to the pub.

Resourceful eh? They think of everything don't they? Probably got an assortment of salted crisps and pork scratchings as well.

"See you later. We're off to have a go on the tombola." I tell him.

"Here ... have this ... I won it earlier." Lenny grins, handing me a Lily Of The Valley talcum powder.

"Oh thanks" ...

My favourite! Does anybody actually use talcum powder any more? Especially Lily Of The Valley. Probably some unwanted Christmas gift donated by one of the W.I ladies.

"There you go Mary. Present for you." I smile, handing it over.

After several attempts, Jack finally gets a winner on the tombola stall. Sadly, the prize is yet another Lily Of The Valley talcum powder.

Where is this stuff coming from? The stall is heaving with it. That and an assortment of jars of home-made jam.

"Over here Cassie! Look! The ducks!" Jack yells, waving me through the crowd.

Yippee! Hook A Duck! Now this is my forte. I am a positive expert in the hooking of rubber ducks. Last year I damn well nearly cleaned out the stall, much to the owners disgust.

"Not you again!" he grumbles, reluctantly handing me a hook.

"Here's a fiver pal. Let her loose!" Jack laughs, handing him the money.

There is indeed a skill involved in the hooking of a duck. Take it too quickly and it's likely to slip off the hook.

You have to approach them with caution and gently snare them as they bob past on the water. I have practised this technique for years and honed it to perfection.

"Got one! Number 3!" I scream excitedly.

"Number 3 ... here you go." Mr Misery mumbles, handing me a bar of gift-wrapped soap.

"Lily Of The Valley ... lovely!" Jack laughs, looking at my disappointed face.

"Let's have another go shall we?"

I'm sure these ducks are weighted down this year. Bet the miserable bugger's put lead in the bottoms. I can barely lift them out of the water.

Here goes. Yes! Number 9!

"Higher number ... bigger prize." he grumbles, handing me a bottle of eau de cologne.

"Great! Lily Of The Valley again!" Jack roars, his face crinkled with laughter.

"What about those teddy bears? What number do I need for one of those?" I ask.

"Any number over nineteen love." he grunts.

"Right! Come on ducks! Move along please!"

I have a feeling that the higher numbers are the ducks floating on the far side so I gently lean across and hook one as it floats past.

Number 18! Oh bugger. Nearly but not quite.

"There you go missus." he snaps, shoving a bottle of shower gel into my hand.

No prizes for guessing what scent it is! Sodding stuff! The entire village will reek of lilies next week. Must be damaged

177

stock or something. I don't think Mary's going to live long enough to use all this.

"Come on Cass, let's get you some hot donuts eh?" Jack smiles, wrapping his arm around me.

I'm sulking now and he knows hot donuts will cheer me up. I really wanted one of those bears.

Levy would have loved it. He's over by the hot dog stall, dribbling. Waiting in the queue with all the other punters.

Silly sod's got no money on him. And a face painted up like a penguin of all things! That's imaginative at least. Not scary. Well not much.

Does look a bit odd though I have to say.

"Jack ... Levy wants a hot dog" ... I tell him.

"Right. Back in a jiff."

I dare not move or he'll never find us again in this crowd. Besides which, this wheelchair is very heavy. Mary is loaded down with Lily Of The Valley products and seems to be dozing.

"Just wheel me over there under that tree, " she suddenly pipes up, "I'll have a little rest."

"Are you sure?"

"Of course! You and Jack go and enjoy yourselves."

"Mary, I don't like to leave you." I tell her, a tad concerned.

"Don't be silly! What harm can I come to? Now off you go" ... she insists.

I'm not entirely happy about this but she has a point. All these people are locals and they wouldn't let anything happen to her. Perhaps she's just tired.

A rest will do her good.

"Where's Mary?" Jack asks, in a panic as I join him in the queue.

"Having a snooze. We'll get back to her in a bit."

"Ketchup?"

"Please."

"No onions for Levy. They give him the wind."

"Thanks for sharing that with me." he laughs.

"He's already had some popcorn. It's all over his chin look!"

I have no idea why but for some reason food eaten outdoors always tastes much better.

We gobble down our hot dogs and make our way to the Tug-O-War tournament outside the pub.

Pete is almost horizontal now and seems to think tying the rope to his left ankle will help.

Lenny is being used as the anchor! They've put him right at the back with the rope tied firmly around his ample waist.

The men in the village take this contest very seriously indeed. This year they're up against a team from The Black Bear and there's no love lost between the two. The Pig & Whistle are a formidable lot. I certainly wouldn't want to upset them on a dark night anyway. Except for Pete of course. He's not a fighter. More of a faller-over.

The lines are drawn and the whistle blows for the start. Lenny looks very determined and grips the rope firmly with both hands.

Pete meanwhile has already fallen over and is about to be dragged to his death by the team on the opposing side. Good job he's wearing leather shorts.

Bit like a motorcyclist I suppose. Give him some protection.

"It's off!" yells the starter, waving a red hankie in the air.

And indeed it is.

With Lenny as an anchor, the other team don't stand a chance. That leg weighs a ton and sweat pours down his smiley face as he digs the leg firmly into the tarmac. Pete is being carried along by the rope, his shorts flapping in the back draft as he hurtles towards the line. At one point, he actually leaves the ground and swings perilously from the rope like a trapeze artist. I can't bear to watch and hide my face in Jack's shirt.

It's all over in minutes, with the Pig & Whistle dragging the Black Bear across the line with ease.

Good old Lenny! And his leg! And the bollock probably had something to do with it as well.

The weight and all that. The crowd roar as once again the local team bring home the prize.

Probably a crate of bloody Lily Of The Valley judging by today's offerings.

"Better get back to Mary." I smile at Jack, leading him away.

"Where did you leave her?"

"Under that tree over there."

"What tree?"

"That one ... outside the library" ...

"Are you sure Cass?" he asks again.

"Oh my life! Where is she?" I cry, scanning the crowd for a wheelchair.

"Calm down. She can't have gone far. Not in that thing."

"Oh Jack! What have I done?"

"Cassie! Get a grip. She's probably chatting to someone."

"What if she rolled away?" I ask, my voice rising in panic.

"Stop it!"

"She could be half way down the motorway by now!" I wail.

"Come on. Let's go look." he sighs, clasping my hand.

"Oh my goodness! What if it gets dark. There are no lights on it!" I wail.

The next ten minutes are spent in a complete panic, dashing from one part of the carnival to another, searching for an elderly lady in a wheelchair.

At one point, we split up and scan the sea of bodies filing along the route desperately hoping Mary will be among them. My heart is racing and I feel quite sick now. God forbid that anything's happened to her. How will I break it to the children?

"Sorry ... we lost your mother ... she was last seen heading along the M5 towards Bristol" ...

I can see Jack across the way and I have to say, even he's looking worried now. His forehead creased with a frown.

Eyes darting frantically around in search of Mary. Oh shit! Trust me to lose an old lady!

"Cassie! She's over here!" he suddenly yells, waving me across to join him.

Thank god! I could never work in an old people's home. I'd be a nervous wreck.

"Now don't kick off!" he laughs, leading me through the crowds.

"Where is she?"

"Just a second. Over there." he tells me, pointing to a row of stalls against the shop fronts.

Guess The Weight Of The Cake. How Many Beans In The Jar? How Old Is This Woman?

Eh? How old is this woman? Oh my life! Two lads have put a sign around her neck.

Buggers!

Look at them! Raking it in I'd say. They've even got a jar with the money in. Little bleeders!

"Oy! Clear off you buggers!" I yell, running towards them.

They scarper pretty smartish as I charge at them, hands flailing in the air.

Well I never! I've seen it all now!

How old is this woman indeed! Mary is oblivious to everything, still dozing peacefully.

Her hands resting serenely in her lap. The cardboard sign dangling from a piece of string.

Jack whips it off and discards it behind one of the stalls. He's dying to laugh I know but he won't.

"They've left the money behind." he smiles, picking up the jar off the pavement.

"Cheeky monkey's!"

"Come on Cass ... it is funny!" he laughs.

"Yes I suppose it is ... but I feel responsible."

"Mary would laugh. If she were awake" ... he smiles.

"Well. That's enough excitement for one day. Let's get her home."

We make our way back to the car park, collecting Levy on the way from the bouncy castle.

Jack is forced to physically drag him away, much to the dismay of the kid he's bouncing with.

He still has his penguin face. And a half-eaten toffee apple stuck to his ear.

"Hello you two." Mary sighs sleepily as we place her into the car, "Lovely day."

"Yes it's been smashing." Jack grins.

"We should try Margate next year." she yawns, resting her head on the dog.

He responds by eating the flower off the side of her hat. Oh well! As long as they've both enjoyed themselves.

***

Chapter Seventeen

... *The Tattooed Lady*

Make a list Tilly said last week. Make a list of three things you've always wanted to do but never had the courage to do. My life! Could be tricky.

Where do I start? I am renowned for my Cowardy Cowardy Custardness as you know so this could take a while. Jack and I spent ages last night trying to cut the list down to just three. At one point we had about seventy-five things on the list.

It would appear that I have gone through life being scared of everything! What a waste! I have never bungee jumped off a bridge. How sad is that? Or not!

I've never done scuba diving either. Or hiking in the Himalayas. What have I done with my life?

Well, raised a family...worked and ... farted around basically. Where does time go to? When I was eighteen I wanted to go to Borneo and see the gorillas.

I get spooked in Oakham Woods if something moves in the trees! Cross that one off the list then.

Along with Formula One driving and abseiling off the top of Canary Wharf.

I never used to be scared. It sort of creeps up on you as you get older. As the years advance you worry about dislocating your hips or strangulating your piles. Attractive eh?

We finally narrowed it down to just three. It took a while but there you go ... and I have the list to prove it.

1) Dance the night away in a club.
2) Go on a cruise.
3) Get a tattoo.

See! How daring is that? Not for you maybe but for yours truly ... a major step for mankind.

I have never been to a nightclub. Honest! And at my age it's highly unlikely they'd let me in.

If I were a dancer I suppose I'd have made the effort but it was never gonna happen was it?

I suppose Jack and I could try one of those over-forty clubs. Or those themed nights they hold at The Rainbow Room.

Seventies stuff and all that. Maybe not. Jack's got rhythm whereas I have not.

It could prove embarrassing for both of us.

And the cruise is out. I'm terrified of being on the water, even though I can swim.

That and the fact that cruises cost roughly a thousand squid per person. What if you hated it?

Can't exactly check out can you? In the middle of the Atlantic Ocean.

That just leaves the tattoo then and even that brings me out in goose bumps. I know they're considered old hat now and everyone's got one but I haven't. Par for the course then.

People are getting theirs removed by laser and I'm just considering getting one done.

Apart from the obvious pain factor ... what about germs?

What if I contract hepatitis and die an agonisingly slow death?

See what I mean? Oh get a grip woman! For once in your life, take a risk.

And now I'm here. Standing outside Body Blast ... our local tattoo parlour. What the fuck am I doing here?

It started off as a whim and now I'm actually here. On my own. Trying to pluck up the courage to go inside. Several people have come and gone while I've been dithering about and they all seemed quite happy ... and healthy. No screams of anguish or blood oozing from their clothes.

Go on girl! Live dangerously for once in your life! Walk through that door!

This place is highly recommended. It has five stars in the local directory. And a certificate for hygiene apparently.

A guy called Josh runs it. He's Glaswegian ... and gay. Bless him.

He has a beautiful butterfly tattoo on his right hand. I noticed it when I stood behind him in the video shop last week. He was renting a copy of Beaches.

Lovely film. He can't be a sadist if he likes Beaches surely?

I'm in now. Step at a time girl. Step at a time. It's not every day you conquer a fear is it?

Sparklingly clean. Everything in here is positively spotless. Even the magazines are crisp and lined up neatly on a pine coffee table.

I can hear Josh out the back somewhere, talking to a client no doubt.

There's a faint buzzing noise but nothing drastic. Could be the tattoo thing ... or a bee.

People tell me it's quite painless nowadays. They rub some sort of freezing agent onto the skin.

Nothing to worry about. Good God girl! You gave birth remember? It can't get any worse.

Here we go! A young lad just came through the curtain. Looks as if he's had one done on his wrist.

He's holding a tiny piece of gauze over it but nothing too bad. He looks happy enough.

Josh follows him out, then turns his attention to me ... hiding under the coffee table.

"Dinna look sa frit lass, " he grins, leading the way into a room at the back.

If I knew what dinna frit meant I'm sure I'd oblige, but I don't so I just follow him instead.

"Aye ... nay wha kin I dufa ya?" he sings, indicating that I sit on one of the stools.

"Sorry, I'm very nervous...I just thought I'd like a tiny tattoo...very tiny." I quiver.

"Nay problem lass ... nay pain ay pramise." he grins at me exposing a gold tooth.

Eh? Oh my goodness! He's a lovely lad but I can't understand a sodding word he's saying.

"Look ... sorry ... can you do me one of those little monster things?" I ask him nervously.

"Aye! Taz ya min?"

Oh gawd! He thinks I mean that Tazmanian Devil thing ... off the cartoons ...

"No. Not that ... erm ... you know ... that little monster ... off the Sprite advert ... the cute one?" I persist...S P R I T E" ...

"Wha?" he looks confused.

"It's sort of squashed. And crinkled. It's on television." I giggle with relief.

"Ay ye sirtin?" he asks, looking perplexed.

"Absolutely! Thank you." I sigh with relief.

"Aye well lass ... if ya sirtin?" he repeats, shaking his head,

I'm getting the hang of this now. After a while you can catch certain words.

"Right here ... just on my shoulder thanks." I tell him, pointing to the spot.

"Nay probs."

I grit my teeth and close my eyes as he prepares the area ... swabbing some sort of cream over the skin and wiping it with gauze.

He is wearing surgical gloves and I can hear them rustle as he grips the dreaded gun in his hand. Too late now!

Surprisingly enough, there is very little pain. Just a mildly uncomfortable sensation as the gun buzzes away at the skin on my shoulder.

I relax slightly and gaze into one of the mirrors on the wall, watching him work. His face etched with concentration. Tiny beads of sweat forming on his forehead.

There's a clock on the wall as well and I mentally tick off the minutes as he continues to scratch away.

"I bet you get some odd requests!" I laugh, looking at some of the weird designs on the wall.

"Aye ... dinna git marny of thees." he babbles in that strange lilting accent.

"Erm ... right" ... I nod, not understanding a word.

Perhaps best not to engage him in conversation. Might make him slip and take off my left ear with that gun thing.

Either that or I'd end up with a tattooed face! Goodness me! That would go down well in the library. They already think I'm barmy because I cannot stay silent when choosing a book. I always get excited when choosing a new read and sometimes that excitement gets the better of me and I make ... erm ... odd noises.

I giggle a lot ... and cough ... oh and burp!

It's not my fault! I think it's nerves. They take themselves so seriously in the library.

And I don't. The more they tell me not to do something ... the more I just have to do it.

Can I help it if I suffer from terminal trumping?

Twenty two minutes now and counting. I'm getting cramp in my legs from sitting still for so long in one position.

Nothing drastic. Bit sore round the old shoulder but I'm sure I'll survive.

I shall be incredibly sore around the ear hole if Ma ever sees this! She would have a fit! I'll have to make sure I cover up in the summer months.

She'd probably cover it with a bandage and tell people I've had an operation.

To remove the hump off my back presumably.

Ma doesn't do tattoos. Or piercings. Or anything else that involves bodily parts. When I was sixteen I longed to get my ears pierced and she demonstrated how painful this could be by clipping me around mine. God knows how she'd have reacted if I'd rebelled and had my nipples pierced.

"Thar ya go!" Josh smiles, placing a piece of gauze over the area.

"Oh ... thanks ... that was quite painless!"

"Aye ... tol yu ... nae baths fur a fu days and eff eet scarbs ... nae pick!" he laughs.

187

Eh? What the fuck was that? Fur a fu? Scarbs? Oh sod it! It's done now.

"Thank you. How much do I owe you?"

"Thirty arite?" he asks.

"Yes ... quite ... thirty pounds ... thanks."

"Cheers lass!" he grins, taking the money.

"Bye!"

Did it! And I didn't faint ... or fart ... which is always a bonus I feel.

***

Two days now and there's been no side effects or anything. I have kept it covered just in case. Wouldn't want any germs to infiltrate and gangrene to set in. Besides which, I'm keeping this as a surprise for Jack Wait until he sees it ... he'll probably faint! Not because it's a tattoo but because I actually plucked up the courage to go and have it done ... on my own!

Now that's what I call brave. Could be a gong of some sort in this for me ... from The Palace.

I'm dying to get a good look at it myself. It's a bit tricky being positioned on my shoulder.

I tried scrunching round in the mirror but couldn't see anything. I'll get Jack to lift me up later in the big mirror in the bathroom.

When he's recovered from the initial shock of course.

Jack is so fiercely protective of me I sometimes wonder what on earth I would do without him.

Granted, I've been ill and a tad spaced out recently but that's nothing unusual.

The Americans have a wonderful expression for Jack's concern.

They call it ... A soft place to fall ... and I think we all need one of those don't you? Just somebody who will always be there for you. Maybe it's Jack who deserves the gong from The Palace after all.

Here he comes now ... pulling onto the drive after yet another twelve-hour shift. I have made a special effort with dinner and actually baked home-made steak pie.

Pastry and everything!

I can tell you're impressed. Let's just hope his teeth are up to it.

"I must be in the wrong house ... I can smell food cooking." he laughs, flopping onto the sofa.

"Cheek! I'll have you know I've made you a pie."

"Apple or mud?" he asks.

"Steak actually."

"Oh Christ!" he grins rolling his eyes.

"You can have new potatoes or chips ... any preference?" I ask.

"Anything. As long as it comes with a stomach pump."

"Fuck off!"

"Yes dear."

See! Patience of a saint that man. Eating one of my steak pies will undoubtedly mean several broken fillings and chronic indigestion but he's never refused any of the atrocious dishes I've put before him.

He did gag at a particularly gruesome liver and bacon casserole once but he ate it just the same.

"I'm ravenous woman! Give me a double portion!" he laughs, grabbing the Gaviscon off the side.

"I've got something to show you first. Close your eyes." I tell him.

"Blimey! Does this involve whipped cream?"

"No, certainly not. Just close your eyes!"

He does as instructed and I take the chance to slip my left shoulder out of my t-shirt.

"There! What do you think?" I ask, edging closer.

"Crikey Cass ... when did you get that done?"

"Monday ... at that place in the village."

"It's ... erm ... very pretty. Is it a Crysanthemum?" he asks.

"Eh?"

"Sorry ... it looks a bit like a little flower. Let's see." he smiles, taking a closer look.

"Like it?"

"Erm ... yeah ... it's very unusual" ...

"I know. I didn't want a rose or one of those cartoon things." I tell him.

"So you opted for a sprout?" he asks incredulously.

"Eh?"

"A sprout Cass! You've got a sprout tattooed on your shoulder!" he laughs.

"Don't be silly! It's that little monster thing off that ... erm ... Sprite advert" ...

"Sprite?" he's repeating himself now.

"Oh no! The tattoo guy ... he's from Glasgow!" I wail.

"Oh Cassie! It could only happen to you!" he roars, incapable with laughter.

I am speechless and probably in a state of shock. Condemned to roam this earth for the rest of my life with a sprout on my shoulder!

How awful! People will think I'm insane.

"Don't suppose he gets much call for vegetables." Jack titters, taking a closer look.

"Oh don't!"

"Come on Cass! It's not too bad. I'll draw a stalk on it. Tell people it's a flower."

"Yeah right!"

"Go back and have some carrots added. Jazz it up a bit!" he giggles.

"Cobblers!"

"My wife ... the vegetable!" he grins.

"Sounds about right."

***

Chapter Eighteen

... *Piling Into The Pound Shop*

It's symbolic apparently. The pound coin. Tilly says it's not the amount she's given us but the decisions on what we choose to buy with it.

Decision making is one of the first things to go when you lose your marbles.

The brain becomes a mish mash of soggy trifle and it's impossible to make a decision about anything. Hence this exercise.

We have all been given a shiny pound coin and now she's sent us out to spend it. This could take a while. Alan's already dithering about which shop to go to and Alicia's stormed off in disgust.

I think it was my suggestion that we pop into Pound World in the village.

Makes sense to me but Her Ladyship obviously thinks it's beneath her. I don't suppose she ever ventures in there. Probably frightened she'll get fleas.

We've only got half an hour so we'll have to make some pretty quick decisions. Maybe that's part of the exercise.

Put the pressure on. Stop us faffing around. Force the old brain into gear.

I do love these sessions. This one in particular as I am positively a Pound World person. I love Pound World!

They really are a delight. Racks and racks of assorted goods and all for a pound!

Okay! So I'm cheap and tacky! Does this face care?

Alan is hovering in reception, fiddling with his privates as he is prone to do in a crisis.

Poor sod. Decision making obviously not one of his fortes. I'll take him with me. We can make plonkas of ourselves together.

"Come on Alan. If we hurry, we can be back in half an hour." I tell him, leading the way.

"Never been in Pound World. Is it expensive?" he asks nervously.

"No Alan. Everything's a pound" ... I laugh.

"Everything?" he looks amazed!

"Yes, everything. Honest. Now come on!"

We walk alongside each other, negotiating the traffic on the High Street. Alan shuffling along in his usual awkward manner. Head down, hands shoved in his anorak pockets. His plastic trainers squelching in the puddles on the pavement.

I could cry just looking at him. I could!

He gives off that awful air of defeat. The look that makes him invisible to passers-by. I long for the day when he'll gain some confidence and have the courage to look people in the eye.

"Here we are! Come on Alan, let's blow the lot shall we?" I laugh.

The shop is empty at the moment. Probably because of the torrential rain earlier. Good job really.

Give us chance to have a quick dash round and choose something. Half an hour isn't nearly long enough. I could spend hours in this shop.

"See anything you like Alan?" I ask, following him down the first aisle.

"Dunno. Can't make me mind up." he sighs, looking perplexed.

"What about some sweets? They've got tubs of marshmallows over there."

"Nah" ... he says shaking his head.

"How about one of those torches?" I ask, pointing to the display.

"I've got electric ... on the meter." he tells me in a serious voice.

Oh dear! I have a feeling this is going to take a while. I'm running out of ideas and besides which, Alan has to make the decision for himself. That's the whole point of this exercise after all.

I leave him in peace and saunter along the aisles, searching for something suitable. Choices you see.

I am spoilt for choice and that's where the decision making comes in. Time is ticking against us and I watch anxiously as Alan hovers on one spot ... panic rising in his face as he struggles to select something.

"Any luck Alan?" I ask, horrified at his inability to perform such a simple task.

"Think I'll get some of them sugared almonds for Tracey." he sighs, picking up the box.

"Lovely! She'll like those I bet. I'm having one of these ... for Levy."

"What is it?" he asks squinting.

"Some sort of suction toy. He loves toys." I giggle, making my way to the till.

Nine minutes left and we have to get back to the unit now. We are forced to break into a slight jog along the High Street, both of us panting as we arrive back with seconds to spare.

Alicia is back already and seated in the counselling suite ... a smug expression on her face.

"Well done everyone! You made it back in time." Tilly smiles, taking a seat.

"We been to the Pound Shop." Alan informs her, taking the sugared almonds out of his bag.

"Excellent!" Tilly smiles fondly at him.

"I got these for Tracey."

"What a nice thought Alan. That was very kind of you." she smiles.

"She's been looking for a present for her bridsmaid. Might give her these." he grins sheepishly.

My life! Are circumstances so dire that he has to give a one pound box of sweets as a gift?

We have no idea do we? Just how hard life is for some people? I am mortified but try not to show it.

193

"That's a lovely idea Alan. Sugared almonds are traditional at weddings you know." I tell him.

"Are they?"

"Yes. Some people give little bags of them to the guests."

"Wicked! I'll tell Tracey." he beams, delighted at his choice.

Alicia is obviously bored with our discussion and I detect a faint sneer of contempt on her face. Nothing new there then! Patronising pillock! Pity she's never likely to have the job of organising her own wedding. With luck, she might choke on a sodding sugared almond! No doubt if and when Wiggy does propose, they'll hold the reception at some country mansion and all the guests will be given boxes of expensive Bendicks chocolates. The Queen hands them out at the Palace apparently.

That would please old arse face.

"Cassie. What did you buy?" Tilly asks, making notes on her pad.

"Oh, just a new toy for Levy. Bit silly but he'll like it." I grin.

"Can we see?"

"Sure. Here you go" ... I smile, handing her the toy.

It is indeed a silly toy but he'll love it. It's one of those suction things that I think you're supposed to stick onto a baby's high chair.

Sort of a plastic sphere thing with a nodding Pope inside it.

Looks a bit spooky really but Levy will love it. He can roll it around on the lawn. He likes anything with movement.

"Lovely!" Tilly says handing it back.

"Not bad for a pound eh?" I laugh, popping it back into the bag.

"And Alicia? How about you?"

"I bought this." she smarms, handing Tilly a copy of The Lady magazine.

"Right. Any particular reason?" Tilly asks, glancing at the front cover.

"William and I are thinking of going on a walking holiday in the Cotswolds. We're looking for some accommodation. Hotels ... that sort of thing" she trills.

Aha! William The Wig! It must be serious if they're going rambling together. Hope he buys a waterproof wig! It can get very wet in the Cotswolds.

"Who's William?" Alan butts in, tactful as ever.

"My intended." she breathes, coming over all Barbara Cartland.

Intended! Fuck me! Nobody uses that expression now. You should get out more love!

"Eh?" Alan blinks, clueless as to what she means.

"My intended! My partner ... the man I intend to marry!" she snaps.

"Are you having sugared almonds?" he persists, confused as ever.

"I doubt it!" she sneers, turning her nose up in disgust.

"The Hogs Head do a nice spread." he persists, never knowing when to back off.

"Really?" old fuck face sneers.

"Harry makes all the sausage rolls himself" ...

"For goodness sake!" she snaps again.

"And the scotch eggs." Alan waffles, on a roll now!

Arse face will puke in a minute. I can tell by the horrified expression on her ugly mug. Sausage rolls and scotch eggs! As if!

Nothing less than caviar and Cristal champagne for that one I should imagine.

In her dreams anyway. William strikes me as a total twat and not one to be dragged up the aisle lightly I shouldn't think.

"So when is the happy day?" I chip in, winding her up even further.

"I have no idea. We haven't got that far yet!" she stutters.

I bet! Only as far as taking his kegs off in the car park apparently.

"Tracey will be selling her frock after our wedding. It's about your size." Alan informs her.

Bless him! That last remark proves priceless as Alicia appears to be about to blow a gasket.

"How ridiculous!" she snorts, her face turning red with rage.

"Got it from the charity shop. They threw in the shoes as well." he adds.

"I've heard enough now!" she rants, sweat forming on her nose.

"What size feet are you? Tracey's a six ... you could have them as well." he offers. Bless that lad! I love him warts and all!

All this over a box of sugared almonds! Worth every penny of that pound I'd say.

Arse face is beside herself with anger, her cheeks juddering with indignation. The ones on her face of course.

Her private life laid bare before us as Alan continues with his interrogation.

"Does Walter need a suit? He can borrow mine if he does" ... he asks.

"It's William ... not Walter ... and he only buys the best!" she rants, losing control.

"Is he loaded then?" Alan persists, hungry for more.

"Oh my goodness! William's a doctor. Now let it rest!" she bawls.

A doctor eh? Bet they met at his surgery. When she was having her face reconstructed.

"Which field?" I butt in, pinning her down.

"Erm ... well ... chiropody actually." she stammers, looking embarrassed.

Chiropody! A doctor? Get real woman! Not exactly neuro surgery is it? Bunions and corns?

"Does he do operations?" Alan asks in all innocence.

"Tilly! Can we move on please!" she begs, desperate to avoid more questions.

"No Alan. A chiropodist only does people's feet." I tell him, smirking over at Arse face.

He looks perplexed for a second then decides he's not interested any more. I think he was expecting some gory details about heart transplants and brain tumours.

"Okay then. You all have your purchases and very apt they are too." Tilly trills.

"Can we go now?" Alicia begs, jumping to her feet.

"Of course, see you all next week" ...

"Does he do verrucas?" Alan suddenly asks, going off on a tangent yet again.

"Give me strength!" Alicia explodes!

"Cos I got a massive bugger. Do you want to see it?" he asks, removing his sock.

"No!"

"Look! I dug the core out but it's still playing me up." he tells her, shoving the foot under her nose.

I fear she is about to faint and my body rocks with laughter.

"Ask Wilfred if he'll have a look at it will ya?"

A bit too much information for Alicia I'm afraid! Her delicate stomach is obviously not accustomed to men's feet. And verrucas.

Snatching her handbag off the chair, she lunges towards the door, desperate to get away. From Alan ... and his verruca.

"Bye everyone!" Tilly giggles, disappearing into the office. I bet she'll miss us when these sessions end.

Must make for fascinating gossip around the dinner table I should think. Alan and his verucca. And me and my psychotic urges to kill Alicia.

"How's the cake coming Cassie?" Alan whispers.

"Oh fine!" I lie, "Don't you worry, it'll be lovely on the day" ...

"Tracey was asking. Only the guests look forward to a bit of cake don't they?"

"Absolutely! How many guests will there be Alan?" I ask nervously.

"About twelve I think. So far. Might be two more if Tracey's cousins can manage to get here."

"Do they live far away?"

"Not really but Nobby's having trouble with his nostril."

***

You know when you do something and you wish you'd never started it? I'm in a right mess ... I've got that ruddy suction toy stuck on my forehead. What a prat! Jack will go mad.

I was only messing around ... the dog thought it was a great game ... me charging round the garden with it glued to my head. Now I can't get the bloody thing off.

It's the suction bit ... it's wedged onto my skin.

Must be some air trapped underneath the rubber I should think. Oh shit! What do I look like with a plastic globe and a nodding Pope attached to my head?

I've tried pulling it off but it won't budge and vaselines no good either. It's quite painful actually.

Every time I yank it, the flesh underneath stings. My life! What if I have to go to casualty with it on? I'd never live it down! They may have to operate. Sod that! I'd rather leave it where it is.

Could prove a bit difficult during dinner parties but there you go.

Oh Christ! There's somebody at the door now! Can't ignore it, it may be urgent.

Looks like a bible-basher. They have that dejected look don't they? From having doors slammed in their faces I should think.

He's spotted me now ... hiding behind the curtain. Oh bugger!

I shall have to front it out or he'll be hovering on the step all afternoon. I open the door wide and grin at him, hoping it will distract his attention away from The Pontiff.

"Afternoon madam. Do you think that the devil ... oh!" he gasps, catching sight of my head.

"Just got back from Rome" ... I tell him, "It's the latest in souvenirs."

"Maybe I should call back another time." he waffles, hurrying away down the drive.

"Bye then!"

That was a result! Thirty seconds to get rid of a Jehovahs Witness. Must be a record.

***

"I like it. It suit's you."

"Oh please Jack! Get the bloody thing off!" I cry.

"Leave it on. It'll make a wonderful conversation piece at parties."

"Stop it!"

"You could join a convent. Sister Silly Arse. It's got a ring to it." he laughs.

"Please!"

"Come here then spoilsport. Let's have a go."

"Ouch!"

"Sorry, but if you will play around with The Pope" ...

"Aargh!"

"Hold onto my waist and pull." he laughs.

"Ready?"

"Pull!"

"Thank god for that! It's off!" I sigh with relief.

"Bless you my child."

***

Chapter Nineteen

... *Is There Anybody There?*

I have to do this. If I don't, then I'll probably go to my grave regretting it. It's taken me forty years to pluck up the courage and that's a lifetime.

All those years wasted because I'm terrified people will say it's shite.

My book that is. I wish I'd had the courage twenty years ago. I truly do.

When you're young you have the confidence to bounce back. My confidence has taken so many knocks lately I'd never get back up again. At the moment, if something upsets me, I simply crawl into the cupboard under the stairs and

hide until Jack coaxes me out. Usually with a bar of Dairy Milk.

I have boxes and boxes of unseen work, all stashed away in that cupboard. When I'm on a downer, I hide in there and browse through it.

Novels ... children's stories ... even a six-part drama series for television.

Writing has been my passion for as long as I can remember but until recently I've been too scared to show it to anyone. And now, here I am, about to attend my very first literary night at the local village hall.

They're a mixed bunch. Mainly retired librarians and bored housewives looking for some outside stimulation. I gather that they review one book a month and on the first of every month they hold a literary evening for local writers.

Well ... I'm local ... and in my dreams I'd like to be a writer ... does that count do you think?

What if they laugh at me? I shall be forced to resort to violence! This book is my baby and I draw the line at people taking the piss out of it ... and me!

It may not be a potential Booker Prize winner but deep down, I am fiercely proud and protective of it. What do I know? A housewife from Oakham?

And a housewife with a history of mental illness now apparently. Doesn't bode well really does it? Perhaps, along with all my other problems, I am delusional. Oh fuck!

Does that mean I could end up believing I'm Catherine Cookson? Heaven forbid!

"Eh up lass ... our Albert's got TB again. Dip lad's vest in lard!"

Something along those lines anyway. Oh whatever! I'm getting into a state again.

How ridiculous! None of these bods know me and I don't know them. What's the worst that can happen? A few sniggers from the back of the hall?

I can cope with that. And Jack has promised he'll be waiting outside for moral support. He wants to come in with me but this is something I have to do on my own. If it all goes pear shaped then it will be down to me.

"Cass ... let me come with you. I promise I'll be quiet." he begs.

"No honest. I'll be fine. Really" ...

"What if you don't like it?"

"Then I'll come home to you." I smile.

"And hide in the cupboard?"

"Yep!"

"Better stock up on the Dairy Milk."

"Good idea."

***

It would appear we have a literary critic in tonight. Just my luck! Some dingbat called Miranda Mowbray. Wonder if she's related to the pork pie people? If I'd have known she was going to be here ... ripping people to shreds I'd have stayed at home. The bitch has already trashed some poor blokes poetry. He looks mortified.

Poor bugger was only on stage for a minute and she stopped him in full flow.

How embarrassing! If she does that to me I shall karate kick her in the head.

Porky Pie Pig has an alice band and an attitude. You know those ridiculous velvet headbands that look cute on a six year old but downright stupid on a grown woman? Well, she's wearing one.

Along with the obligatory Country Casuals tweed suit. And a set of pearls.

Quite appropriate really ... what's that expression ... pearls before swine?

"We really must move along ladies and gentlemen." she drawls from the stage,

"Who's next?"

Not me mate! I'm hiding at the back, trying to make myself invisible behind one of the pillars.

If I breath in and hunch my back over she might miss me completely. Either that or she'll think I'm a cripple and leave me alone. Oh fuck it!

Weeks and weeks of psyching myself up for this and now my bottles gone.

Well and truly. My bottle is half way up the M6 heading for Leeds as we speak.

"Come along! I don't give up my evenings for nothing!" she snaps into the mike.

Oh yeah? What do you normally do of an evening? Polish your hunting helmet?

Ginny, the girl who runs the group ... looks exasperated. A room full of people and we are all too shit scared to get up on stage.

The bloke with the naff poetry is still sulking in the corner.

It wasn't that bad. Well...I've heard worse. At least he was having a go. It's not every day you get a version of something entitled Post-Impressionist Pat.

I drifted off half way through but the gist of it was about some postman who longed to be a painter. Bless him!

"Come on Juliet ... will you go next?" Ginny calls to a hungry looking woman at the front.

Juliet appears to take all this very seriously and approaches the stage carrying several large folders under her arm, her glasses suspended on a chain around her neck and she's carrying a Vic nasal spray.

Could be in for a long session with this one.

"I shall read from This Beating Heart. My latest novel." she whines, adjusting her glasses.

Oh gawd! Another Mills & Boon addict. That's the third one tonight. What is it with these women?

All this thrusting of bosoms and ripping of bodices can't be healthy can it? I suspect that in reality Juliet has never thrusted her bosoms at anyone and there lies the rub so to speak.

"Tarquin gazed longingly into her eyes ... his manhood stirring with passion." she breathes.

Eh? His manhood stirring with passion? What's all that about then? I shall have to ask Jack if his manhood stirs with passion when he looks at me.

Highly unlikely but there you go.

"Take me Tarquin! she gasped, clinging onto his muscular thighs" ...

Oh fuck off! Take me Tarquin? What a ridiculous name! Shag me Syd would be more realistic.

I don't do slop. And let's be honest here. This is slop. Fantasy stuff about women who start out as a kitchen maid in some Scottish castle and end up marrying the master. Bollocks! Give me real life any day.

It generally stinks but at least it's true.

"Thank you Juliet. That was quite good but it needs work." Miranda yawns.

Juliet looks quite miffed and her cheeks flush with embarrassment as she packs her papers away.

"Yes, well ... my reading group voted it a winner at our last session" ... she protests feebly.

"I'm sure darling but you have a long way to go yet." Porky Pie sneers.

"But" ... Juliet tries again, determined to have her say.

"Move along please!" Mouthy Mowbray snaps, cutting her off in mid-flow.

Oh dear! Yet another deflated ego. How rude! She could at least try to be tactful.

Poor Ginny looks mortified. All this effort and the group are being mauled by Mrs Mowbray. I wonder who she writes for anyway?

Don't think I've ever seen any of her work. Probably does a column in the Pigeon Fanciers Gazette. Silly tart! And that's the saddest part of all this.

We don't know her from Adam but because we care so much about our work we're prepared to listen to her opinion. If the rest of this group are anything like yours truly, they'll be extremely shy about their scribblings and ultrasensitive to criticism. It's a writers thing. Rejection being the norm or so I'm reliably informed.

Melton Mowbray mush is preparing to leave. Anxious to get back to the factory no doubt for a slice of pie. I remain seated at the back of the hall, my work unread in the folder I am clasping protectively to my chest. Fuck it! Failed again! Maybe I'm just not ready yet. This writing game takes nerve and courage and I have very little of either at the moment. People begin to file out dejectedly leaving just me and Ginny who is gathering up her papers from the table at the front.

I stay silent at the back wishing the floor would open up and swallow me.

Try as I might I appear to have lost the use of my legs. It will pass. Just sit here for a month and I'll be fine. Lost my nerve ... lost all sensation in my lower limbs ... oh shit! Is this what anxiety does to you? Tilly has discussed the overwhelming fear associated with panic attacks in our sessions. Maybe I am in the middle of just such an attack. Or maybe it's a stroke? Either way I'm doomed.

"Oh hello! I thought everyone had gone." Ginny smiles, heading out of the hall.

"Actually I'm here for the next group." I lie convincingly.

"Lovely" They should be here in a minute. Starts at 8 on the dot." she giggles.

"Great! I'll just wait here then" ... I grin back.

"Night." The heavy oak door clangs behind her and I remain frozen to my chair.

Levy will find me. He should have been a Search & Rescue dog. He can sniff out a biscuit from a five mile radius. I expect he'll be here any minute. Carrying a barrel of brandy and a Mars to revive me.

"It went well I take it?" Jack's voice whispers behind me.

"Awful" I wail, "Total and utter wubbish.." ...

"Did you read them your work?"

"Never got the chance! Mrs Pork Pie was vile!" I cry.

"Next time eh mate?" he reassures me, wrapping his arm around my shoulder.

"Maybe. We shall see. Better get going before the next group arrive." I sniff.

Too late! The hall doors bang open and an enormous throng of bodies surge through them. Jack and I are trapped by a sea of people all clamouring for seats. Within minutes the hall is packed to capacity with not a seat to be spared. A mass of chattering bodies who all seem to know each other well.

Greetings are given. Hands shaken in friendship and numerous boiled sweets passed around amongst the crowd.

"Any ideas?" Jack laughs.

"None whatsoever!" I grin, searching the sea of faces for clues.

We don't have to wait long as an incredibly tall woman takes centre stage and the group fall silent. She must be over six feet tall with her hair pinned up into a bun on top. Her clothes circa 1970. Lots of frills and a long flowing skirt with a poppy pattern on it. She is wearing a silk pashmina and tosses it dramatically across her shoulders before she speaks.

"Good evening everyone. Welcome again to our monthly spiritualist session."

Oh blimey! It's a meeting of Ghostbusters! And we are both walled in on both sides by believers!

"We have some new faces in the room tonight. Let's give them a warm welcome." she gushes homing in on Jack and I.

"Welcome and may the spirit's be with you." she beams, exposing a set of enormous quite frightening gums.

I am mortified but Jack remains calm and casually waves to the audience.

"I shall prepare for the visitors now." she whispers and the room falls silent.

Visitors?? Are the aliens coming?? My life! What have we got ourselves into now?

A guy at the back dims the lights and Dolly Acorah takes her place on the stage.

Closing her eyes she takes several deep breaths and emit's a little moan from the back of her throat. Fuck me! If ectoplasm starts pumping out of her gob I shall do a runner! Jack grasps my hand and I can see his eyes dancing with glee. I should have stayed at home. No ghosts or aliens there. Only Levy.

"I am sensing a Charlie." she shouts, making me visibly jump.

"I am sensing a room full of Charlies." Jack whispers.

"He is hovering very close now. He has very big feet. Possibly an eleven."

Eh? Did I hear that right? Size eleven feet? And hovering? What bollocks!!

"Charlie passed recently. He is in turmoil. He is looking for a Fanny."

No sorry!! That's just too much for me to bear and I collapse into fits of giggles. Jack squeezes my hand tightly in an effort to shut me up.

"Are there any Fanny's in the room?" she trills, "This man is desperate!"

Jack loses it now and we both hunch forward in an attempt to stifle the noise.

"My Uncle was a Charlie but he never had a Fanny." A woman behind us shouts.

Jesus Christ! Are these people for real? I am convulsed with laughter and Jack is much the same.

"He was married to a Pansy!" she shouts excitedly, getting into the zone.

"Charlie is fading." Dolly tells her. The moment is obviously gone.

A ripple of disappointment wafts around the room as Charlie heads back up to the big Fanny Finder in the sky presumably. Jack and I are in bit's and incapable of moving at the moment. Dolly girds her loins and closes her eyes again. The room falls silent for what seems like ages until the oak door bangs open again and we all jump this time!

"Sorry. Had trouble getting a taxi." a woman gasps, struggling into the room on two walking sticks.

Poor sod! All that effort for so little. We watch as she heaves her gnarled body wearily to an empty seat at the front. Almost toppling over as she let's go of her sticks.

"I feel a spirit close by. She is concerned about someone." Dolly shouts.

We wait with baited breath for the spirit to make itself known.

"You will have to speak up my dear." she shouts into thin air."Yes ... yes ...I have it now. I will pass on your message."

Her eyes rest on the poor old girl who has just arrived late. Fixing her with an icy stare she says, "The spirits are worried about your health. You have problems with your mobility do you not?"

No shit Sherlock!! I could have told you that! How ridiculous!

"It's all in the detail you see. They tell me you had a cat at home." she says.

"I did have a cat but he went missing." the old girl sighs.

"He is still with us." Dolly smiles, "But he lives in Leicester now."

The old dear seems quite relieved to hear this and dabs at her eyes with a tissue.

"He has found a new home and he is happy." Dolly waffles unconvincingly.

"Have you got the address?" The old dear asks in all innocence, "I'd like to know he's being looked after." she sighs.

"Sorry... they are fading. It's difficult to hear them." she lies.

Fading fast! So is my patience! Jack shakes his head in disbelief and gives me a look that says DO NOT KICK OFF! Message received and understood. Who am I to burst their bubble? Poor deluded sods. Desperate for a message, however vague and unimportant from those they have lost. Clutching at straws I feel. Dolly is gathering herself together at the front and launches into another rambling monologue.

"As you regular believers will know the cost of the hall has risen quite substantially recently. In order to raise funds for the group we shall be holding a raffle at the end. Tickets are £5 and the prizes are on the stage. Just token prizes as you can see. The aim is to raise funds and I hope you will all dig deep for the cause." she warbles.

Jack and I crane our necks to get a look at the goodies. We are underwhelmed to say the least! £5 a ticket! Dolly must have a villa in Portugal to pay for!

Dolly appears to have emptied the contents of her kitchen cupboard for prizes. A tin of Ambrosia Rice Pudding. A roll of black refuse bags. A teapot in the shape of a Christmas pudding and a jar of Duchy Organic marmalade! Scandalous! And the poor sods are actually buying tickets!

A queue has formed at the front with Dolly shoving the fivers into her skirt pocket! Methinks she will be passing over to the other side very shortly if I get my hands on her throat! Jack senses that I am about to implode and grasping my sweaty hand leads me along the line of plastic seats out towards the back door. The cold night air hit's us both and we gulp in its freshness. Relieved to be out of the stifling atmosphere inside.

We can hear the excited voices chattering as we make our way along the lane. My blood pressure is calming down and we both giggle at the events we have just witnessed.

"Ambrosia Rice pudding!" I rant, "Bloody con merchant!"

"Ah well ... if they get some sort of comfort out of it." Jack sighs.

"Charlie looking for Fanny!" I squeal, dissolving into giggles.

"And him marrying a Pansy!" Jack laughs, "Unbelievable!"

Back home Levy is waiting up for us with one of my bra's around his neck. He is a devil for clean laundry! If I don't hang it up he will wear it. Jack's scarf ... my underwear ... the odd sock or two. I untangle the bra and he dives onto my lap on the sofa. He weighs a ton and I am pinned underneath his bulk now until bedtime.

"Jack. When I die ... I'll try to send you a message." I promise him.

"Erm ... okay. Any idea what sort of message?" he grins.

"Let's have a code! Each choose a word that only we will know!" I cry.

"Right. Let's think. A code. Got it! My word will be breasts!" he shrieks.

"Funny!"

"Seriously Cass! You'd know it was me if the word breasts came through!"

"True!" I agree laughing.

"What will yours be?" he beams.

"Boo!" I cry.

"Very funny!"

***

Chapter Twenty

... *Kenny & The Cornflakes*

I was only waiting in the queue for a Walnut Whip and managed to get myself a job instead! How did that happen? Never know what's round the corner do you? In my case it's the corner shop and Mr Raj who owns it has just offered me work! Bless him! He has no idea what he's letting himself in for! Poor guy has a severe staff shortage which is a measure of his desperation I feel! It's only a small shop but the racks of shelving are crammed to capacity with stock. You can buy anything there. From a needle and cotton to a course of driving lessons with his cousin Deeph who does a package of ten lessons for three hundred quid. And he throws in a car waxing kit as well. Bargain!

Raj was telling me about his staff problems as I paid the paper bill and I felt sorry for the guy. The shop opens at 6a.m and closes at 8p.m. That's a fourteen hour day! And now two of his staff have done a runner taking two hundred Benson & Hedges and a crate of Carling with them. Disgraceful! The man is distraught! The staff in question were late-nighters who went in after the shop closed to stack the shelves. Needless to say he is wary now of leaving anyone alone in the shop ... hence the job offer. He knows me and seems to think I will fit the bill. After a long time of being unable to work I am delighted that he has confidence in me. He must know that I am barking mad but seems prepared to give me a go. Can't let him down can I? That would be rude!

It's all very casual. A few hours here and there when required which suit's me. I start tonight! Just two hours after the shop closes to fill up on stock. I can do that! The pay is shit but hey-ho! I might just earn enough to buy Levy a crate of dog biscuits. And I'll be treating Jack as well. He has supported me for years and never batted an eyelid. If I save my salary for roughly a year I should be able to buy him a nice shirt! Like I say ... the pay is shit!

Jack is working in Sheffield today. Damn! I wish he were here! He will be gobsmacked to know I've got a job! I shall have to leave him a note. I expect it will be about 9p.m before he gets back and I have to be at work for eight.

I won't ring in case he's driving. God forbid I should be the cause of a pile up on the M6.

Jack I have a job! Raj at the shop asked me.

Stacking shelves 8 till 10. Meet me from work.

Dinner in oven. Gaviscon in drawer.

Cass xxxx

Raj is waiting for me as I arrive. Anxiously jangling the shop keys in his haste to lock up.

"Evening Raj."

"Lovely ... lovely." he grins, ushering me inside.

"Where shall I put my bag?" I ask, looking around the deserted shop.

"Hang it on that door." he smiles, pointing to a hook on the door.

"Right! I'm ready! Where shall I start?"

"Kenny will be here any minute." he tells me, "He main man" ...

"Kenny?"

"Stock controller! Very important job." he informs me.

"Oh right."

"Kenny knows everything about stock. He'll show you what to do."

I am relieved that somebody will show me what to do. I know it's not rocket science ... stacking shelves ... but there must be some sort of structure involved. Good old Kenny. Whoever he is. I have no idea but am about to find out. There is a sharp rap on the shop door and Raj unlocks it to let Kenny in.

Kenny looks about thirty. He also looks incredibly grumpy. Which is probably not the best word to describe him as Kenny is also a dwarf. At a rough guess I'd say he is about

3 feet 4inches tall. I am vertically challenged at just over five feet but he is positively tiny in comparison.

"Kenny this is Cassie." Raj tells him."She gonna help you out tonight."

"Whatever!" Kenny growls, obviously impressed.

"I'm hoping you'll show me the ropes." I smile encouragingly.

"I got enough to do without babysitting you!" he bites.

My gut instinct is to punch the little shit in the face but I refrain and instead count to ten and focus on calming down. Rude bastard! I don't care if you have got problems mate! No need to lash out at me! What the fuck did I do?

"I gotta go" ... Raj grins looking embarrassed, "The missus will be waiting."

With that he gathers up his keys and jacket and heads for the back door.

Kenny remains rooted to the spot, glaring at yours truly. I glare back.

"Don't get in the way. Just follow what I do. Got it?" he barks.

My back is up now! How rude!

"Look mate! I know your career in Star Wars was short lived but hey ... no need to be so sodding obnoxious!" I bite back.

"Fuck you! He snarls walking away.

"Right back at ya pal!" I shriek.

Jesus! This is turning out to be a nightmare. Where does all that anger come from? I am trying to be sympathetic but he is bristling with bitterness.

"Raj want's the cereals filled." he snaps, pointing up at the top shelf.

"No problem. Have you got a ladder?" I ask in all innocence.

"You taking the piss?" he snaps.

"No! Honestly. Unless you are prepared to climb onto my shoulders then we'll need a ladder." I tell him.

"I'll go up the ladder. You can pass me the boxes." he grunts walking away.

Oh great! It's late at night. I'm alone in a shop with a psychotic dwarf and nobody knows I'm here. Kenny reappears dragging a stepladder behind him and wedges it against the display.

"Grab that box of Weetabix." he snaps and I do as I am told. Watching in admiration as he vaults the steps in seconds.

We work in silence. Me passing him the boxes and he arranging them neatly on the shelf. As we work I am drawn to his body language. Aggressive! His every movement sharp and snappy. I get the distinct impression Kenny is not to be messed with. And that's fair enough. I imagine he's had a lifetime of abuse and that must make you defensive. And angry. I get it. My comparing him to R2D2 probably didn't help but he asked for it. A bit of respect goes a long way and so far he has shown me none.

"Bit old to be doing this aint ya?" he growls from above.

"Bit short to be taking me on aren't you?" I retort.

"You got a problem with short people?" he asks.

"Only those who are downright rude!" I tell him.

"Bothered!" he smirks, adopting that awful expression used on TV.

"Whateeeeeeeeeeever!" I rant back, stooping to his level now.

This is absurd! I've only been here half an hour and am at breaking point. Never in my life have I experienced such animosity from someone I hardly know. Attitude does not come close with this lad!

"Cornflakes!" he barks, pointing to a carton on the floor.

I attack the cardboard with a vengeance, tearing at the tape in order to open it. Wishing in my head that it was Kenny's throat!

"Seen you about with that big dog." he snaps, "Comes near me and I'll av im!"

"He's got squeaky toys bigger than you at home." I inform him, fuming.

"Yeah well, just saying. Dogs don't like me."

"Neither do I so that comes as no surprise." I add.

"Bit feisty for an old bird!" he smirks.

"Bit short for a hard man"! I snap back.

I can't do this! Spend another hour and a half being insulted by this twat. If he were the same height as me it would be a fair fight but he's not. All this for a few pounds an hour? Fuck that! If Jack were here he'd have taken him on. And the other six dwarves come to that. No contest! For the first time in a long time I am forced to make a major decision. No fannying around now Cass. Either deck the little shit or walk away. You deserve better than this girl!

"Listen mate. It's been a blast but basically life's too short. I'm off!" I tell him , dropping the carton of Cornflake boxes onto the shop floor.

"I aint said you can go yet!" He smirks, his face twisted in anger, "We got all these boxes to do tonight."

"Tough! I suggest you get on the phone to Dopey and Sleepy, they might be able to help!"

"Raj will sack ya"! He snorts.

"Too late! I sacked myself!" I grin, "I suggest you get a proper job mate. The panto season starts soon. Beats stacking shelves!"

"Coffin dodger!!" he bawls.

"Ewok!" I bawl back, stomping towards the door and letting myself out. Christ!

Is this what working in the real world is like now? Insults and anger? It's been a while since I was employed but not THAT long ago! When I did work we all showed respect to each other. We were friends as well as colleagues. What happened? Did the world go mad? Obviously! I am shaking with anger! Coffin dodger? Where the fuck did that come from? I'm not that old! No wonder elderly people feel threatened and afraid in society today. I've got a good mind to go back and challenge him but what's the point? Kenny has a problem. Height aside his attitude stinks! All that festering anger and bitterness! It must be tearing him up inside. Tilly would have a job dealing with all that shit and she's trained for it!

I wander back home dejectedly. That went well! Just over an hour and I'm unemployed yet again! I am jinxed! Trust me to get a job with a demented dwarf! As I cross the road to home Jack pulls on to the drive. He seems startled to see me out alone after dark without Levy.

"Hey Cass! What you doing out on your own?" he grins getting out of the car.

"Don't ask! Raj gave me a job and I blew it"! I wail.

"A job eh?" he looks puzzled.

"Stacking the shelves. But Kenny hated me! He's vile! Called me a coffin dodger!" I sob pathetically.

Jack's face clouds over and I am beginning to regret the whole incident.

"Kenny? Who would that be?" he asks in a soft voice.

"He's a dwarf! I've never known such rudeness Jack! And now I've left my bag in the shop! Kenny will probably take a pee in it"! I shriek.

"Go inside Cass. I'll go and get your bag." he smiles.

"No Jack! Leave it!" I beg, seeing the anger in his eyes.

"Inside Cass. Put the kettle on. I'll be back in a minute." he smiles, walking off in the direction of the shop.

I wait indoors. Terrified that police sirens and an ambulance will come racing up the lane. Jack is a big guy and does not take kindly to dwarfs who insult his wife. Oh heck! What have I done? I pace the lounge floor with Levy pacing along with me. He knows when I am stressed and clings to my side protectively. After what seems like an eternity Jack's figure appears in the distance with my bag swinging carelessly at his side. Thank God! I open the door and wrap my arms around his neck as he gets inside.

"Thank God Jack! I thought you'd been arrested!" I wail.

"Whatever for?" he grins, "Going to get your bag?"

"No silly! Beating a dwarf to death"!

"No need Cass. Kenny knows what the score is now." he smiles gently.

"How come?"

"Could take him a while to get out of that cardboard box but he will I'm sure."

"You didn't"! I cry.

"I did. Now where's my dinner woman!" he laughs, heading for the kitchen.

Real world you see. Jack lives in a world where you NEVER insult a woman. A world where you ALWAYS show respect to your elders regardless. And a world where men make a stand for their women. Old fashioned maybe but safe. Maybe Kenny will think twice before he vents his spleen at a woman again. Or anybody else for that matter.

Chapter Twenty One

... Love Thy Neighbour

Fiona and Henry are back. Oh joy! I watched them pull onto their drive last night. Their brand new Audi convertible laden down with Louis Vuitton luggage and duty free bags. I wonder if they've bought me some fags? Unlikely I should think since she hates me and the feeling is quite mutual! They both look well. Mind you – you would after weeks of lying on an exotic beach being waited on by a flunky wouldn't you? I think they've been snorkelling with dolphins or snowboarding with seals or something. Whatever. No doubt they will invite us round later to look at the photo's ... NOT!!!! Fiona is always immaculately dressed in designer gear. I am always covered in dog snot and fag ash. We are worlds apart and I suspect the divide will never be breached. She has her pubes waxed I bet every month. I struggle with my moustache.

It's her loss anyway. I like to think that I'm a good neighbour but suspect Fiona will never call on me to unblock her U bend. She'll have a man in to do it. Like she has a 'little woman' in to do her cleaning. And another one to do her ironing. I wait for the day when one arrives to wipe her arse! Lazy cow! Fiona is most definitely a lady who lunches! An early morning latte at Cafe Nero followed by a session at the gym. Lunch at Quatro in the village with friends. Hair and nails at 3pm then back home to shower before dinner down at the Quays.

No wonder she's exhausted! Although I suspect she's tired from carrying the weight of her new tit's around. I swear honestly! When they moved in she had – well – normal sized boobs. And now – well! Dolly Parton would be jealous! Quite obviously a boob job of gigantic proportions. Must be at least a 36GG! Silly cow! I'm amazed they didn't implode on the flight and bring the plane down.

I wonder if Henry's had his bollocks done as well? Maybe the clinic had an offer on. Buy one get one free. Whatever. Henry's face resembles one big bollock anyway. He encourages her and frankly deserves all he gets. He calls her daaaaaaaaaaaaaaaaaaaaaaaaaaaaahling! She calls him precious. I call him prick. His facial expressions amaze me! A sort of mixture of contempt and disgust whenever anyone of a lower class dares to invade his air space. That's me mainly. Bless him! All that ego confined inside such a small brain. He'll learn.

Life has a way of kicking you up the arse when you get to big for your boots. In Henry's case the boots would be made from rare wombat hide – hand stitched by Aborigines in the outback.

Even their recycling boxes are crammed with designer labels! I quite often have a mooch through on collection day just to see what they have been wasting their money on. Bollinger bottles of course – in the glass tub – and Pinot Gris Reserve. Even their marmalade jars have Harrods labels! It's amazing what you can discover about people from their rubbish. I have discovered that I am a stalker and seriously disturbed but hey-ho!

Henry just left for the office wearing his Bluetooth earpiece in case the Prime Minister rings for some financial advice I imagine. He was also wearing a rather natty tweed jacket and brown loafers. Very Gary Barlow! Pete staggered past as well on his way to the shops. Pete was dressed more like Ken Barlow. A chunky cardigan teamed with brown crimplene trousers. Bless. He obviously woke up to find the cocktail cabinet empty and is on his way for supplies. You can buy booze at almost any hour of the day or night now. Pete is in heaven! No more withdrawal symptoms waiting for the pub to open. I often wonder what it must be like to be in a permanent state of pickledness. Painful I imagine. And costly! How Pete manages to afford all that alcohol I do not know. I suppose if you have an addiction you do whatever it takes to satisfy the craving. In Pete's case by breeding guinea pigs and salvaging stuff out of skips to sell.

Busy morning out there today. A van just pulled up with Claws & Paws painted on the side. Some pet service by the look of it. Oh blimey – Crawford's back! Fiona's pussy so to speak. Looks like he's been on holiday as well. Some luxury cattery I bet. Now that's service for you! Delivered back home in a crafted cat carrier complete with cushion. Poor sod! Bet he'd love to roam the lanes like Bilbo used to but not much chance of that happening. He is Fiona's child substitute and she dotes on him. He has outfit's! I swear it's true! She actually dresses the poor bugger up in ridiculous cat clothes! On Halloween he was sat in the window wearing an orange pumpkin hat on his head! The expression on his face said it all really. Clothing for cats! How absurd! Imagine if I tried to get Levy into a Santa outfit? He would object most strongly and fair play to him! Animals are already dressed – in their own fur. I have an overwhelming urge to kidnap Crawford and set him free. Free to stay out all night and rummage through bins scavenging for scraps. The shock would probably kill him so maybe not.

Oh gawd! Fiona Of The Fuckwit is coming up our drive! Oh hell! What did I do? Can't remember! They've been away for weeks. Innocent your worshipfulness. I sprint to the door, opening it before she has chance to ring the bell.

"Hi there! Nice holiday?" I ask, grinning like an idiot.

"Super!" she trills, handing me an envelope.

"Oh – what's this then – a restraining order?" I laugh.

"Henry and I are holding open house tonight. Bit last minute. Thought it might be nice to meet all the neighbours" ... she twitches, looking nervous.

"Great! What time?" I giggle.

"It's all on the invite ... must dash ... get these delivered."

And with that she's gone, rushing away as if she'd just discovered I had smallpox. She has a mass of envelopes in her hand and I watch fascinated as she rounds the bend and pops one through Pete's door. Oh joy! There is a God after all! She obviously has no idea about any of the occupants hereabouts. Too busy having a weekly vajazzle I suppose. Craning my neck around the door frame I can just about make out her suntanned legs as she positively sprints up and down the surrounding paths delivering the invites. Mary has one. And even Bolak!

My cup runneth over!!

The notepaper is expensive of course. And scented. Vanilla I think. And the message beautifully hand written in purple ink ...

Henry and Fiona
Would like you to join them tonight
For an open house evening
At Number 15
8 till late.

My life! Open house? What exactly does that mean I wonder? Can we go in and swipe all her freshly laundered towels? Jesus! Pete will have a field day! Hope they have a lock on the booze cupboard. And in my case the chocolate cupboard. I don't think Fiona does chocolate. Too many calories. How sad! Never to have experienced the sheer joy of devouring a giant slab of Dairy Milk! I must phone Mary. See if she's planning on going.

The phone rings out for ages and I am beginning to get concerned when suddenly she picks up ...

"Hello?"

"Hi Mary. How are you today?" I ask, "Did you get your invite?"

"Invite?" she asks "What invite?"

"Open house at number fifteen." I tell her.

"Oh that ... who's Harvey?"

"Henry." I laugh, "They have that cat Crawford ... remember?"

"Oh I forgot." she giggles, "The cat with the hat."

"Exactly!" I sigh, relieved that she seems to be having a good day. A day when she remembers who I am and a day when she doesn't attempt to walk along the M6 in her nightie.

"Shall I come and fetch you later. You can come with Jack and I."

"That would be nice. Thanks."

"I'll be over at about eight then ... I'll bring some wine as a gift."

"No need Cass. I've got them a house warming present." she assures me.

"Oh right ... lovely."

"They can have my mop. Every house should have a mop." she tells me.

"Erm ... lovely." I waffle, trying to think of a suitable response.

"See you later Cass. I must find my high heels."

"Eh?"

"Thought I'd doll up a bit. Wear those heels and my wedding suit." she sighs.

"Tell you what Mary. I'll be over about seven. Help you get ready."

"You're an angel. See you later."

"Bye."

Not such a good day after all then? Mary got married in 1949. Her wedding suit was pale blue and roughly a size 8 judging by the wedding photo on the dresser.

She was wearing heels. At this precise moment in time she is a size 20 and wears slippers most of the time due to her grossly swollen feet. Bless her! All we need now is for Pete to turn up to the party wearing his Speedo swimming trunks and a pair of welly's!

The party is in full swing by the time we finally arrive at eight thirty.

Mary was in her nightie and hairnet when I went across. The party a dim and distant memory in the recess of her confused brain. This daily deterioration is heart breaking and Jack clasped my hand tightly as tears welled up in my eyes.

Between us we manage to get her kitted out in a pretty lime green floral dress and cardigan and gently squeeze her swollen feet into a pair of dark red slipper boots. Jack discreetly hid the mop which she had propped up against the front door earlier. It was wrapped in several pages of the Radio Times.

The drive to number fifteen is rammed with cars, all parked at obtuse angles with not an inch to spare between them. BMW and Audi being the majority with one lone Lexus gleaming in the glare of the security lights. Serious money here I think! The windows are thrown open and the chatter of polite conversation drifts through the night air. As we approach the mahogany front door a security beam floods the front step with light.

"What's that on the front door?" Jack asks sounding puzzled.

"Probably a note telling us to piss off!" I laugh.

He peers closely, blinded by the light and seems perplexed.

"What does it say?" I ask, holding onto Mary's arm.

"Bloody cheek!" he spit's, reading it aloud.

Please go around to the back gate.

We have new Brinton carpet throughout.

The party is being held al fresco!

Thank you.

I thought it was too good to be true! How rude! Invite people to a party then refuse them access to the house!

"Cheeky bastards!" I snap, "Better go round to the tradesmans' entrance then."

"Unbelievable!" Jack laughs." Come on ladies. Mind your step."

"Hold on to me Mary. This path is a bit dodgy."

We make our way along the alley surrounding the house and after almost losing Mary in the hedge, finally make it into the garden. Jack is still laughing and I have a sprig of privet in my hair. The other party guests look quite startled as we stumble through the back gate. I am somewhat startled too by the sheer volume of expensive dental work and blingtastic jewellery on display. And that's just the men! The women appear to be extras out of the Stepford Wives. All dressed in flowing maxi dresses – their hair backcombed to within an inch of its life. I am wearing a pair of Levi's and a white shirt. What's that expression now – a fish out of water? Yep. That's me! A trout in a turban so to speak. I would be slightly perturbed but for the fact that Pete is here, leaning against the conservatory looking worse for wear. He is wearing a pair of Bermuda shorts with a shark pattern on and a string vest. I love that man!! He lifts my spirit's and right now I need them lifting big style. Lenny is sitting on the patio, his ballooning leg and bollock resting on what looks like a very expensive ornate garden urn. One of those terracotta things that people have imported from Morocco.

"Over here Jack!" Pete bawls, waving frantically.

Lenny waves but remains seated bless him. Probably glad to get the weight off I should think.

"Hi Pete. So glad you made it." I grin.

"You know me and a party." he laughs, scratching his bum.

That's my boy! You know where you stand with Pete. I like that.

"Cassandra ... Jack ... you came!"

It's Fiona, trying hard to mask her annoyance that we showed up! I bet she'll be on Mogadon for months after this.

"Of course we came." Jack smiles, "We are neighbours after all."

"And this is Mary. I don't think you've been introduced." I tell her.

"Oh of course. Mary. The house with the damson tree out front?" she grins somewhat rigidly. Old Fiona looks terrified. As if aliens have landed in her garden and are threatening to probe her with surgical instruments. The grin frozen on her face making it seem quite garish in the harsh lighting.

"Erm ... do make yourselves at home." she warbles, wandering off.

Rude! Rude! Rude! Not a kind word for Mary ... or the offer of a drink ...or even a seat for goodness sake! Poor old sod will keel over in a minute. Lenny comes to the rescue and like the true gentleman he is, drags the plastic chair he was sitting on over to Mary.

"There you go. Have a seat Mary." he offers, helping her onto the chair.

"Thanks Kenny." she smiles.

Lenny ... Kenny ... whatever ... I need a drink and quick! Henry must have read my mind as he suddenly appears at my side carrying a tray of drinks. I say drinks in the lightest possible way. Bottles of beer for the men and glasses of white or red wine for the ladies. Oh well. It's a start I suppose.

"Nibbles are set out over there." he gestures"The pig roast will be here soon."

"Pig roast eh? Great! I could eat a ... well ... pig." Jack grins.

"We have a guy up from Stroud. A whizz with a hog roast." Henry guffaws.

"Fantastic!" Pete slurs, farting loudly with all the excitement.

Henry catches the brunt of Pete's explosion and I have to say he looks appalled.

He almost drops the tray of drinks in his rush to escape and I lose sight of him as he disappears into the crowd. The crowd that appears to have formed a divide since we arrived. Them and us so to speak. Them on one side of the garden. Me ... Jack ... Pete ... Lenny and Mary on the other. The battle lines have been drawn.

I suppose it was inevitable really, two completely opposite worlds colliding in a suburban garden. They are what they are and we are what we are. We are ordinary folks just getting by on a daily basis. They exist in a parallel universe of privilege and Prada. To each his own I say. There is absolutely NO reason why we shouldn't mix together tonight but sadly I know it's never gonna happen. They have clocked Pete's shorts and Mary's red slipper boots and the disparaging looks say it all. Shame. If only they could drop the attitude and come over and say hello. Fuck um! We are here now and I intend to enjoy myself. Mary is oblivious to it all and slowly sips on the glass of red wine she took from the tray. Not sure it's a good idea to mix alcohol with all her prescription medicines but one won't hurt I'm sure. Let her enjoy herself.

"This beers piss poor!" Pete grimaces loudly, draining the bottle.

"This wine's not much better." I agree.

"No worries. The pig roast will be here soon." Jack whispers optimistically.

"Yay!" Pete bawls, sliding down the wall and ending up in a heap on the patio.

Eyebrows are raised to say the least on the other side of the lawn. My life if they think that's bad wait till he gets into his stride. It's early yet. I have seen him unconscious on the roundabout at two in the afternoon. Now that's shocking!

"Nibbles anyone?" Jack asks, heading for the food table.

"Please. I'm starved." I plead.

"Just butter on mine thanks." Mary tells him.

"Sorry?" he stops, mid stride.

"Just butter. On my toast ... thanks." she smiles at Jack.

"Got it Mary. No problem." he grins, playing along.

Sounds like ... roast ... toast! Bless her.

"He's here! He's here!" Fiona shrieks, suddenly running amok amongst the crowd.

Who would that be then? Elvis? The Pope? David Beckham? I suspect she means the pig man from Stroud as the crowd of party goers bray excitedly along with her.

True to form, the pig man arrives to a roar of approval from the throng. Fuck me! Have they never eaten before? Okay ... it's a pig ... chill out man!

I almost expect a fanfare of trumpets as the hog is wheeled into the garden by a very rotund little man wearing a chef's hat and an apron with The Happy Hog emblazoned across it. He seems like a man who is happy in his job. Although the hog itself looks anything but happy I have to say. It's head unceremoniously speared with a spike. It's mouth gaping open in the last throes of death. Oh dear. I was ravenous a few minutes ago but that head has somewhat turned me off pork for the time being.

The prospect of free grub proves too much for Pete and in a flash he is on his feet and heading for the front of the queue. Several guests look on in alarm as he elbows them out of the way, anxious to eat. His shorts flapping in the breeze which I have to say is now whipping around the garden like a minor tornado.

"Jack ... it's freezing out here. I'm worried about Mary." I shiver.

"I'll nip back and get a throw from the lounge." he offers, dashing off.

Mary is looking a bit frail ... and pale ... not surprising really considering her age and the fact that she's being asked to sit outside in the garden ... in a hurricane! How sodding rude and inconsiderate is that? Rude bastards! I imagine all the other guests keep warm by all the hot air that's wafting around the gazebo. Inane chatter that spouts forth like verbal diarrhoea ... all of it meaningless and aimed to impress...

"Nailed the bonus Julian! Expecting at least 500k in October!"

"Considering buying another property in Provence?"

"Wise move I feel!"

"Should double in value in under a year!"

Fuckwit's! And the women are no better! Circling each other like prey, comparing designer dresses and diamonds. Shallow does not come into it! The air kissing and false smiles! Pass me a bucket please I feel quite sick!

"There you go Mary." Jack is back with a woollen throw.

"Thanks mate." I smile, as he gently wraps it around her shoulders.

"Got you something to warm you up as well." he grins, handing me a JD bottle.

"Now you're talking!"

I dispose of the wine which actually tastes like vinegar by lobbing it into the bushes and crack open the Jack Daniels. Pete instinctively hears the opening of a bottle and lurches towards us carrying two trays laden with roast pork cobs.

"Blimey Pete! Feeling a bit peckish?" Jack laughs.

"Fill your boots!" he grins, ramming a whole cob into his mouth.

"Drink?" I ask, offering him the bottle.

"Don't mind if I do!"

I have to concede that the hog is indeed delicious. Melt in the mouth delicious with just a smattering of crunchy crackling to round it off. Silence descends as all five of us devour the contents of the trays. Silence apart from Pete's continuous farting! Jesus! He certainly is windy tonight and I'm sure all that pork will only make the problem worse.

"Pardon me!" he burps apologetically after letting another one rip.

"Granted!" Lenny laughs.

"And once more with feeling!" Pete roars, losing control altogether now.

My life! I have no idea why I find farting so funny but I do! Childish I know and incredibly immature but it never ceases to make me collapse in a fit of giggles. I am incapable now, leaning against the garden wall for support, tears streaming down my face.

"Steady Cass! No laughing allowed at this function!" Pete giggles.

"The party police over there will arrest you in a minute." Lenny laughs.

I can see what he means. We are attracting some attention from the others.

Their faces wrinkled in disgust as we titter and trump in the corner. Pete has started to sway now ... always a bad sign. It takes a fair amount of alcohol for Pete to sway. Remember he generally starts drinking at around eight in the morning so by now he's been drinking solidly for roughly thirteen hours! Enough to put you or I into a coma. Lenny is also past the pickled stage and for some bizarre reason has decided that now would be a good time to dance. A sudden rush of food gone straight to his brain I should think.

The sounds of Adele reverberate around the patio and considering his size and infirmity Lenny is surprisingly light on his feet. His hefty frame gyrating quite nimbly to the beat. Pete is incapable of actually dancing but his swaying movements are quite rhythmic and I watch fascinated as they gain momentum, the thumping beat of Set Fire To The Rain urging them on to a frenzy.

"Impressive!" Jack laughs, clapping along to the beat.

"It will end in tears!" I grin, anticipating what is to come.

And come it does! At the precise moment that Lenny throws caution to the wind and tries to do a high kick, his leg gives up the ghost and he topples forward, grabbing on to Pete as he falls. To be precise, he actually grabbed Pete's

Bermuda shorts which end up round his ankles. And he would have chosen tonight to go commando! His considerable arse exposed in all its glory to the horrified crowd. The milky white cheeks glimmering in the glare of the security lights.

"Oh my life!" I cry, helpless with laughter.

"Time for a sharp exit!" Jack grins, helping Lenny to his feet.

Pete appears oblivious to all the fuss and without batting an eyelid, bends down quite gracefully to retrieve his shark infested shorts and lets rip with yet another earth shattering fart. A fart that ricochets around the garden like a cruise missile. I swear people actually dived for cover! He certainly knows how to make an impression!

"Thanks for having us!" Jack yells, taking Mary by the arm.

"Cheers!" I add, following on behind, desperate to get away.

Lenny is a few steps behind me, dragging his bad leg painfully along the lane.

As I look back Pete is helping himself to yet another tray of pork cobs. And a pack of beers. That will be his breakfast for the morning no doubt. Bless him. He is harmless. Just incapable.

Rounding the bend behind the lanes I swear I can her Fiona sobbing. Be a while before we get another invite I expect. I can live with that.

***

Chapter Twenty Two

... *Alan & The Anti-Christ*

Alan has a black eye! Oh my life! How on earth did that happen? He is such a sweetie. I can't imagine anyone wishing to do him any harm. He just arrived ... late ... for our weekly session. Stumbling into the room carrying a battered old suitcase. Christ! He's been evicted! And the wedding is less than a month away. They will have to come and live with Jack and I. Homeless on your honeymoon! I couldn't let that happen. Dear God give this lad a break please!!

"My goodness Alan!" Tilly squeaks, shocked at his appearance.

"Soz. Saw this in the charity shop. Be great for me honeymoon." he grins.

"Is everything okay Alan ... your eye" ... I whisper.

"Yeah. Some kids tried to rob me chips last night." he sighs, sitting down.

Bastards! I am incensed on his behalf. All that violence for a bag of chips!

"Shoved me saveloy in me pocket. They never got that." he grins.

Oh bless! Why is the world so cruel? What harm has this lad ever done to anyone?

"I was waiting for the number 17 bus. On the wall outside the chippy." he sighs.

"That's terrible Alan. What is the world coming to." I rant indignantly.

"Have you put anything on that eye Alan?" Tilly asks.

"Got no steak." he laughs, "Slapped a slice of corned beef on it!"

"How ridiculous!" Alicia snorts, obviously annoyed at the attention being diverted away from her.

"It's meat aint it?" Alan snaps, offended and quite rightly so.

"Butt out Bollock chops!" I rant, forgetting I am inside a mental health unit.

Tilly flushes with embarrassment and I am forced to back down. This is her group and quite frankly she has enough to deal with without me inviting Alicia outside for a fist fight.

"Shall we proceed?" Tilly sighs in an attempt to regain control.

"Sure. Sorry." I smile.

"Today we need to discuss moving forward." she smiles back.

"Eh?" Alan asks looking perplexed.

"Moving forward Alan. I need to know what you have gained from our sessions."

"Crikey. That's a whole bag of worms!" I laugh.

"Indeed." Tilly agrees, flicking through the diary on her lap.

Alicia remains silent and stoney faced. Her ample bosom heaving in anger.

"Let's take a minute in silence to think about the question." Tilly suggests.

"What question?" Alan stammers in a panic.

"Oh for goodness sake!" Bollock chops bites back in disgust, "Stupid boy!"

Now I did try to warn her didn't I? You'd think she would have learned after all this time that I have a zero tolerance policy for her attitude. Especially where Alan is concerned. He brings out that mothering instinct in me. Well, somebody has to stand up for the lad.

He's one of life's losers. He has no family. No money and an air of defeat about him that is quite tangible. He is weak and Alicia in her capacity as one of life's bully boys always tries to put him down at every opportunity. Bullies are like that. They spot a weakness and go in for the kill. Not today love!

"Were you dropped on your head at birth?" I rant at her, my eyes blazing.

"What?" she shouts back, looking down her fat nose at me.

"You heard! Just trying to work out why you behave as if you're brain damaged!"

"Ladies please!!!" Tilly begs, looking decidedly upset.

"I have never been spoken to like that in my life!" Alicia Anti-Christ sobs.

"Don't get out much then do you!" I laugh.

"Our Billy got dropped on his head once." Alan suddenly chips in.

Bless that lad! I have no idea where he gets his timing from but it's classic.

"Sorry?" Tilly asks, swivelling around in her chair to face him.

"Our Billy. His Mam was a drinker. Hanging the washing out and dropped him."

"Oh my life!" I cry, aghast at the thought of it.

"He was fine. Landed on top of the dog. Big bugger he was. Alsatian."

"Thank goodness!" Tilly giggles.

"Went into care in the end." Alan sighs sadly.

"Oh dear ... that's sad Alan." I sympathise.

"Nah. He got adopted. Good family too." he tells us.

"I like a happy ending." I smile, relieved.

"Shame he got killed in a car crash on the M6." he adds wistfully.

"Oh no! Sorry to hear that." Tilly tells him.

"Coppers was chasing him. Robbed a BMW in Manchester" ...

I should have known. It was never going to have a happy ending was it? The stereotypical story of abuse, abandonment and the inevitable outcome. Sad.

"Is this session ever going to get under way?" Alicia suddenly snaps.

"Of course. Sorry. Let's get on shall we?" Tilly apologises.

"What was the question again?" Alan grins.

"Moving forward Alan. What have you gained from coming here?" Tilly sighs.

We all remain silent. Racking our brains to come up with a suitable response. Me personally? I have learned that the Anti-Christ is alive and well and living in Oakham and wears clothes from the Per Una Collection.

"I got Tracey didn't I?" Alan suddenly pipes up."I never come over this way normally but I went into Tesco for some sardines and Tracey was there."

"Erm ... okay." Tilly giggles.

"I usually go to Spa. The woman on the till there's got no teeth." he tells us.

"Okay Alan. And apart from Tracey, what has helped you in these sessions?"

"Cass!" he grins excitedly, "She's been great! Even doing me a wedding cake!"

I am blushing now. Partly because of his kindness. Mainly at the thought of the cake! The clock is ticking and every single one of my attempts has been disastrous. If only he knew.

"No worries!" I grin, with fingers firmly crossed behind my back.

"So you've gained friendship Alan? Is that what you mean?" Tilly tries again.

"Sure." he nods, his face blushing a scarlet pink.

"Friendship is important. Where would we be without friends." Tilly sighs.

"Be a Billy No Mates!" Alan laughs, his bruised eye glinting in the light.

"And so, in conclusion, now we have to think about moving forward."

A logical conclusion really. We have been coming here to the Crumpled Clinic for almost two years now. That's a long time to be in therapy ... for free! I think the average length of treatment is about a year but not surprisingly we have exceeded the norm! The sessions just seem to have continued without anyone questioning their validity or value. God bless Tilly I say! She deserves a mention in the Queen's Honours List! I have gained a lot from these visit's! Anger management aside, I have met Alan and he truly is priceless. And Tilly of course, goes without saying. Alicia can go fuck herself.

"So how do you propose we move forward?" the fucked one suddenly asks.

"Good point. We should chat about what you can do next." Tilly replies.

"We could have a day trip." Alan pipes up, "Weston ... or Blackpool."

"Sorry?" Tilly asks looking puzzled.

"A day out! We aint done that. We could go on a coach." he grins.

Bless him! He has interpreted Tilly's words literally. She's talking about where we go from here ... when the sessions end ... but he's in full flow now.

"The Co-Op do day trips. Pick you up on the corner by Aldi." he informs us.

"I don't think I can bear much more of this." Alicia sighs, losing all hope.

"Great idea Alan! Maybe after the wedding" ... I laugh.

"Probably best wait." he agrees, "We got a night in Worcester booked."

"You and Tracey?" I ask.

"The honeymoon. Staying in a caravan." he tells us excitedly.

"Lovely!" Tilly and I chorus together.

"Nobby's got a van by the river. He's letting us have it for the night."

The Anti-Christ appears to have lost the will to live, her head slumped casually back against the headrest on the chair. Her eyes glazed and off somewhere in the clouds. We are obviously boring her to death. Good!

"I have learned that you get what you pay for!" she snaps, "If you want decent healthcare you have to pay for it!"

Tilly looks shell shocked! How rude! What a bitch! Tilly has devoted hours and hours of her time and tears to all three of us. Enough already!

"You obnoxious cow!" I rant, "Tilly has been kindness itself to all of us!"

"I ... erm ... sorry." she stammers, regretting the previous outburst.

"Cass it's fine. Alicia is entitled to her opinion." Tilly sighs dejectedly.

"No! She's NOT entitled to slag you off! I won't stand for that!" I shout.

"Sorry. I really am. I don't know what I was thinking." Alicia wails.

"Let's all calm down shall we?" Tilly begs.

"I will, when she apologises properly!" I glare at Alicia, daring her to reply.

"Tilly. Forgive me. I am truly sorry." she whines.

"Apology accepted. Now let's move on please." Tilly whispers.

My heart goes out to that girl. Barely out of university and overwhelmed every day with a case load of loons like us! Can't be easy can it? I am seething and take several deep breaths in an attempt to control my anger. I wish Alicia would fuck off to a private clinic! Do us all a favour love and do one!

"Cassie. Your turn. What have you gained from these sessions?" she asks.

"The ability to stand up for myself!" I laugh, glancing over at Alicia.

"Right. That's a positive don't you think?" she grins.

"Absolutely! A few years back I was a doormat. Now I don't go there and that's all thanks to you Tilly! Thank you!"

"You're welcome." she smiles, "Glad I could help."

"I forgot!" Alan suddenly shrieks making me jump, "Me new tumble dryer!"

"Eh?"

"I got meself a new tumble dryer cos of these sessions. A woman called round from some charity. I told her I was depressed and she asked me why. Told her I couldn't dry me pants properly. They go all stiff on the radiators see. She got me a grant. For a new tumble dryer!" he blurts out excitedly.

Only Alan eh? Only Alan could turn this conversation round to stiff pants! Bless that lad! I'd love to have been a fly on the wall when that woman came calling.

"So ... let's wind this up for today shall we?" Tilly stops him in mid flow.

"Hallelujah!!" the elephant in the corner sighs.

"I just want you all to think about the future. About what lies ahead."

"Got it. Bit scary but we have to I suppose." I nod.

"Nah ... don't be scared Cass. I'll come on the big rides with ya!" Alan grins.

"Blackpool?"

"Yup!"

I bet Tilly's got a headache. I've got a corker. It started in my left temple and now it's crushing down on my forehead. What a session! Came close to actually punching Alicia's lights out today. And Alan! With his pants and his black eye! It's exhausting!

"See you all same time next week?" Tilly trills, gathering up her stuff.

"Absolutely! Three more sessions and Alan will be a married man!" I laugh.

"Exciting!" Tilly giggles, gently stroking his sleeve.

"Can't wait! Cake and a night in Nobby's caravan!" he grins, walking away.

My life! Poor sod is actually looking forward to my cake! I shall have to get a grip and get the ruddy thing sorted. That lad's had enough disappointments in his life. I refuse to add another one to the list.

CAKE CRISIS V

Purchase 16 expensive fruit cakes from Waitrose.
Attempt to glue them together with jam & marzipan.
Watch in horror as the cake topples to the floor.
Ring BBC2 and demand Paul Hollywood's address.

Chapter Twenty Three

... Mazel Tov Mrs Morgenstein!!

Not a good day to be wearing a swimsuit and slippers. Autumn is fast approaching and there's a definite nip in the air. I even detected the faint whiff of a ground frost when I got up this morning. You know that distinctive crisp smell that hit's your nostrils on a cold morning? Mary is oblivious to the seasons apparently. She thinks it's summer and that we are in the middle of a heatwave. I popped in earlier to find her sitting in the kitchen dressed for the beach. I am the one who is drowning! Drowning in a tidal wave of anxiety and despair at just how quickly this disease seems to be overwhelming her. Call it what you like ... dementia ... senility ... old age ... she has it with bells on.

How quickly the brain decays in cases such as this. It's less than a year since she became a bit forgetful and now ... well ... every day brings yet more signs of the downhill decline. It began with the odd blip when she struggled to remember the names of people she had known for years. And objects. I was intrigued one day when she asked me to pass her the flippers. She meant scissors. Silly things that seemed funny at the time. Details that I put down to her age. I'm not even fifty yet and there are days when I forget my own name!

Then there were the household bills. Mary is old school and always paid her bills the minute they plopped through the letterbox. I was aghast one day to find a huge pile of unopened post rammed behind the dresser in the kitchen. It took Jack and I a week to sort it all out. Michael took over at that point and he settles all the bills now through the bank. Power of Attorney I think it's called. Think I'd better get Tom to do that for me soon!

And the dress sense! My life, that goes out of the window straight away! She has always been immaculately turned out.

Classic suit's from Debenhams and House of Fraser. Natty little handbags with shoes to match. And always sparkling clean with a faint whiff of Estee Lauder wafting in her wake. Not now. This morning it was swimwear. On Monday it was a Christmas jumper with Rudolph on the front combined with a pair of big pants. Nothing else. No skirt or trousers.

Heartbreaking.

She would be mortified is she were aware. A dignified, fiercely proud Dubliner who has spent her entire life being a good soul. Her kids idolise her and so do we all. Dementia is indeed a cruel illness. I'll go further than that and say it's a bastard! It creeps up on you slowly and with a vengeance and before you know it you're in Asda wearing your pyjamas and attracting unwanted attention from the security guards. Maybe it's a good thing she's not aware. She doesn't venture far these days so most of her episodes are confined to the house. Like today. I coaxed her into changing into some warm clothes eventually. It took a large packet of Maltesers but we got there in the end. There seems to be a very childlike element to this illness. As if the roles have been reversed. Mary will do anything for a Malteser! I always keep a bag handy just in case.

When I left, she was sitting at the kitchen table tearing pages of The Independent into squares. I have no idea. Don't ask! Michael is driving up from Oxford later today. He rang me last night. He is bringing a colleague with him from the hospital. Some guy who specialises in geriatric medicine. The dreaded day has arrived when Mary is to be assessed for her competency. I am struggling with all this and praying that I can hold it all together. Otherwise it could well be yours truly who ends up being assessed!

Today is one of those days when I have had to talk to myself in the mirror. See! Analyse that! You know ... those dark days when you just have to try and be strong for everyone when in reality your heart is breaking and you just want to crawl under the duvet and hide? I read somewhere that if you face yourself in the mirror and give yourself a stern talking to then that will give you the strength to overcome everything. I have tried this method lots of times and basically ... it's bollocks! It never works for me! Must have read it in Cyclists Monthly or something. Twaddle!

A much better method for yours truly is to tell Levy. That poor dog has absorbed all of my worries and woes over the years and never once told me to shut up! Impressive! His huge eyes simply gaze adoringly into mine as I rant and sob ... his wet nose nuzzling my face as the tears inevitably fall. That's my method. He has even been known to raise an eyebrow at times as if he is actually interested! God bless black labradors I say! Who needs a therapist? Well ... me actually! Tilly is fantastic but I can't very well romp through the woods with her on a wet windy day can I? People would talk.

***

Michael has just pulled up outside. My heart literally missed a beat when I caught sight of the silver Volvo. I have worked myself up into such a state and she's not even my mother! God forbid that some doctor will ever try to assess Ma! She'd have him tied up in knots ... no worries! Mary has been such a big part of my life for such a long time I feel as if we are related. Granted most days now she thinks I'm Deidre Barlow but hey-ho! Better get over there and offer some kind of support ... if that's possible in my fragile mental state.

"Cass! Thanks for coming over. Lovely to see you again!" Michael smiles, opening the door for me. He suddenly grabs me in a bear hug and I can sense that he is dreading what is to come as well.

"No worries." I tell him, "She'll outlive the lot of us!"

"She's a tough old stick." he sighs, leading the way into the lounge.

Mary is sitting upright in her favourite chair, thankfully fully clothed but sadly wearing a knitted tea cosy on her head.

This does not bode well and I am unsure as to whether to laugh or cry.

"Hi Mary. Surrounded by handsome men again?."

"Cassie! This is Dick ... a friend of Michael's." she grins, gesturing to the middle aged man sitting opposite her on the sofa.

"It's Adek actually Mary." he laughs, getting to his feet and shaking my hand.

"Nice to meet you." I smile back and he gestures for me to sit down.

"Michael asked me to come along and check you over Mary." he says, taking her hand gently in his own. This simple gesture of kindness overwhelms me and I am already struggling to hold it together.

"He tells me you've been a bit out of sorts lately?"

"Well I am seventy three"! She giggles, "Not bad for my age eh?"

Seventy three? Oh my life! Add another twenty years and you'd be right. Oh dear.

"Indeed. You look well. I just need to ask you a few questions if that's alright with you Mary. Just see if we can get to the bottom of it all eh?" he smiles.

"Whatever you think best Derek." she sighs, looking tired.

"Lovely! It won't take long. Shall we get started?"

Michael and I remain silent, both holding our breath in anticipation of what is to come. He explained on the phone last night that this is known as a Cognitive Impairment test. It's standard in dementia cases and gives a rough idea of just how impaired the sufferer is. Fascinating. He also filled me in on the literal translation of dementia. Latin. The root of mind madness or something similar. He lost me in the translation. Thank God for the medics of the world. Whatever would we do without them?

"Mary. Can you tell me what the date is today?" Adek asks, taking notes.

"August the thirty-third." she replies without hesitation, a huge grin spreading across her face. Michael smiles gently and grasps my hand. I have a lump in my throat the size of a satsuma but daren't let Mary see I'm upset.

"And what would you say this is Mary?" he asks, holding up his pen.

She hesitates briefly at this then suddenly shrieks"Silly sod it's a spoon!"

"Excellent! Just a few more and we are almost done." he smiles.

"Doing well Mammy." Michael sighs sadly, "doing well!"

"Mary, I'm going to say three words and I'd like you to repeat them."

"Lovely." Mary nods, playing along with the game.

"Penny ... table ... and apple." Adek repeats slowly, still taking notes.

Mary looks suddenly perplexed and I ache to repeat the words for her.

"Erm ... Mabel ... is that right?" she giggles nervously.

"Fine Mary fine. Can you remember the other two?"

"Give me a second." she whispers, her face deep set in concentration.

"Take your time Mammy, no rush." Michael reassures her.

"No ... it's gone. What was the question." she sighs.

"That's fine Mary. You're doing really well." Adek smiles again.

This is worse than I thought. Her attention span appears to be fading fast.

Gone are the days when we would wrestle with the crossword in the Daily Mail.

"Can you tell me who the Prime Minister is Mary?" Adek asks.

"Of course! David ... erm ... David." she stutters, struggling with the name.

"No rush. Take your time."

"Beckham!" she suddenly blurts out, her face flushed with the effort.

Oh gawd! My heart sinks and I can see that Michael is struggling to remain in control. There is no going back from this. The disease itself or the dreadful consequences that it brings crashing down onto the sufferer and the family. I suppose it's like staring death in the face ... but an incredibly slow death without any dignity.

"Just one last question Mary. When were you born?" Adek whispers.

"September 14th 1919!" she grins excitedly.

"Well done Mammy!" Michael beams, thrilled that she got that one right.

"I think that's it for now Mary. How about a cup of tea?" Adek grins.

"Lovely Dennis. Nine sugars please." she sighs wearily, closing her eyes.

Silence hangs over us all, the grandfather clock in the corner ticking like the time bomb that's apparently fizzing inside Mary's fuddled head. Adek is still scribbling away in his notebook. Michael and I are still holding hands.

"Shall we adjourn to the kitchen?" Adek whispers, "Have a chat?"

"Sure. Cassie ... come and join us. Let Mammy have a nap." Michael sighs.

I follow, closing the lounge door quietly behind me. I really do not want to hear what this lovely man has to say but running away won't help anyone, least of all Mary, so I busy myself making the tea, spooning out several large heaps of sugar into Mary's favourite china tea cup.

"Not good is it my friend?" Michael suddenly asks Adek.

"Classic signs Mike. You know what the score is." he whispers gently.

"So what now? I mean, I know where this is leading but"

...

"If she were my mother ... I'd prescribe tender loving care." Adek smiles.

"No intervention?" Michael asks, his eyes resigned to the inevitable.

"Absolutely not Mike. Would you want to put her through all that?"

"No. For what purpose? Nothing can reverse the condition can it?"

"Well ... there are clinical trials. Drugs that may slow it down but" ...

"It's unlikely she'd even get funding for those at her age." Michael sighs.

"Indeed."

"And I don't want her going through any scans or hospital procedures."

"Fair comment. Be bloody traumatic at her age."

"Hard to believe ... my Mammy ..." Michael sobs, "Where did the years go?"

I am supposed to be making tea but the kitchen surface is now awash with my tears. I knew this was coming ... we all did ... but that doesn't make it any easier to hear. Michael is distraught and my heart aches for him. I have never seen him lose control before. He's a consultant. An educated man in his sixties who has always remained calm and in control. He is also a son. A son faced with the prospect of watching his Mammy fade away before his very eyes. The grieving starts now.

"Mary has all of us for support Mike. Take comfort in that." Adek whispers.

"I know ... I know ... I need to get a grip." Michael suddenly smiles.

"And you can count me in! And Jack!" I offer, tears sploshing onto my chin.

"Cass, you've got snot on your nose." Michael laughs.

"Tissue?" Adek grins, pulling a packet from his coat pocket.

"Oh my life! How mortified am I?" I giggle, wiping my nose.

"We're medics." Adek laughs, "We've seen a lot worse!"

Michael suddenly leans across the confined space in the tiny kitchen and wraps his muscular arms around me in a bear hug. We stand stock still for what seems like forever, his warm embrace sending out shockwaves of compassion and comfort. It's a testament to his strength that at a time like this HE is comforting me.

Adek carries on where I left off, busying himself with cups of tea. Carefully laying out the cups on the tea tray. Opening cupboards in search of tea spoons and saucers. Doing what people do best in a crisis. Carrying on.

"Any biscuit's about Cassie?" he grins, "I'm ravenous!"

"Should be. I did a shop yesterday." I tell him, letting go of Michael.

"Oh ... here they are. In the washing machine!" he roars, laughing.

"Sounds about right!" I giggle, "She put a loaf in the dishwasher last week."

"God love her." Michael smiles, blowing his nose.

"You can get through this Mike. And so can Mary. Chin up eh?" Adek tells him.

"Sure ... sure ... she's always done the best for us. It's our turn now."

"Role reversal." Adek nods, "These things always come full circle."

"And that's the nature of the beast" ... Michael sighs distractedly.

"Now let's go back through. See if Mary would like a biscuit." Adek grins.

Mary is awake now. Studying the rose pattern on the wallpaper. Her face wrinkled in thought. The tea cosy still perched on top of her head. Her face breaks out into a fabulous grin as Michael takes a seat opposite her.

"There you go Mammy ... a nice cup of tea." he smiles, handing her the cup.

"And a chocolate biscuit." Adek grins, offering her the packet.

"Lovely!" she beams, "Thank you dear. I'm partial to a biscuit."

"You're welcome."

"And a drop of Guinness." she laughs.

"And why not Mammy! You can have anything you like." Michael grins.

"I'll have a sweet sherry then please ... and Cass will have a Jack Daniels."

She is somewhere else again. One minute quite lucid and seemingly normal and the next away on another planet. In another place altogether. The two worlds colliding even more frequently of late. This is how it will be. There is no turning back. Dementia destroys healthy brain cells, turning them into mush. The damage is irreversible and the repercussions catastrophic. Adek is quite right. What Mary needs now is tender loving care. And pretty soon she will need that care 24/7. As if reading my thoughts, Michael suddenly whispers in my ear, "Better look for a care home with a bar!"

***

I manage to hold it all together and even wave enthusiastically as Michael and Adek drive away. As the Volvo disappears along the lane I lose it completely and stand at the end of the drive sobbing like a baby. Oh Mary! If only I could turn the clock back and transport you back to when you were in your prime. A healthy, robust woman in full control of your life and your faculties. I miss you! The Mary who never failed to make me laugh when I was down. The Mary who rocked Tom to sleep with a knack that I never quite mastered. The Mary who knew who the Prime Minister was ... and the entire Cabinet as well. I have to stop this! Stop looking back. Time to look forward now. To the future and what's best for Mary.

Michael has said he will research some care homes locally. Find out which would be the best for her. Private of course. Money really isn't a consideration. And sad to say that a vast majority of council run care homes are merely God's waiting rooms nowadays. Caring for the elderly is big business. The emphasis being on business not caring. Mega fortunes are made every year from a section of the population that has little or no say on exactly what levels of care are dished out in these institutions. He will do what's right by his Mammy. A fact that offers me some comfort on such an dark day as this.

Better get inside. Standing outside wailing like a banshee. This isn't helping anyone ... especially Mary. This is not about me and how I feel. It's about her and what we can all do to help. We can do this. As a community I mean. Until a suitable place is found for her we shall have to pull together and make sure she's safe and well. Pete will muck in. And Lenny. And countless other friends who think the world of Mary. I shall cross Fiona and Henry off the list. God forbid that Fiona should have to do anything remotely related to real life! I expect she's signed up to be cryogenically frozen when she gets old. No change in the facial expression then?

Levy is waiting anxiously in the bay window for me. He's been bonking that bloody bear again! The lounge is plastered with bits of stuffing. Strands of it wafting across the ceiling, gently spiralling down onto the wooden floor.

Bonking Bear has now lost another ear and the will to live apparently. It's dishevelled form lying prostrate on the rug, legs akimbo, it's one remaining eye turned inwards as if in shame. Time to root around the car boot sales and find a replacement. This will be Bonking Bear number 3! You have to admire his stamina!

"The vet could sort you out with an op!" I laugh, stroking his huge head.

He strides off, farting loudly and with feeling. Point taken.

***

Michael and I are on our way to Ashford. It's a little village about five miles away from Oakham. Pretty little place I'm told with a thriving craft centre and a steady stream of coach tours that take in the medieval church and glass blowing barn. Fair play to Michael. Less than a week ago he was here with Adek to assess Mary and now he's back with a glossy brochure for a care home he thinks may be suitable. I gather

Adek has been a major player in all this. Bless him! Apparently he's been working round the clock to find the best place in the area and this, we hope, is it. Esther Blumenthal House. A fabulous home which specialises in dementia care. Michael tells me an ordinary care home just wouldn't be enough for his beloved Mammy and I am inclined to agree. She will need specialist care and you don't get much better than this. The brochure is fabulous with numerous colour photographs of the facilities on offer along with lots of happy, smiling pics of residents enjoying a swim in the Olympic size pool and sitting in the conservatory enjoying afternoon tea. Mary would like that. The afternoon tea ... not the pool ... she can't swim.

"I do hope it lives up to the brochure." I sigh, staring out of the window.

"It will Cass. We've done a lot of research into this." Michael smiles.

"Of course. Sorry. It's just that I worry ..."

"Bless you for that." he sighs, "Mammy found a good friend when you moved in."

"Ditto! She's been a rock to me for years" ... I stammer, biting back the tears.

"Come on Cass. We have to stay strong." he smiles gently.

"Sorry. Girding my loins as we speak!" I laugh.

"Besides, I may need you to back me up when we get there." he grins.

"Eh?"

"It's a home for elderly Jewish people Cass and Mammy is not Jewish!" he laughs.

"Oh crikey! Does it matter? What faith she is I mean?"

"We'll find out soon enough." he giggles, "Just follow my lead!"

"Right! Consider it done! We can do this. Whatever it takes eh?" I laugh.

"Absolutely! And Cass ... Mazel Tov!" he giggles, pulling into the driveway.

"Oh Lord!"

I am stunned by the sheer opulence of this place. A vast Georgian style mansion surrounded by an avenue of laburnum trees swaying gently in the breeze.

This is impressive! No sooner have we pulled up at the entrance than a jolly looking man appears by the car door and opens it for me to get out. Now that's what I call service! He appears to be in his fifties, with a mass of black curly hair and a smile as broad as his belly. I am liking him already.

"Welcome! Marty Weinstein." he grins, shaking my hand.

"Cassie. Nice to meet you ... and this is Michael ... Mary's son" ... I waffle.

"Michael! Good to meet you in person at last. Come on in."

"Good to meet you too. Thanks for fitting us in for a viewing." Michael grins.

"No worries. This is a difficult time ... we try to smooth the way."

He leads the way into the foyer. And what a foyer it is too! I swear some of the best hotels in London would have a job to match this place. Marble abounds in the ornate pillars that support every corner of the reception and the desk itself. The carpet is so thick you can actually feel yourself sinking into the pile. And the furnishings are to die for! Sumptuous sofas and Sanderson drapes giving the place an air of elegance and refined dignity. And most importantly, from my perspective anyway, a distinct lack of the smell of pee! The aroma wafting around this place is that of jasmine and bergamot oil. Thank god for that! I went with Ma once to visit one of her neighbours in a care home that demonstrated no care whatsoever and the smell of stale urine actually made me gag!

"Would you care for some tea or coffee before we start?" Marty asks us.

"Cass? How about you?" Michael asks, turning to me.

"I'm fine. Maybe later." I smile, anxious to begin the tour.

"Right. Let's take a look at the guest rooms shall we? This way."

We follow, trying to take in every tiny detail as we are led towards the lift.

A lift which is roughly the size of my back garden. The sort of lift you would normally find in a major hospital with enough room for roughly thirty people ... or possibly a dozen wheelchairs in a place like this.

"It's voice activated." Marty informs us, "Level 2 please."

"Impressive!" Michael beams, as the lift ascends upwards.

"Some of our guests have problems with technology so it's easier for them."

What will they think of next? I am liking this place more by the second.

"We have two floors. The less mobile guests are situated downstairs of course."

"Makes sense." Michael nods.

"And for those who can still samba we have this upper unit." Marty laughs.

"I like it!" I laugh, "Mary always loved to dance."

"Well, she still can. We have weekly dances here ... and piano sing-a-longs."

"Fabulous!" Michael beams, "Mammy will be in her element!"

"Dementia isn't an immediate death sentence. There is life after diagnosis."

"What a refreshing outlook!" Michael smiles, thankful for Marty's kindness.

"And here we are. To the left folks. We have a room ready if you are."

"Ready as I'll ever be." Michael sighs and we both follow Marty out of the lift.

The corridors are spacious and airy with brilliant sunlight pouring in from the vast expanse of windows along it. The carpet just as luxurious as that in the foyer and every wall adorned with the most beautiful paintings. Paintings of days gone by ... of steam trains and days at the seaside and one of a woman selling pots and pans from the back of a horse and cart. Each individual guest room as Marty calls them, has a wooden plaque bearing the name of the occupant in bright bold lettering, delicately carved into the wood. Ruth Abelman ... Levi Rosenthal ... the names actually feel as if they are alive. Alive and vibrant. Human beings who belong here. Somewhere where they actually matter.

"Ah ... here we are. This is the one." Marty smiles, opening the door.

We step inside and Michael and I both gasp in unison at the sheer warmth of the room. The overwhelming feeling of being at home. Nothing institutionalised about this room! Every single detail thought out with love and care. Spacious. Light. Immaculately clean and furnished to an incredibly high standard. Every piece of furniture heavy oak and polished to perfection.

"This is wonderful!" Michael beams, looking out of the window into the garden.

"It's beautiful." I whisper, overwhelmed again.

"We aim to please!" Marty grins, "We believe our guests deserve the best."

"I can see that. A helluva lot of love has gone into designing this place."

"This home was built out of love. Esther Blumenthal's husband had the house converted when she was first diagnosed with dementia. He wanted her to have the best and this is it. Esther died ten years ago but she died happy. Her husband died a few months later and left the home to us to continue the good work. I think he'd be pleased with what we've achieved since." Marty tells us.

"Indeed!" Michael nods, still gazing out onto the lawns below.

"This is the bathroom. As you can see there's a hoist just in case."

"That's marvellous! Mary does have a problem getting into the bath now." I nod.

"And we have a strict gender policy here. Our female guests are cared for by female assistants. And the men get a man to assist with their personal needs."

"Thank God! Mammy would have a fit if a man tried to undress her!" Michael laughs.

"Exactly. Dignity is vital to all our guests. We insist on it."

"A rarity these days I gather in the care home community." Michael sighs.

"Sadly. But you have no worries on that score with us." Marty assures him.

"I can see that. Marty I'd like to thank you for putting my mind at rest."

"Shall we take a seat? You can ask me anything you like. Except my age ... and my weight!" Marty laughs, gesturing for us to sit down on the sofa.

"Will Mary be able to bring some of her own things?" I suddenly blurt out.

"Of course! Anything she likes. Most of our guests bring all their memories along with them ... you know ... photos ... trinkets ... nik naks ... that sort of thing. Anything that holds a connection to the past. We encourage it!"

"Sounds good." Michael nods again, "A part of their history I suppose."

"Totally. You'd be amazed at how good their long term memory is yet if you ask them what they had for breakfast today they'd be stumped." he smiles.

"And her clothes? I worry that she'll end up in somebody else's dress!" I cry.

"Not here Cassie! Mary will have all her clothes laundered in house and returned to her ready to wear. We take personal care very seriously here."

"Wow! Any chance I could move in with her?" I laugh, relieved.

"Maybe not for another thirty years!" Marty laughs too.

"And I know the medical care is first rate. I'm almost ashamed to say I ran some checks on this place." Michael says sheepishly.

"And why not!" Marty grins, "I'd do the same if it were my mother!"

"I feel a bit silly now ... seeing how much you all care" ... Michael sighs.

"Nonsense! You more than anyone have a right to protect your mother's interests. And being a doctor you are obviously aware of the shortcomings in certain care homes. I'd be upset if you hadn't bothered to check us out."

"Fair comment." Michael agrees, getting to his feet, "Where to next?"

"We'll take a stroll down to the day room. This way folks."

The day room again is light and airy and awash with tiny crystal vases filled with fresh flowers. A huge chandelier hangs from the ornate ceiling, sparkling in the late afternoon sun. About a dozen residents ... or guests ... should I say, are sitting around a central area listening to a man playing the piano. His fingers deftly stroking the keys in a rendition of Moonlight Sonata. We stand at the back of the room, fascinated as the notes reverberate around us. Every face entranced and every eye sparkling with delight. This is most definitely NOT a waiting room for god! This is a place where the spark of life still burns.

"I think I'm going to cry!" I whisper to Michael.

"You are allowed." Marty laughs, bending forward to whisper back.

"Don't you dare Cassie! I may have to join you!" Michael laughs.

"I'll organise some refreshments." Marty says and wanders off into the distance.

The pianist plays on and Michael and I quietly take a seat behind the group. As my eyes scan the room I am surprised to see that there are several carers amongst the audience. Quietly sitting on the side lines, unobtrusive apart from their crisp laundered uniforms. Pale blue stripes for the ladies and a darker blue stripe for the men. All of them transfixed by the music, every now and then reaching out to gently stroke the hand or the arm of a resident.

Michael gently nudges my arm and gestures to the far side of the room. One of the male carers is on his feet and escorting a frail old lady into the middle of the room. Her steps are faltering but the expression of joy on her face is a pleasure to see. He gently takes her by both hands and slowly guides her across the floor as the words of that wartime song echo around the room ...

I'll be seeing you in all the old familiar places ...

Carers and residents alike join in the chorus and the room is uplifted with song. Never forgotten words that each and every one of them seem to remember.

Transported back to the war perhaps and the memories this song evokes.

That this heart of mine embraces ...

Michael is singing along too, tears streaming down his face at the poignant picture being played out before him. How awful must this be for him? The stark realisation that his beloved Mammy will soon be living here and being cared for by strangers.

"Let it go Michael. A bloody good cry does you the world of good!" I tell him.

He is incapable of speaking and simply buries his head in his hands and sobs.

There is nothing I can do. Nothing any of us can do to change the inevitable. Mary is ill. She needs constant care and none of us can offer that. Every single one of her seven kids have wrestled with their own guilt over this and I have too. In an ideal world we would all have the time and energy and space to look after our own. Sadly, that's not practical in today's society. We all have families of our own. Jobs that exhaust us. Bills that need to be paid. And yet still we carry that guilt. I don't have the answers. Nobody does.

"I think you could do with a strong cuppa!" Marty says softly to Michael.

"Thanks ... that would be much appreciated." he sniffs, blowing his nose.

"Come on. The ladies in the dining room have laid us out some tea."

Again, we follow behind this lovely man who knows exactly what Michael is going through right now. He must have seen it a hundred times before and yet still has the compassion to care. The dining room surpasses all my expectations. Each and every table covered with an expensive linen cloth with napkins to match. The cutlery sparkling and laid out in precise rows. Each table decorated with a large church pillar candle in the centre. Fine dining indeed! No wonder Michael chose this place.

I thought we were about to have a cuppa and perhaps a biscuit but goodness me! The ladies in the kitchen certainly have laid us out some tea. Plates of sandwiches with the crusts delicately cut off. A mountain of cakes oozing with fresh cream and a large china teapot delicately patterned with red poppies.

"Please let me move in Marty!" I joke, playfully linking arms with him.

"I'll think about it!" he giggles, gesturing for us to sit down.

"I'll pour. You two look a bit shell shocked." Marty grins.

"I never expected this place to be so ... well ... wonderful!" I gush.

"Well thank you!" he grins back, pouring the tea.

"We just have one obstacle to overcome" ... Michael suddenly pipes up.

Marty and I both stare at him, waiting anxiously for him to continue.

"Mammy's a Catholic Marty. I understand this home is for those of the Jewish faith ... is that correct?"

"Jewish ... Catholic ... whatever! Does it matter?" I gabble, feeling nervous.

"That was the original intention when the home was started" ... Marty nods.

"Well...we'll convert her if necessary! Change her name to Morgenstein!" I cry.

"Cass ... calm down" ... Michael laughs, "We can work around this I'm sure."

"Please don't ban her because she's a Catholic!" I plead, hysterical now.

"Listen folks ... we have a room ... you have a loved one who needs our care. That's good enough for me!" Marty laughs, taking a cream slice off the plate.

"Oh my life! Thank goodness for that!" I wail, sweat forming on my nose.

"Now drink your tea. And try one of these cakes. Delicious!" Marty laughs.

"I thought I was going to have to blag that one Marty!" Michael grins, "I would have sold my soul to the devil to get Mammy a place in here."

"No need. Like I said, originally the rooms were intended for the elderly from the local Jewish community but now we are much more flexible. It's not down to us to exclude people because they follow a different faith to us is it?"

"That's a lovely philosophy." I gabble, biting into a cream horn.

"So. What's the verdict? Do you think Mary will like it here?" he asks Michael.

"I'm sure she will. The question is do you have room for another guest?"

"We do." Marty nods, "The room you just saw is vacant ... and ready."

"Better bite the bullet then eh Cass? Get the ball rolling."

"Mazel Tov!" I shriek, desperately trying to remember any random Jewish words.

"It's no good pretending you're Jewish!" Marty laughs, "Too late!"

"I couldn't afford to live here. I shall end up in an asylum!" I giggle.

"Talking of money ... shall we discuss fees?" Michael chips in.

"Sure. Come through to my office. Cassie ... have another cake."

I watch as the two men disappear into the distance, Michael's body language now relaxed, as if all the earlier tension has been washed away. I truly do believe he would have sold his soul to the devil to secure a room here for Mary. In fact, I'd go as far as to say he'd probably have even been circumcised if necessary! I feel as if a huge weight has been lifted from my shoulders too. I so wanted today to be good and it's actually been great! Last night I tossed and turned for hours, visions of Dickensian institutions cramming my thoughts...and instead we found this haven of peace and dignity. It was meant to be. Up there somewhere, an angel is watching over Mary and today that angel did good!

"More tea dear?" a voice suddenly asks, jolting me back to reality.

The voice in question belongs to an elderly man, who is now sitting opposite me.

"No ... erm ... thanks. I'm fine." I tell him, smiling back at his kindly face.

"Are you sure? I know how you love your tea." he giggles.

"Really. I'm fine. Can I get you a cup ... or a cake perhaps?"

"No cake for me Gilda. I'm diabetic remember?"

"Oh ... right. Of course." I grin, playing along.

"Time we were off to bed my dear. It's getting late." he sighs, standing up.

Bit tricky this one! I'm facing a slight dilemma here! If I refuse and try to explain that I'm not Gilda he might get upset and I'd hate to inflict that on him. He seems like a proper gentleman. Immaculately dressed in a suit with a waistcoat and a fob watch hanging from the pocket. His shoes are polished to within an inch of their life and he has a tiny gold signet ring on his little finger with the initial S on it. He has the kindest eyes I have ever seen. How could I possibly shatter his illusions?

"Samuel! There you are! I was wondering where you'd got to."

A young man in the obligatory navy stripe approaches and sits down next to us.

"Gilda and I were just going to bed. She gets tired you know." Samuel smiles.

"I know. Why don't you join me for a drink then we'll get you settled."

Samuel hesitates briefly then nods in agreement.

"I'm Elliot." the carer smiles, "Samuel is one of my lads."

"Nice to meet you Elliot. You arrived just at the right time." I tell him.

"Gilda. I'll see you upstairs. Don't stay up too late my dear." Samuel grins.

And with that he wanders off, his tiny frame shuffling towards the exit door.

"He'll be fine. A nice glass of wine and he'll be tucked up in bed." Elliot reassures me, "Enjoy your tea and cakes!"

"Thanks. Look after him eh?" I plead, wishing I could take Samuel home.

"I will!"

Mary will like Samuel. He is obviously a gentle soul in search of his Gilda.

I wonder where Gilda is? Long dead probably and yet still her memory remains inside his head. I wonder if Jack will still be searching for me after I'm gone?

Probably not! After a lifetime of living with me I imagine he'll be relieved to get some peace.

"I think we're done Cass. Are you ready to go?" Michael asks sitting down.

"Everything sorted?"

"All done! The room's ready. Mammy can move in as soon as ..." he sighs.

"Oh Michael. I feel for you, but it's for the best, we know that."

"I know. I'm still trying to get my head around it all."

"Let's make a move shall we? It's getting late."

"You won't forget her will you Cass? When she moves here?" he pleads.

"As if! I shall be here probably every day ... I may even move in!" I grin.

"Yes but Cass ... you're not Jewish!" he laughs, suddenly brightening up.

"I could be ... if necessary! I can butter a bagel with the best of them!"

"I bet!"

"And the beard thing. The Rabbi look. I could do that."

"Enough!" he giggles.

"Enough already you mean!!"

"Stop it!"

"Don't think I could live without pork pie though." I whinge.

"You're doomed then ... to a life in an asylum apparently."

"Klutz!" he suddenly blurts out, roaring with laughter.

"Kiss my tokhis!" I laugh back.

"Cassie! You are a star! I'm so glad you came along today."

"Michael ... shalom!"

"Get in the car!"

"If I were a rich man ... fiddle diddle diddle diddle diddle dum" ...

***

Chapter Twenty Four

... *Don Corleone & Date Expired Food*

Alicia can't make the session today. Having a personality transplant I expect.

Tilly has decided we are safe to be seen out in public and arranged to meet us at the new ice cream parlour on the High Street. We are to have an outing! Yay!

Just the three of us ... Alan ... Tilly and I. Methinks that Alicia would rather have her nipples pierced with a hot poker than be seen out in public with us so she has declined the invitation. Silly tart! Her loss! I was so looking forward to shoving a mocha chocca cornet into her fat face.

Alan is beside himself with excitement. You know he has a fascination with ice cream so this will be a real treat for the lad. Tilly knows her stuff. If she'd suggested we go to the Natural History Museum he would have run a mile. I think these exercises are meant to build your confidence and lord only knows Alan needs some of that. Social situations are not something he copes well with and I think this may be just the sort of thing he needs.

Look at him! Waiting outside already and it's only midday. I had intended to pop into Boots before we met but I can't leave him hanging around on his own outside like that. He looks petrified. Hopping from one leg to another, his hands shoved deep inside the pockets of his anorak. Oh! He's wearing a tie! Bless him! I could weep but I won't. He is making progress and that's good.

"Hi Alan! You're early. And looking very smart eh?"

"Cass!" he grins, still hopping about, "I need a wee!"

"Oh right. Let's go inside then. They have wash rooms here."

He almost knocks me over in his panic to get to the loo and I watch fascinated as he heads towards the back of the premises in search of relief so to speak.

His spindly legs splaying out in all directions in his haste. Several startled diners duck for cover as he hurtles past.

"He's with me." I tell a bemused barista, "We'll order in a while."

I manage to find a table by the window and check my watch. 12.14 ... Tilly will be here any minute. She said 12.30 but she's always early.

"Gawd I needed that!" Alan sighs on his return, "Nearly gambled and lost then!"

Oh dear! That's a mental image I could do without but still, no damp patches on his trousers so that's a bonus.

"Take a seat." I smile, "The menu looks great!"

"Can't believe they do all these different ice creams." he beams excitedly.

"I can't decide which one. How about you?" I ask.

"Depends ... on how much" ... he squirms, looking embarrassed.

How stupid am I? It never even entered my head to think Alan might struggle to find money for a treat like this. A treat ... however small ... has to come out of the meagre pittance he receives in unemployment benefits. I feel ashamed!

"Alan ... this is my treat. Have what you like." I whisper, not wishing to add to his embarrassment. "Go on! Pick whatever you want."

"You sure Cass? Bit pricey you know ... five fifty for a sundae!" he squeaks.

"I'm loaded Alan!" I lie, "Stop fretting and pick one!"

He relaxes and studies the menu with great concentration. His eyes totally focused on the list of delights before him. Peppermint bark cornets ... strawberry shortcake sundaes ... and even one appropriately named banana brain freeze! Excellent! At a rough count I'd say they have over fifty varieties to choose from so this could take a while.

I sit back in my chair and study Alan who is still engrossed in the choices. I can't help but draw comparisons between him and Tom. Similar age ... similar height and weight ... and a whole world apart. Who decides eh? Who throws the dice and determines that one should have everything and the other barely anything? That's a bit too profound for a Friday afternoon in an ice cream parlour I know. Still, it's a subject that does fascinate me. I don't have the answers. Life just seems to be incredibly random. Alan got the short straw.

This time round. I pray that next time he's here on earth he'll be a millionaire rock star ... with attitude ... and contact lenses.

"Afternoon everyone!" Tilly sings, suddenly appearing at our table. She looks relaxed today, her face glowing in the late summer sun.

"We're still trying to decide." I grin, pointing at the menu.

"I know, so much choice! Franco certainly knows his ice cream." Tilly smiles.

"Think I'll have the banana brain freeze." Alan suddenly blurts out.

"Good choice!" Tilly laughs, "How about you Cassie?"

"Erm ... Affogato" ...

"Forgot what?" Alan asks looking perplexed.

Tilly can't contain herself and rocks with laughter, her head thrown back in a fit of giggles.

"It's an ice cream Alan." I giggle, "Espresso poured over vanilla ice cream."

"Oh right. Soz. Thought you'd gone all Italian on us." he grins.

"I'll go and order." Tilly laughs, getting up, "These are on me."

"Are you sure? I said I'd pay." I offer, looking for my purse.

"No! Honestly Cass. We have a budget for outings." she insists.

"Fair enough. Maybe a week in Sicily next year then." I giggle.

"Where's that then?" Alan asks, looking puzzled again.

"Italy Alan. It's where the Mafia originated from." I tell him.

"What ... Marlon Brando and that lot?" he smiles.

"Sort of. Only the real Mafia. The Mob."

"Perhaps Franco's one of The Mob." he suddenly grins, "This place could be a front for bootleg booze."

"Highly unlikely Alan. They only sell coffee and ice cream." I laugh.

"Aah ... could all be down in the cellar." he insists, getting carried away.

"I ... erm ... I doubt it."

"Might have a stash of machine guns hidden down there." he continues, letting his imagination run riot.

"Alan! This is Oakham ... not Chicago!" I giggle.

"And a big vat of spaghetti with a horses' head boiling in it!" he yells.

"Whoa!! Alan ... here's Tilly with the ice creams." I'm relieved to say.

"There you go. Banana brain freeze. Affogato ... and a sundae for me." she grins.

"Alan thinks this place is a front for the Mob." I tell her, giggling.

"Unlikely." Tilly grins, "Franco was born in Barnsley."

"How do ya know that?" Alan blurts out, his mouth full of whipped cream.

"Franco and his family moved in next door to me last month." Tilly tells him.

"So you know him?" Alan squeaks, obviously impressed.

"Sure. He's a lovely guy. And no Mafia connections!" she beams.

"Delicious ice cream!" I tell her, trying to divert the conversation away from The Mob before Alan goes off on one again.

"So Alan. A week on Saturday eh? Are you nervous?" Tilly asks him gently.

"Nah! Everything's done. Just gotta get me haircut." he smiles.

"Where will you have it cut Alan?" I ask, licking my spoon.

"Elsie at the chip shop's gonna do it for me."

"Eh?"

"She used to have a barbers but she works in the chippy now." he informs us.

"Oh. That's useful." Tilly stammers.

"Two quid for a cut. Extra pound for a shave." he grins.

"That's reasonable." I stutter, aghast at the thought of anyone having their hair cut amongst the deep fat fryers.

"Says she'll throw in a piece of haddock for me supper." he laughs.

"Bargain!" I giggle, losing the plot.

Only Alan eh? Only that lad could negotiate a haircut, shave and a fish supper for three quid! We really don't have any idea do we? How some people survive I mean? Every day a struggle to make ends meet. Gotta admire his skills.

"And Tracey. Will she be having some beauty treatments?" Tilly asks agog.

"Sure! I got her a face pack from the car boot ... and some rollers." he grins.

"She'll look beautiful Alan. She's a very pretty girl." I reassure him.

He blushes and his whole face lights up with joy. Bless that boy!

" You will both be there won't you?" he asks, his eyes almost pleading.

"Of course! Wouldn't miss it for the world!" I tell him, grabbing his hand.

"Absolutely! I have a new hat!" Tilly giggles, stroking his arm.

"Besides. I'm bringing the cake ... and the balloons!" I laugh nervously.

The fact that I have less than a week to prepare and bake a wedding cake had escaped me until now. Faint beads of sweat begin to form on my forehead at the thought.

"We got the room from eleven Cass. Harry says you can take the cake in early."

"Good!" I giggle somewhat hysterically, "Leave it with me."

"So, it's registry office at midday then The Hogs Head." Tilly asks.

"Yeah. Nobby's running us down to the caravan after the pub closes."

"Is he a relative?" Tilly asks, scraping ice cream from the bottom of her dish.

"On Tracey's side. Nice bloke. Runs a scrapyard in Mapleford."

"Bet he's loaded! There's big money to be made in scrap these days." I laugh.

"Mega money!" Alan squeaks excitedly, "He's got a yard and two donkeys!"

"Sorry?" Tilly squeaks, almost choking on the last spoonful of her sundae.

"Keeps um instead of guard dogs. Says they make more noise." Alan grins.

"Goodness! I bet a donkey bite would be painful!" Tilly stutters.

"Bloody is! One of um bit me first time I went there with Tracey."

"Oh blimey!" I gasp, horrified at the thought.

"I still got the scar." he tells us, rolling up his trouser leg and exposing a quite noticeable scar about three inches long running down his shin bone.

"Ouch! Nasty!"

"Not as nasty as the dog he used to have. Bleeder bit his nose off!"

"My life!" I cringe, mortified at the very thought.

"Doberman it was ... devil dog."

"Is Nobby alright now?" Tilly asks nervously.

"Fine. They rebuilt his nose. Got just one nostril now though."

"Eh?"

"Had to reconstruct the nose. Left him with one big nostril."

"Oh right."

"He can still smell stuff. Just gets a bit messy when he's got a cold."

Tilly looks visibly pale and I am struggling to take in all this news. I really do exist on a parallel planet! Devil dogs and giant nostrils! Whatever next!

"He's over the worst. Be there suited and booted on Saturday." Alan smiles.

"I'm glad to hear it!" I smile back, amazed at the tenacity of this lad.

"And what about after the honeymoon?" Tilly asks, regaining composure.

"Be moving in with Tracey's Gran. Then I gotta get a job." he sighs.

"Something will turn up Alan. Life has a way of working out." I reassure him.

"Keep those positive thoughts going Alan!" Tilly says, "Be open to good stuff."

Could be a bit difficult that but bless her for trying to jolly him along. He's unemployed. Skint. About to move in with his wife's gran. No prospects. A plaster on his broken glasses and a donkey bite on his shin but hey-ho ... keep smiling!

"Tracey tried to get me in at Tesco's but I failed the test."

"What test Alan?" Tilly asks, her voice full of concern.

"Role play. Had to pretend I was helping a customer and I blew it."

"In what way?"

"They got a pretend shop and I had to serve a vegetarian."

"And?"

"She asked me for party food and I give her sausage rolls."

"Oh dear." Tilly sighs, her face pink with embarrassment.

"And they said I shouldn't have given her mince pies either."

"Sorry?"

"Mince pies. They got stuff in vegetarians can't eat."

"Bloody vegetarians!" I rant, thoughts of my night out at The Nut Hut still raw.

"Onwards and upwards Alan. There are other jobs out there." Tilly sighs.

"Might try Burger King after the wedding. Bet they don't do vegetarian."

"Good idea!" Tilly giggles, "Anyone fancy a slice of cake?"

"Great! Thanks Tilly!" Alan and I both chorus together.

"I'll go ask what the special is today." she beams, getting up again.

Not for the first time do I hold this lad in my heart and send out prayers to anyone who is listening to give him a break. Just one break that could well make the difference between his survival or his demise. Not much to ask is it?

A few hours a week, working in a job that would bring him some much needed confidence and a few quid to restore his pride. If there's anybody up there get a move on and send him a lifeline please!!

"Tiramisu all round?" Tilly asks, joining us again at the table.

"Lovely!"

"It's coffee cake Alan. I think you'll like it." Tilly tells him seeing the blank look on his face.

"I'm starving. I love cake! Chocolate's me favourite." he gushes.

"Did you have breakfast?" I ask, knowing what the response will be.

"Only had a bag of Wotsits in the cupboard. Gotta do a shop later."

Oh Lord! I knew it! How does he survive ... on random bags of crisps and the odd fish supper courtesy of Elsie? Thank goodness he's getting married next week.

At least Tracey and Ruby will see he gets fed.

"Where do you shop Alan? Not much choice on the High Street." Tilly sighs.

"I got a routine. Got it all wrote down on me fridge." he tells us.

"A routine?" I'm really confused now!

"Yeah. I knows what shops reduce the stuff late at night" ...

"Oh I see." Tilly responds, looking blankly at me.

"Mortons the cake shop do theirs about five ... and Todd the butcher ... he trays up the leftovers about half five. Got a massive tray of chicken wings last week. And the Co-Op course ... you can get a loaf there for twenty pence just before they close"...

Did you hear that? That was the sound of my heart breaking! Right here in Franco's Parlour on Oakham High Street! My heart just literally broke into a million tiny fragments. I can't speak and Tilly, as ever, saves the day.

"Well done you! How clever to save your pennies like that." she sings, "With the cost of food nowadays I'd say you're onto a winner there Alan!"

"You want me to look out for stuff for you?" he asks, "Bit hit and miss. You never know what's gonna be on offer but" ...

"No honestly Alan. You concentrate on feeding yourself." Tilly whispers gently.

"Go Alan!" I squeak, still reeling from this latest revelation. Trawling the shops late at night searching for food reductions. Stale bread and cakes and very possibly potential salmonella in that chicken! No wonder he's prone to boils and infections.

"I better get going. Gotta meet Tracey from work at three." he grins.

"Are you sure you don't want anything else to eat ... or drink" ... I ask.

"Nah! I'm stuffed." he laughs, getting to his feet.

Tilly and I both jump up at the same time and simultaneously attempt to hug him.

He looks quite taken aback for a second then relaxes as we form a group hug.

"See you next Saturday then" ... Tilly smiles, breaking away.

"Yeah! Twelve at the registry office." he grins.

"Don't you worry about the cake ... or the balloons" ... I lie.

"Thanks Cass! And thanks for the grub Tilly. It's been ace!"

And with that he disappears from view, dashing along the High Street to meet Tracey. His gangly legs working at a furious pace. His arms flailing at his sides in that familiar weird walk that endears me to him even more.

As he rounds the corner into Loxley Lane I notice the sole on his right shoe is flapping in the wind. Totally unglued from the base. And to add to the mental image he has a huge hole in his sock. Is anybody up there listening to me?

***

CAKE CRISIS VI

Head straight for Pete's and ask Lenny if he'll make the cake.
Cry with relief when he says yes.
Discuss designs over drinks.
Fall into privet on way home.
Tell Jack all about it as he bathes scratches on face.

Chapter Twenty Five

Here Comes The Bride ...With Ken Dodd By Her Side

I cried when I saw it. The cake that is. I knew Lenny was a great baker but he has surpassed all my expectations on this one and even stayed sober it seems in order to get it right! Jack and I popped over last night to collect it and I stood in the kitchen sobbing like a baby. Such a sumptuous creation wouldn't be out of place in a Hello photo shoot! Three towers of rich dark chocolate cake smothered in chocolate ganache ... and the decorations! Well! I am absolutely gobsmacked. Tiny little gerberas and pansies all sculpted out of fondant icing in various shades of ivory and white. The detail! Never in my wildest dreams did I imagine he was capable of creating such a fabulous cake. I hugged him so hard he actually started wheezing and I had to let go.

Jack came up trumps with the balloons as well! He drove out to some industrial estate in Beechwood and did a deal with a guy who owns a lock-up full of party gear. We have two hundred balloons in cream and ivory ... some speckled with gold glitter and others wishing the bride and groom good luck. Job done! What would I do without these guys? As an added bonus Jack splashed out and got a blow up bride and groom as well for the top table! He refused to tell me how much it all cost. I insisted on paying him back but since I only had four quid in my purse he declined my offer.

I'm not sure I was this nervous when Tom got married! At least then there were a whole team organising things and family and friends as well. Alan doesn't have that support so I'm praying everything will be fabulous for him today. Just one day God! Please!!

The cake is sitting safely on the top table at the Hogs Head with Harry keeping guard. God forbid that anyone should go near it! Harry has a glass eye from the result of a bar brawl years ago and even I would think twice about taking him on. Jack and I arranged the balloons and Pete and Lenny even pitched up with a few boxes of that wedding confetti that you sprinkle on the tables. When we left, I have to say the room upstairs was looking lovely. Even Harry got all emotional and I swear I saw him wiping away a tear ... from the good eye.

I have never been to a Registry Office wedding before. I've been to a few civil ceremonies held at hotels but never one actually inside the Registry Office.

"It's a bit funereal Jack isn't it?" I whisper as we take our places in the room assigned for the ceremony.

Half a dozen guests are already seated and Jack, Pete, Lenny and I scramble to sit together near the front. I would hate to miss a second of this. Alan really has become a big part of my life over the past two years. We have laughed, cried and farted together. That's friendship in my book.

"All council buildings are the same." he smiles, "they buy the paint in bulk."

He's right I think. Magnolia walls and huge purple drapes at the high windows.

I seriously expect a coffin to be wheeled in any second. Even the flower arrangement on the table is lilies! Oh gawd! Are we in the right place?

"No sign of the groom yet?" Pete whispers in a worried tone.

"He'll be here. Alan's always late!" I giggle.

And as if he heard me, the groom suddenly appears, crashing through the double doors, his face bathed in sweat.

"Got me pants caught in me zip." he gasps, struggling for air.

That's my boy! Nothing changes, even on a day such as this!

"Oh dear!" Lenny laughs, his ample belly wobbling with mirth.

"Had to get the scissors on um!" Alan wails, running down the aisle of seats.

"I see what you mean. I'm filling up already." Jack grins, shaking his head.

"God love him! What can I say."

"Let's hope that zip holds up during the ceremony."

"Stop it!"

"Could have been worse ... could have got his todger caught in the zip!"

"Jack!"

"That would have knackered his wedding night!" Pete roars, joining in.

"Enough!"

Glaring at them has no effect whatsoever and I'm relieved when the registrar arrives and the schoolboys I'm sitting with stop giggling and try to regain their composure. Not for long sadly. The reason for this being that the registrar is a dead ringer for Ken Dodd! Except he's black! Nigerian I'd say but my life ... the hair ... the teeth ... the goggle eyed expression! An absolute dead ringer for the man! If he opens his mouth and a Scouse accent comes out I shall lose it I swear.

"Ladies and gentlemen. Take your seats please. The bride is in the foyer." he booms ... thankfully not in a Liverpool accent.

The entire room appears to be focused on the vision before them. Every single one of the guests staring transfixed at the man about to conduct the ceremony.

Alan is hopping again. He must be a nervous wreck poor sod! I hope he can hold his water until it's all over or we may have a leak from that broken zip.

"Are you thinking what I'm thinking?" Jack whispers along the row.

"Yep!"

"Yeah!"

"Me too!"

"And me!" A voice from behind suddenly chips in.

I would love to turn round and get a look at the face but I'm afraid to move.

"Ladies and gentlemen ... the bride." the registrar booms and as if by magic music suddenly blasts forth from speakers secreted somewhere in the ceiling.

I'M LUCKY I KNOW ... I WANNA GO HOME ....

Bless these two! Michael Buble! I know Alan's nan was a big fan ... bless them ... what a lovely choice... she would be proud!

We all stand and turn in unison to get a glimpse of the bride and what a glorious bride she is! Her rich auburn hair freshly curled, her face sparkling with sheer joy. Her tiny frame elegantly dressed in a floor length cream creation. Go Tracey! The dress looks as if it were made especially for her, the waist nipped in and delicately embroidered with tiny diamante studs. She looks stunning and my mascara is already starting to run!

"Please be seated." Ken roars, his voice reverberating around the room.

Alan has stopped hopping and even taken his hands out of his pockets. I have to say he's scrubbed up well too! Nice navy blue suit with a pale blue shirt and a lovely silk tie with a cream stripe. I could actually burst with joy for both of them!

Not surprisingly, Tracey has chosen her Gran to walk her down the aisle. Good old Ruby! Flushed and flustered, looking good in a pale pink dress with a matching jacket. And a fabulous hat in a deeper shade of pink with a black brim. Ruby looks as if she is bursting with pride and fair play to her. Who would ever have thought that these two would ever make it down the aisle today? Life has dealt them both a cruel hand but hey ... they've fought back and look at them now! Standing in front of Ken Dodd and about to be married.

"I think we are ready to begin ..." Ken smiles, and a hush falls over the room.

Tracey slips her hand into Alan's and a small sob escapes from the back of my throat. Oh gawd! Give me the strength to get through this without making a total prat of myself. I can see Tilly sitting two rows in front, her head tilted to one side in concentration. No sign of Alicia and Wiggy! No loss there then! Not sure I could contain myself if she pitched up full of sarcasm today. I don't normally brawl at weddings but I'd make an exception in her case.

Ruby takes a seat on the front row next to a couple who I imagine are family.

Must be Nobby and his wife. Nobby is a big lad, his massive frame struggling to perch on one of the tiny plastic seats. He's filming the ceremony! I'm so glad! I was wondering if they could afford a photographer and even considered offering to pay for one but Nobby's got it covered. Nobby's wife looks like a game old bird! She's wearing a lycra boob tube and has a tattoo of an eagle on her shoulder. I shall show her my sprout later! Bet she'll be impressed!

You know that American expression … There's a lot of love in the room … well I have to say there IS a helluva lot of love in this room today! It's quite palpable. Granted, I guess there are roughly twenty guests here but every single one of them is wishing Alan and Tracey all the luck in the world. We can do this! Get together and support them and show them that life isn't all that bad.

"You okay Cass?" Jack whispers, taking my hand.

"Fine. Just a bit emotional" …

"I wouldn't have guessed." he laughs, "Only the trail of snot gave it away."

I might as well just give in and accept the fact that I am a blubbering wreck.

Let it all go and sit with an ice pack on my face at the reception.

Ken is on full throttle now, his teeth clattering quite badly as he speaks …

"Marriage is a very serious commitment and with that in mind …"

Some of Tracey's workmates are here. Sitting on the row to my left. I only know that because one girl has her Tesco uniform on. Must have dashed here in her lunch break.

There are two elderly ladies directly in front of us. Probably friends of Ruby.

Both kitted out in the obligatory Marks & Spencer autumn coat and comfortable shoes. And the shopping bag of course! What is it with old ladies and those tartan shoppers?

Nobby is in full swing now ... kneeling down in the aisle to get the best camera angle. Hope he doesn't get a shot of the inside of Ken's nose. I swear the likeness is remarkable! All we need now is for a dance troupe of Diddymen to burst through the doors.

"Is he still alive?" Pete whispers across the row of seats to Jack.

"Who?"

"Ken Dodd!"

"Erm ... I think so."

"Wonder if he knows he's got a half-brother?" Pete asks in all seriousness.

I am vaguely aware of the conversation taking place around me but fascinated by something that just caught my eye. The two sensible shoes ladies are eating ... chips!!! Surely not! I saw the wrapper and you can hardly mistake that aroma can you? Jesus! A bag of chips during a wedding ceremony? Do elderly people have no boundaries at all? Apparently not!

"And so it gives me great pleasure to pronounce you man and wife ... you may now kiss the bride ... I think a round of applause would be appropriate." Ken laughs.

The room suddenly erupts into a frenzy of clapping and cheering as Alan sheepishly kisses his bride lightly on the lips. Crikey that was quick! I've been to a few Catholic weddings and aged considerably during the service!

We are all on our feet whooping with joy for them. Alan grinning like the proverbial cat that got the cream. Tracey being bear hugged by Nobby who has handed the camcorder over to his wife. She really is a game old bird ... she has an even bigger tattoo on her left breast of an elephants head!

"They look good together." Jack grins, "Alan finally got his happy ending."

"Look at his little face." I sob, "And him with his flies broken!"

"Oh dear. Never mind. Tracey will sort him out." Jack laughs.

Only Alan could go through his wedding ceremony with a broken zip in his trousers. He never changes and I'm glad. That's Alan. What you see is what you get and I wouldn't have him any other way.

"Chip anyone?" Pete asks, shoving the greasy wrapper under my nose.

"No thanks."

"Cheers Elsie." he grins, handing back the packet to the woman in front of us.

Ah Elsie! Now it's beginning to make sense. Elsie the barber and cod batterer.

God only knows who the other woman is ... I do hope she doesn't work in the pub or Pete will be offering round pints of bitter next. He looks sozzled already but why am I surprised? It's almost one-o-clock after all. Considering that his day begins with a can of Strongbow for breakfast!

I weave my way through the seats and manage to catch Alan on his own. He is hopping again and I have a job to keep up with him.

"Congratulations Alan ... you make a lovely couple!" I beam, hugging him.

"Thanks Cass! Looks great don't she?"

"Wonderful! And you've scrubbed up well yourself!" I giggle.

"Have you got a safety pin Cass?" he blushes, holding his flies together.

"I'll find you one. Just pull your shirt over them for now."

Ken suddenly appears at my side and vigorously shakes Alan by the hand.

"Every happiness for the future." he grins, "I have to be going" ...

"Thanks mate!" Alan smiles back, "Wanna join us for a drink?"

"Thank you but I have another ceremony at two."

And with that he's off, teeth exiting the room before he does. Nice man. He could get work with one of those lookalike agencies. Although I'm not sure they are big fans of Ken Dodd in Nigeria.

"Ladeeeees and gents!" Nobby bawls from the front of the room, "Thanks for coming and can we all make our way to the Hogs Head. Anyone needing a lift I've got the mini bus out the front!"

A clamour of people make their way to the exit doors led by Alan and Tracey who link arms and form a sort of procession out into the marble foyer. Tracey is carrying a tiny little sprig of fresh flowers, made up of cream and white roses and as we file out into the street she suddenly tosses it up into the air much to the delight of the guests. The young girl in the Tesco jacket leaps to grab it but is beaten to it quite surprisingly by Elsie's friend, who I have to say is incredibly agile for an elderly lady.

"Eh Phyllis ... your turn next!" Elsie laughs, slapping her on the back.

Oh bless! Phyllis ... off the pastie counter at the Esso garage! It's making sense now. She had Alan's post after he bit the postman! See, my addled brain does retain some information. Not much granted but still.

Nobby is still filming and seems determined to get everyone in on the act. We all form a sort of group with the tallest at the back and me at the front next to Ruby who is of a similar height.

"What a lovely day!" I grin to Ruby, "They make a lovely couple!"

"They do." she nods, "Now where's that ruddy mini bus, my piles are huge today!"

***

I have to say Tracey looks thrilled at the balloons and the cake. Her tiny elfin face lighting up with joy as we all file into the reception room upstairs at the Hogs Head. Harry has kept his word and the room remains intact. The late afternoon sun giving the tables a golden glow. Lenny's masterpiece standing proud and magnificent on the top table. I never thought it would all come together and it has! Oh ye of little faith!

Alan was quite right regarding the numbers. I just did a rough head count and there are indeed twenty guests. Plenty of cake to go round then! And sausage rolls by the look of the buffet table! My life! Trays and trays of them, all glistening in the afternoon sun. And cobs of course. Huge big crusty cobs with layers of cheese and onion rammed inside. And black pudding. Oh and a veritable mountain of salted peanuts and crisps in plastic dishes. Proper grub! None of your mamby pamby cucumber sandwiches with the crusts cut off! Jack will be delighted. He is partial to a cheese and onion cob. I estimate that Harry has allowed roughly six cobs per guest so Jack could be eating them for a while.

Pete is already getting stuck in and has half a sausage roll sticking out of his mouth. Lenny meanwhile is making some final adjustments to the cake, gently turning it to the left so that it's completely central. He really has saved the day and Jack has promised him several large drinks later. Could prove to be an expensive night!

"Penny for them." Jack whispers, taking a seat next to me.

"Just thinking how lovely it all looks. I'm so happy for them."

"They'll be fine Cass. You need to stop fretting now. He has Tracey."

"I know. Maybe now he'll get some decent food and socks without holes in."

"And someone to wash his pants!" he laughs, "Bless him!"

"Well, judging by the gifts on that table, they'll have plenty of Persil!"

"Sorry?"

"The gifts ... over there ... someone's got them a giant box of Persil." I giggle.

"Oh right. Still, it's a practical gift." Jack smiles, looking around.

"Absolutely! More useful than a toast rack."

"There's an industrial sized pack of toilet rolls as well!" I gasp.

"Oh blimey!"

"And a four litre bottle of Lenor!" I tell him, scanning the gift table.

Our list of household cleaning products is interrupted mid-flow by Alan who suddenly appears at our table, his face glowing with pride and perspiration.

"Cass! The cake's ace!" he grins, grabbing me in a bear hug."Thanks!"

"No worries. Glad you like it. Lenny made it you know."

"Magic! Tracey loves it ... and the balloons!" he gabbles excitedly.

"Ah ... you have Jack to thank for those."

"Cheers Jack!" he beams, shaking Jack vigorously by the hand.

"Congratulations to you both." Jack smiles, "She's a lovely girl."

"Nobby's setting up the decks in a bit. We can have a dance Cass!"

"I'll look forward to it!" I giggle, remembering our previous efforts.

"Better go and get my speech ready." he grins, rushing off.

"Now do you see why I worry?" I tease Jack.

"I might have to adopt him myself." he sighs, biting into a cheese cob.

***

Alan, Tracey and Ruby are seated at the top table along with Nobby and his wife. I have no idea what her name is as we haven't been introduced yet. She looks like a Rita ... or a Sharon. The bride and groom are holding hands and it's a joy to behold. Every bride blossoms on her wedding day but that girl is positively glowing. Alan has a huge mountain of food piled onto the plate in front of him. Bless! Tracey fetched it from the buffet for him. The signs are looking good.

Pete is pissed already and got up to dance a few seconds ago ... on his own ... much to the amusement of Nobby who cheered him on with shouts of encouragement.

Lenny is sat with his leg elevated on an empty seat, munching on a bowl of nuts.

Elsie and Phyllis have taken off their winter coats and chosen to sit away from the music system in the corner. They appear to be well prepared ... Elsie has already been up to the buffet table twice and Phyllis has just sneaked a bottle of gin out of her shopping bag and hidden it under the table.

The Tesco crew are immediately to our right and seem like a nice bunch. The mystery of the cleaning products has been solved anyway. I overheard Tracey thanking them for the Persil and the toilet rolls. Bless! She has a good practical head on her shoulders that girl. I spend a fortune on cleaning products every week and that table is groaning with the stuff! Nice one!

"Thanks for coming!" Alan shouts, tapping his glass with a spoon.

We all swivel round to face the top table and he blushes a deep crimson colour.

"Tracey and me want to say thanks for all the stuff"...

"And for coming to share the day with us!" Tracey grins, standing up.

"Tuck into the grub and we'll cut the cake in a bit." he giggles.

"Let's raise a glass to this lovely couple!" Nobby shouts, "Alan and Tracey!"

"Alan and Tracey!" The whole room echoes as we all get to our feet, "Cheers!"

Nobby's nostril is fascinating. They've done a marvellous job with the surgery it's just that he has a huge gaping hole in the centre of his face. It sort of draws you to it making it difficult to look away. I do hope he doesn't suffer from hay fever in the summer months. That could be messy!

"I'd like to welcome Alan to the family. Raise your glasses please!" Nobby shouts, lifting a pint of bitter high above his head, "To Alan!"

"To Alan!"

"And I know you'll all join me in wishing them well. Now it's time for that first dance!" he grins, clapping furiously as Alan and Tracey make their way to the floor. The saga of the first dance has rolled on for a while. After hours of trawling through my CD collection Alan eventually chose that stunning track.

More Than Just Skin Deep by Go West. For a while it looked as if they might begin married life dancing to Star Trekking Across The Universe but common sense prevailed.

As they take to the floor, Alan seems to lose his awkwardness and falls into a gentle swaying rhythm with his new bride. Maybe not Strictly Come Dancing but close enough! Bless that lad!

You & I ... See Magic In Each Other's Eyes ... Years Go By But The Magic Still Remains ... You Can Count On Me I'm Where I Wanna Be ...

"I really am optimistic for those two!" I tell Jack, blowing my nose.

"They'll be fine Cass. His flies are open but still" ... he smiles.

"Oh Lord!"

"You dancing?" he grins, taking my hand.

"Does the Pope wear a funny hat?" I giggle, following him onto the dance floor.

Within seconds the dance floor is full of bodies, all swaying together in time to the beat. Except for Pete who appears to have taken a shine to Elsie and has her gripped in a tango like stance, swirling her round the floor like someone possessed. I'm amazed he's still upright at this time of day but hey-ho!

"I think Pete's pulled!" Jack laughs, twirling me around.

"Ah well, at least he'll never go hungry. She works in the chippy." I giggle.

"What more could a man ask for? An endless supply of pickled eggs!"

"The woman of your dreams eh?"

"Not quite. Is that a panty liner sticking out of the back of her skirt?"

"Oh shit!" I gasp, "I'd better go tell her. She'll be mortified!"

"Leave it Cass. The rate Pete's swinging her round it will end up on the buffet table!" he grins, pulling me closer.

I watch fascinated as the offending article dangles precariously from the waistband of Elsie's pleated floral skirt. Must have worked its way up with all the vigorous moves Pete's put her through. Phyllis must have clocked it as well as she suddenly leaps to her feet, sweeps past them and snatches it with the agility of a finely tuned athlete. Swerving to avoid a collision with the happy couple she is back in her seat in seconds. I'm impressed! That's what friends are for eh?

"Where did your shrink disappear to?" Jack asks, scanning the dance floor.

"No idea ... maybe she had nutters to see."

"On a Saturday?"

"Mental health doesn't do Monday to Friday." I tell him.

"Fair point."

She does seem to have disappeared. I caught sight of her briefly at the Registry Office. She was sitting quietly just in front, unobtrusive as ever, her face calm and serene taking in every detail. And she kept her promise to wear a hat! A stunning hat at that! Chocolate brown straw with a gold organza ribbon around the brim. Lovely! I wish I could do hats but I invariably end up looking like a mushroom so I don't.

"The drinks are on me!" Nobby suddenly announces, dancing closer to Jack and I.

"That's very kind ... thanks!" Jack smiles, shaking his hand.

"No worries mate! Tracey tells me you and your wife have been golden to them."

"Honestly. There's no need. They're nice kids." I blush.

"No arguments! We look after our own!" Nobby's wife grins, "I'm Vera."

"Nice to meet you Vera. I was admiring your tattoo earlier." I tell her.

"Got an ape on me arse!" she giggles, "And a tarantula on me" ...

"Vera! Enough with the bodily parts! Get these people a drink!" Nobby grins.

We follow as instructed not wishing to offend Nobby who I feel could quite easily take on the whole room in a fist fight and not even raise a sweat.

The bar is heaving so Vera clears the way and finds us an empty table.

"Nobby will get them in. What's your poison?" she asks, sitting down.

"Pint of Coors for me and Cass will have a Jack Daniels please ... no ice."

"Nobby get a bottle. Cass and me will share!" she laughs exposing a set of perfect bleach whitened teeth.

"A woman after my own heart!" I giggle, "Saves making trips to the bar."

"We got a driver coming later. Take us home. You're welcome to a lift."

"I might take you up on that." Jack grins, "Not for us...for the happy couple."

"What was that?" Vera shouts, trying to make herself heard above the music.

"Cass and I have booked them a night at the Black Swan in Mapleford" ...

"Oh how lovely is that?" Vera cries, coming over all emotional.

"It's only one night. Nice hotel though. Everything's paid for." he blushes.

"Leave it with us. We'll make sure they get there." she whispers in my ear.

"Drinks?" Nobby yells, fighting his way from the bar carrying a vast tray of glasses and a bottle of Jack Daniels. This could be a long night.

"I'll get you some of those cobs Cass." Jack grins, "Line your stomach."

What delightful people they are! And that's not me wearing my beer goggles!

They truly are lovely folk. Kind and generous and incredibly funny. Nobby has a laugh that can light up a room and Vera quite obviously adores him. Within the space of an hour she has given me the name of her cosmetic surgeon and the salon she goes to for hair removal! I could do with a bit of help in that area! The hair removal, not the cosmetic surgery!

Vera has Botox apparently every six months. And the cellulite on her thighs zapped! I don't think there's a machine big enough to zap the cellulite on my thighs! Her nails are crafted by a manicurist and even the blonde hair tumbling around her shoulders is the result of expensive extensions. There must be some wonga in scrap metal!

And yet despite all the surgically enhanced looks and the nails and the hair, Vera is one of the most genuine people I have ever had the pleasure of meeting. No side to her. No airs and graces. Just straight up ... in your face reality.

Works for me! And Jack by the look of it. He and Nobby have been roaring with laughter for the past hour. I think Jack is hammered. I definitely am.

"Ooh it's the conga!" Vera suddenly shrieks, "Come on get in line!"

Lenny is leading the long snake of people all weaving their way around the pub.

Lenny has the advantage of the leg to balance him on the bends. I watch from behind as he swings it out in time with the music, the sheer weight of it acting as an anchor so he manages to remain relatively upright. Fascinating!

Pete meanwhile has given up the ghost and succumbed to the vast amount of booze he has consumed today. Well, not just today of course ... the last twenty years possibly. He is fast asleep with his head draped drunkenly on top of a table.

He has a balloon tied to his wrist and a chicken drumstick sticking out of his shirt pocket. That'll be breakfast then!

The Tesco crew are tagging on the back of the line and I can see Elsie and Phyllis up ahead. Phyllis has her arms wrapped around Lenny's waist and is laughing so much I fear she may need to borrow that panty liner soon.

Lenny suddenly decides this conga will travel and leads us all outside on to the main road. The cold night air hit's me like a shovel and I suddenly feel incredibly light headed. Good job Jack is behind me holding me up. I may need a piggy back home later.

"Aye aye aye aye conga ... this line is getting longer!" Jack giggles in my ear.

I swivel round and am amazed at the number of people following us. Must be people from the pub I should think. Oh crikey! A guy just ran out of the Chinese Takeaway and tagged on the end! See! People do love a conga! Old fashioned maybe but a great way to get people together.

"Aye aye aye aye conga ... that Nobby's got some wonga!" he sings loudly.

"Jack!"

"Tell Lenny to head back to the pub. I'm knackered!" he laughs.

Alan and Tracey are waiting at the oak doors, laughing hysterically as the giant throng of people spill back inside.

"We're gonna get off in a bit!" Alan beams excitedly, hopping on the spot again.

"Been a long day." Tracey nods, "Lovely but long."

"Don't dash off yet. Jack's got something for you." I tell them.

"We've booked you a night at the Black Swan. It's all paid for, breakfast and lunch tomorrow." he beams, "All you have to do is enjoy yourselves."

"Wicked!" Alan grins, barely able to contain himself.

"Thanks! That's great!" Tracey laughs, grabbing Jack and hugging him.

"Ladees and gentlemen! The happy couple are about to depart!" Nobby shouts across the packed room.

A round of applause echoes around the rafters as friends and strangers alike gather together to see them off. Tracey is carrying a tiny overnight bag. Needless to say Alan has his trusty Lidl carrier bag!

Everyone forms a line and they proudly walk along the centre, shaking hands, exchanging kisses and hugs as they go. Elsie shoves a five pound note into Alan's hand and as they reach the end of the line Nobby steps forward and discreetly shoves a packet of Durex into Alan's top pocket.

"Too late for them Nobby! She's having a baby!" Alan grins, "Ace!"

**

"Cass … would you like a glass of water?"
"Please."
"And some Nurofen?"
"Thanks."
"What about a bucket?"
"No ... I'll be fine."
"Early start in the morning?"
"Yep!"
"Mothercare?"
"Yep!"
"Thought so ..."

**

End

Also by Sue Brown

Crumpled

Cassie Ryder is middle-aged - married - and slowly losing her marbles as she struggles to cope with the chaos around her. Two elderly, confused parents - several insane neighbours and a demanding job, eventually drive her over the edge and into therapy sessions at the local Mental Health Unit - or Crumple Clinic as she calls it. Cassie refuses prescribed medication and tries alternative therapies - Leg Stretches With The Living Dead in the village hall to name just one. And all the while fighting the preconception that anyone with a mental health problem dribbles a lot and howls at the moon!

About Sue Brown

Sue Brown is still living in Harborne with her long suffering husband.

She continues to scribble determined to demonstrate that there is humour in every subject however sensitive. Enjoy!!

Printed in Great Britain
by Amazon